Brain Games For

Word Game Hints

If your puzzle of choice is a word search, word scramble, or cryptogram, keep the following tips in mind. And turn to Chapter 2 for more information.

- ✔ Use a straight edge to guide your eyes if necessary, and check each row or column for the first letter of the word you're looking for.

- ✔ If you get stuck on a word scramble, write the letters in as many different orders as possible until something looks familiar.

- ✔ Look at one-, two-, and three-letter words first, and always use a pencil — you're likely going to make some guesses before arriving at the solution.

Crossword Hints

If you're new to working crosswords, keep the following tips in mind. For more strategies, see Chapter 2.

- ✔ Keep key resources, such as the following, on hand (whether in electronic or hard-copy form):
  - • A dictionary
  - • A slang dictionary
  - • A thesaurus
  - • An atlas
  - • An almanac

- ✔ Work in pencil. When you're an old pro, you may insist on working in pen to up the challenge.

- ✔ The phrasing of the clues determines each puzzle's difficulty, and it may take a while to get familiar with a puzzle's particular phrasing.

- ✔ Look for fill-in-the-blank answers first; most people find them among the easiest to solve.

Brain Games For Dummies®

Cheat Sheet

Logic Puzzle and Riddle Hints

When you tackle logic puzzles or riddles, you're pitting your wits against those of the puzzle constructor. Keep the following in mind, and check out Chapter 2 for more details.

- ✔ If you can think of more than one answer that makes good sense, chances are you've outwitted the puzzle constructor!

- ✔ Your job is to study the language and figure out what's being hidden. Sometimes a single word can crack open the solution.

- ✔ If you're stumped, you're better off stepping away than turning to the answer page.

Sudoku Hints

If you're ready to join the ranks of sudoku devotees, keep the following information in mind. Chapter 3 details some key sudoku strategies.

- ✔ It's harder than it looks! Even with the easiest puzzle, you won't fill in a sudoku grid in a matter of minutes.

- ✔ Each puzzle has a unique answer; you can't find multiple ways to solve it.

- ✔ Start each puzzle by locating obvious, definite answers — those that you can solve simply by looking at what else falls within a particular row, column, and 3-x-3 box.

- ✔ When you've exhausted the obvious answers, you need to find a systematic way to explore the less-obvious (but still definite) answers.

- ✔ Myriad advanced strategies exist that aren't covered in this book. If you search for *killer, advanced,* or *extreme sudoku* online, you'll find countless Web sites that contain strategy suggestions for the toughest of puzzles.

For Dummies: Bestselling Book Series for Beginners

Brain Games

FOR

DUMMIES®

by Timothy E. Parker,
with Joan Friedman

Wiley Publishing, Inc.

Brain Games For Dummies®

Published by
Wiley Publishing, Inc.
111 River St.
Hoboken, NJ 07030-5774
www.wiley.com

Publisher's Acknowledgments

We're proud of this book; please send us your comments through our Dummies online registration form located at www.dummies.com/register/.

Some of the people who helped bring this book to market include the following:

Acquisitions, Editorial, and Media Development

Project Editor: Natalie Faye Harris

Acquisitions Editor: Tracy Boggier

Senior Copy Editor: Sarah Faulkner

Editorial Program Coordinator: Erin Calligan Mooney

Technical Editor: Denise Sutherland

Editorial Manager: Christine Meloy Beck

Editorial Assistants: Erin Calligan Mooney, Joe Niesen, Jennette ElNaggar, David Lutton

Cartoons: Rich Tennant (www.the5thwave.com)

Production

Project Coordinator: Kristie Rees

Layout and Graphics: Reuben Davis, Kathie Rickard

Proofreaders: John Greenough, Betty Kish

Publishing and Editorial for Consumer Dummies

Diane Graves Steele, Vice President and Publisher, Consumer Dummies

Kristin A. Cocks, Product Development Director, Consumer Dummies

Michael Spring, Vice President and Publisher, Travel

Kelly Regan, Editorial Director, Travel

Publishing for Technology Dummies

Andy Cummings, Vice President and Publisher, Dummies Technology/General User

Composition Services

Gerry Fahey, Vice President of Production Services

Debbie Stailey, Director of Composition Services

Table of Contents

Introduction

• •

Sure, puzzles are fun. They're a great diversion when you're sitting on a plane or getting sneezed on in the waiting room at the doctor's office. And if enjoyment is your one and only reason for picking up this book, you'll get no argument from me. (After all, I enjoy a good puzzle myself!)

But here's the great news: This kind of fun is actually good for you. Specifically, it's good for your brain. So welcome to the mental gym, where the equipment is portable, your exercise area is private, and the after-workout shower is completely optional.

About This Book

I bet that when you were a kid, you didn't schedule physical exercise into your day. You kept your body strong by doing what felt natural: riding your bike, skipping rope, climbing trees . . . But these days, to stay in shape, chances are you're much more deliberate. You probably don't climb trees the way you used to, so you have to actively seek out exercise or accept that you'll be a little weaker and slower with each passing year.

The same goes for mental exercise: When you were young, you were bombarded with things that stimulated your brain, even when you weren't sitting in a classroom. Every time you learned a new song, played a new board game, or tried a new sport, you gave your brain the stimulation it needed to stay sharp.

Maybe you have a job that gives you ample mental stimulation and helps keep your brain in the game. But not everyone is so lucky. Adults are often rewarded for repetition — not for trying new things. We have to perform consistently at work, create routines for our families, tackle the same household chores again and again . . . and our brains feel the effects by getting just a little weaker and slower with each passing year.

That's where mental exercise comes in. Countless articles, books, and Web sites are now devoted to the idea that if you don't want to lose it ("it" being your mental sharpness), you'd better use it ("it" being your brain). And sure, you could give your gray matter a decent workout by dusting off that anthology of 19th-century literature that's been sitting on your shelf since college, but doesn't a puzzle sound like more fun?

That's why I created this book: to give your brain a challenge you'll really enjoy, so you can get on the path to greater mental fitness and truly enjoy the workout.

Conventions Used in This Book

In a couple of chapters, especially in the Part of Tens, I include a handful of Web site addresses so you can explore additional resources if you'd like. The Web addresses appear in `monofont`, which makes them easier to locate if you want to go back and find them after you're done reading.

Keep in mind that when this book was printed, some Web addresses may have needed to break across two lines of text. If that happened, rest assured that I didn't put in any extra characters (such as hyphens) to indicate the break.

So, when using one of these Web addresses, just type in exactly what you see in this book, pretending as though the line break doesn't exist.

What You're Not to Read

If you're in a hurry to get to the puzzles and already know how to do them, you can skip over the chapters in Part I (of course, I hope you'll read every bit of this book, but I won't make you promise to go back and read them later). If you do read the Part I chapters, you don't have to read the text preceded by the Tip icon in order to understand the subject at hand. You'll also see sidebars, text in gray boxes. Sidebars are merely asides; the information is interesting but not critical to the text. You can safely skip it.

Foolish Assumptions

I try not to make any assumptions about how much experience you have with working the types of puzzles that appear in this book. That's why I include the chapters in Part I, which help you get familiar with each type of puzzle and how to solve them. That's also why I include puzzles of varying levels of difficulty throughout the book. Whether you're a novice or an expert at sudoku, you'll find puzzles to give you the challenge you need. The same goes for crosswords, cryptograms, and the other types of puzzles I include here.

My only assumption is that you want to have fun and stimulate your brain at the same time. Oh, and that you bring two critical tools with you: pencils and patience!

How This Book Is Organized

The bulk of this book is devoted to what you came look-ing for: puzzles (and their answers). But in case one or more of these puzzle types are new to you, I first spend some time explaining each and suggesting some strate-gies for working them.

Part 1: Preparing Your Puzzle Strategies

My first task in this part is to introduce you to the reasons for spending some quality time with this book. I explore what recent research says about the importance of mental exercise and the impact it can have on your cognitive abil-ities — including your memory — as you age.

I then introduce each type of puzzle that appears in this book and provide tips for solving it. From crosswords and word games to Sudoku and logic puzzles, I help you pre-pare for the workout that's coming.

Part II: Getting a Complete Puzzle Workout

Here's what you've been waiting for: the puzzles them-selves. For each type of puzzle, I offer various levels of difficulty; the easier puzzles come first, followed by fairly tough puzzles, and then by downright treacherous ones — the kind that will keep you awake until the wee hours, cursing my name!

Part III: The Payoff: Checking Your Answers

Pretty please, no matter how much you're tempted, don't look at this part until you've spent some quality time with Part II. Think of it as exercising your willpower at the same time you're pumping those brain cells.

Part IV: The Part of Tens

I include two chapters in this part: one that introduces ten types of puzzles not featured in this book that you may want to check out, and one that offers ten strategies for becoming the best puzzler you can be.

Icons Used in This Book

In the Part I chapters, you'll notice two icons in the margins that help you navigate the text:

When you see this icon, know that the text next to it contains a helpful hint for solving puzzles.

This icon points out information that you want to tuck into your mental filing cabinet — it's worth holding on to.

Where to Go from Here

That depends entirely on you. If you're new to the world of puzzling, I recommend that you cozy up with the chapters in Part I before putting pencil to paper. If you're already a puzzling pro and picked up this book knowing exactly how to tackle each type of puzzle included here, feel free to jump directly into the good stuff: the puzzles themselves in Part II.

My only rule is that you can't go directly to Part III! But I assume that because you've taken the time to read this Introduction, you're not going to spoil your fun by looking at the answers before making an earnest effort to solve the puzzles yourself. After all, the effort is the whole point: Your brain will thank you for it.

Part I

Preparing Your Puzzle Strategies

The 5th Wave   By Rich Tennant

"Well, Mr. Humphrey, it appears that working on puzzles for hours on end certainly DOES have some side effects."

In this part . . .

In Chapter 1, I introduce you to the myriad reasons for scheduling some quality puzzle time into your day. You can fight mental flab by doing something that you enjoy anyway — what could be better?

The remaining two chapters in this part introduce you to each type of puzzle featured in this book. Each chapter contains tips and strategies so you can hit the ground running when you crack open Part II.

Chapter 1

Puzzling for Your Health

• •

In This Chapter

▶ Taking a peek inside your brain

▶ Storing up ammunition against Alzheimer's

▶ Getting your body and mind in tip-top shape

▶ Choosing your puzzle poison

• •

*B*e honest: Do you feel as mentally sharp today as you did when you were 20? (If you're 20 now, or even younger, indulge me for a moment while I address your elders.) Can you retain information as easily as you did at that age? Or do you suspect that you don't learn as quickly as you once did, and worry about occasional fuzzy moments when you can't recall things that used to be second nature?

If you're in the "fuzzy" category, even on rare occasions, you may feel a bit anxious about the changes that seem to be taking place in your brain. And you may wonder what, if anything, you can do about them. I suspect that may be why you're reading this chapter right now, as opposed to jumping straight into Part II of this book and trying your hand at the puzzle of your choice.

As an isolated activity, working a crossword puzzle or untangling a word scramble may not dramatically change anyone's cognitive ability. But combined with other lifestyle changes, working puzzles — or doing other types of mentally stimulating activities — may have profound long-term effects on memory and overall cognitive ability. That's why I devote this first chapter to the big picture of working puzzles: why they're potentially beneficial, and what else you can do to try to recapture your twenties (if only in your mind!).

Pumping Up Your Synapses

You may suspect that *I'm* the one who needs some mental help, writing about synapses in a puzzle book. But bear with me — I'll try to demonstrate that I haven't gone around the bend.

On the off chance that you aren't a neurologist, let me start with a couple definitions. *Neurons* are cells that control your central nervous system: your brain and spinal column, and the nerves connected to them. *Synapses* are tiny gaps between the neurons in your brain. When synapses are working correctly, they allow your neurons to communicate with each other, which keeps your nervous system functioning the way it should.

Your nervous system must function properly in order for you to learn new things, retain information, and use your powers of logic and reason.

You're feeling some love for your synapses now, aren't you?

You have about 100 billion neurons in your brain. And you have literally trillions of synapses — possibly even a *quadrillion* (that's a 1 followed by 15 zeroes). It sure seems like you have plenty to spare, but as you age, your synapses deteriorate. And because your brain activity takes place courtesy of synapses, their deterioration equates to a decrease in your brain function, including memory.

The take-home lesson here is that if you want your mind to live to a ripe old age, you need to do more than just take care of your body (although that's crucial too, as I explain later in this chapter). You need to keep your synapses in top condition. How do you do that? Keep reading!

Building a Cognitive Reserve

In the late 1980s, a study published in the *Annals of Neurology* raised questions about why some people develop symptoms of Alzheimer's disease and some don't. Autopsies were conducted on 137 former nursing-home patients. As expected, the brains of those who had demonstrated symptoms of Alzheimer's were filled with *plaques* (brain deposits made up of dead cells and proteins) and *tangles* (nerve cells that had become tangled together) — characteristic physical signs associated with the disease.

Here's the unexpected part: The brains of ten patients who *didn't* show any symptoms of Alzheimer's contained the same level of plaques and tangles. If the physical reasons for the disease were present in those people, why didn't they get the symptoms?

There was another twist as well: The ten patients in question had heavier brains and more neurons than they should have given their age.

What made these ten people different from their peers?

As a result of this study, a new theory emerged: the *cognitive reserve* theory. It essentially says that people who have a larger reserve of neurons and stronger cognitive abilities can tolerate some brain deterioration without showing symptoms. In other words, the more you use your brain, the greater your chances of avoiding symptoms of Alzheimer's.

Strong stuff, huh?

Obviously, no one is offering guarantees here. I can't promise that anything I suggest in this book will add X number of years to your life, and that those years will be free of any symptoms of memory loss or other mental decline. But study after study in the past two decades has shown that mental activity can — and often does — have a positive effect on your quality of life in the long run, and I can't argue with that.

How do you build a cognitive reserve? The same way that you keep your synapses happy and healthy. Keep reading — the following section offers specific suggestions.

Taking a Whole-Body Approach to Brain Health

The great news about the steps you can take to improve your chances of long-term cognitive health is that many of them are the same steps you take to keep your body healthy. You need to add just a couple items to a list that's probably already familiar. And the new items are fun — promise.

Here's the familiar stuff:

- ✔ **Reduce stress.** If you've heard this advice from your doctor in relation to a physical condition, you now have double the reason to heed it. Research shows that stress causes synapses to malfunction.

  Long-term stress can cause a *neurotransmitter* (a chemical that carries messages between nerve cells) called glutamate to build up in your synapses. If enough of it accumulates, it can become toxic and interfere with your memory and your ability to learn.

- ✔ **Get aerobic exercise.** Aerobic exercise can help you manage and resist stress, which is enough reason to make it part of your daily routine. But among its many other benefits, studies suggest that it stimulates the creation of new neurons and strengthens the connections between them.

- ✔ **Eat a diet rich in antioxidant foods.** If your physical health alone hasn't inspired you to stock up on blueberries and spinach, do so for your mental health. Foods rich in antioxidants may help counteract effects of free radicals in your brain. (*Free radicals* are molecules that contain oxygen that attack cells throughout your body. They have been linked to cancer and heart disease, as well as brain deterioration.)

- ✔ **Control high blood pressure and diabetes.** A study published in the journal *Neurology* in 2001 showed that the mental abilities of participants with high blood pressure or diabetes declined more rapidly than those of other participants. High blood pressure is a risk factor for a condition called *vascular dementia,* in which a series of tiny strokes can affect memory and other cognitive abilities.

Early diagnosis and tight control of these conditions may help prevent some of the ill effects on your cognitive health.

Ready for the steps that may be new on your to-do list?

✔ **Get lots of mental stimulation.** Ahhh, *this* is where the puzzles come in — finally!

You may be hard-pressed to find a scientist who would claim to know exactly how much mental stimulation the average adult of a certain age needs, or what types of mental activities are best for a certain population. The science is fairly young, and I guarantee you'll hear a lot more about it in the years to come. But the general consensus is this: Mental stimulation of any kind can have positive effects on warding off memory problems and other declines in cognitive function. And lack of stimulation is a serious factor in mental decline.

So, how should you use your brain to get the maximum results? Only you can answer that question. That's because whatever you do, it has to be enjoyable enough to truly stimulate you and to keep you coming back for more, day after day. We're talking about running a mental marathon here — not winning a sprint. So you have my permission to read *War and Peace* or pull out your old calculus textbook, but only if thats what you really *want.* Otherwise, I suggest you look for other types of activities that will keep you interested in the long term. (Anyone for Sudoku?)

The bottom line: If there's a hobby you love that you haven't made time for in years, make time for it. If there's an activity you've been meaning to do but have put on the back burner because it seems less important than folding laundry, do it. If there's a subject you've been curious about for ages but haven't had time to study, study it. And if anyone (including your conscience) pesters you about how you're spending your time, memorize your new mantra: *My brain needs me.*

✔ **Stay curious.** This is an extension of the previous point. If you've buried your curiosity about the world around you because you haven't had time to explore it since childhood, now's the time — no matter how old you are or what your life circumstances are — to rediscover how curiosity feels.

Whatever activities you choose to help keep your brain stimulated, you need to enjoy them enough to do them regularly. You can't get your body fit by working out three hours in a row and then ignoring your health altogether for two weeks (because you're so sore from the marathon workout that you can't move for the first five days!). You benefit much more from working out consistently for shorter amounts of time — for example, every day for 30 minutes, or four days a week for 45 minutes each time.

The same seems to be true of mental exercise. Your goal should be to make time for mental stimulation at least several days a week, if not every day. If you can't devote time to working a crossword every day, no problem. But don't let a month go by between mental workouts. You have to invest the time if you want the results (see the sidebar "A puzzle constructor's dream").

A puzzler constructor's dream

An article published in *The New England Journal of Medicine* in 2002 reports on potential connections between leisure activities and the risk of dementia. Here's a quote:

> *Participation in leisure activities is associated with a reduced risk of development of dementia, both Alzheimer's disease and vascular dementia. The reduction in risk is related to the frequency of participation. According to our models, for example, elderly persons who did crossword puzzles four days a week . . . had a risk of dementia that was 47 percent lower than that among subjects who did puzzles once a week . . .*

Now, I swear I did not author this study! But I will tout it gladly to support the idea that spending quality time with this book, *The New York Times*, or any other source of quality crosswords may pay valuable dividends.

Chapter 2

Playing with Letters and Words: Logic and Word Puzzles, Riddles, and Crosswords

In This Chapter

▶ Rediscovering good learning habits

▶ Tapping helpful resources

▶ Employing tips and strategies

Some people adore puzzles that allow them to play
with words: Crosswords, logic puzzles, riddles, word
searches, word scrambles . . . They just seem to have the
knack for solving them. Others don't have the knack and
wouldn't recognize it if it smacked them in the forehead.

So, how do you get the knack? If you want to be able to
look a puzzle squarely in the face and say, "You're not
keeping me awake tonight!" what can you do (other than
keep the answers handy)?

Many of us started working puzzles in elementary school,
when our teachers had us fill in puzzles that reinforced
our spelling, reading, science, or social studies lessons of

the day. Chances are you've been familiar with the structure of most of these puzzles for a long time, and you've probably had at least some experience working them.

But that doesn't necessarily mean you're comfortable with them. In fact, you may feel downright nervous when you sit down to work a crossword these days. After all, what better way is there to test how much knowledge you've accumulated — and retained — over the years? And what better way to feel like a complete moron than to find yourself staring blankly at clue after clue?

Maybe you've long avoided some of these puzzles precisely because they point out how much you don't know. And maybe you're now ready to overcome your fears. As I point out in Chapter 1, the benefits of working puzzles are potentially great. Plus, they're a lot of fun — after you get past the fear and frustration.

Getting Logical

Logic puzzles can take a variety of forms. They may involve words, numbers, or images, and — like all puzzles — they may be fairly easy to solve or extremely difficult.

Preparing to solve logic puzzles isn't like preparing to solve a crossword (see earlier in this chapter) or sudoku puzzle (see Chapter 3). You don't need to understand how the puzzle is constructed or what the rules are. You don't have many specific strategies to consider. However, you should keep the following in mind:

- ✔ As with other puzzle types, each logic puzzle has a unique answer. The puzzle constructor doesn't intend for you to be able to solve one puzzle in multiple ways.

> ✔ In many cases, the person writing the puzzle is intentionally veiling the answer. The way the puzzle is written may be deceptive to some degree — the degree of deception being one determinant of its level of difficulty.

Logic puzzles are a varied lot. You'll likely find that some answers spring to mind as soon as you've read the puzzle — your own logic will make them seem obvious to you. But others will be much more diabolical.

If you spend a good amount of time studying one puzzle and just can't seem to figure it out, walk away and come back later. A fresh look may be your best bet, or you may want to enlist help from a friend or family member.

Another thing to keep in mind is that the more puzzles you solve that are written by the same puzzle constructor, the better your chances of figuring out whether (and how) that person is trying to deceive you.

For that reason, I encourage you to start with the easy logic puzzles in Part II, even if you don't find them very challenging. They give you a sense of who I am and how I write logic puzzles. That information may help you when you reach the toughest of the tough. By that point, you may have some insights regarding my use of language and my thought processes.

I also encourage you to keep the answer pages closed until you've given each puzzle a good effort. You want the best workout your mind can get, and sometimes that means allowing for frustration.

Fiddling with Riddles

If logic puzzles appeal to you, riddles likely will as well. These two types of puzzles are close cousins, but riddles are often shorter than logic puzzles and involve plays on language. For example,

> What becomes larger the more you take away from it, and smaller the more you add to it?

The answer is *a hole in the ground.* The reason this riddle works is because it forces you to think in a new way — to realize that not everything gets larger when you add to it.

As with logic puzzles and other puzzle types, each riddle should have just one unique answer. If you can think of two or more reasonable answers to the same riddle, chances are you've outwitted the puzzle constructor!

Riddles are a great way to introduce kids to the joy of playing with language. And for adults, they're a great way to keep the mental gears cranking even when you have only a short time each day to devote to puzzling.

Decoding Cryptograms

Cryptograms are more complicated than word searches and word scrambles, and they'll almost certainly require more of your time. But solving a cryptogram is really satisfying — it makes you feel like a master detective — so the extra time is well worth it.

A cryptogram is a sentence or phrase that's *encrypted* or *enciphered.* What does that mean? Each letter has been substituted with a different letter. (In some cases, non-letter characters — such as numbers — are used as substitutions as well, but in this book I use only letters.) So within the sentence or phrase, for example, every A may be replaced with an N, and every S replaced with a P. In order to figure out what the sentence or phrase says, you have to figure out each substitution — not an easy task!

I'll be honest: Even with the following strategies in mind, sometimes solving a cryptogram is tough. Your best bet is often just to make guesses and see what sticks. But the tips I offer here should at least help you refine your guesses!

- ✔ Use a pencil. Because you're bound to be making guesses at least some of the time, you want the ability to erase and guess again if you discover you've made a mistake. And keep scrap paper close by!

- ✔ Know this: No letter substitutes as itself in a cryptogram. The puzzle constructor won't try to trick you by using an A to represent an A, for example.

- ✔ Know this also: Only one solution is possible for a cryptogram. Part of the puzzle constructor's job is to make sure the sentence or phrase is long enough that the solution must be unique. In other words, you can't come up with two or more logical solutions to the same puzzle.

- ✔ If a hint is provided, look at it first. In this book, I offer hints that indicate, for example, how often a certain letter appears or where you may find a certain letter (at the start or end of a word).

Other puzzle constructors may give you a different type of hint. For example, a hint may be a phrase that's only partly encrypted, such as MICKEY PRTIN. When you figure out that PRTIN represents MOUSE, you then look for instances within the encrypted sentence or phrase where you can substitute M for P, O for R, and so on.

In other cases, the puzzle constructor may show you a few letters in the solution itself.

✔ Your next step is to look for one-letter words (if there are any), which have to be either I or A. (You could find an instance of a single-letter word being O, but that's pretty rare.)

✔ Two- and three-letter words should be your next targets. Consider common two-letter words such as *an, as, at, by, in, is, it, no, of, on, or, so,* and *to.* Frequently used three-letter words are *and, but, for, the,* and *you.*

✔ If you see an apostrophe in the encrypted text, you can guess that what follows it is an S or T. (D is also possible, but contractions such as *he'd, they'd,* and *we'd* aren't that common.) If you see more than one instance of an apostrophe, and the letters before and after each apostrophe are the same, you can guess that you're looking at an N before each apostrophe and a T after it. (Think *can't, don't,* and *won't.*) If you don't see that repetition before and after multiple apostrophes, you're likely looking at possessives (ending in S).

✔ Double letters are also good places to focus. For example, say you see RR in an encrypted word. You may not immediately know whether you're looking at an ll, an ee, an ss, or some other double-letter combination, but you can guess that R doesn't substitute for letters that aren't commonly doubled (such as A, I, H, Q, and U).

You can also consider how frequently each letter appears in the cryptogram. You can assume that if you see a letter only once, for example, it's probably not an E, T, A, O, or N.

But going much deeper with *frequency analysis* (considering how often certain letters typically appear in the English language and comparing that with how often the encrypted letters appear) is pretty complex stuff and may suck the fun out of solving the puzzle. My hope is that the tips in the bulleted list help you solve a handful of letters, which in turn help you make educated guesses about a few of the words, which give you solutions to more encrypted letters, and so on.

If you get stuck, make some guesses based on what you've figured out so far. And walk away if you need to — it's better to come back to the puzzle with fresh eyes later than to get frustrated!

Straightening Out Word Scrambles

You can play word scramble puzzles in various ways, including the following:

- You look at a group of letters placed in random order and rearrange them into one word, using every letter. The words to be rearranged may be rather short — between five and eight characters. For example, unscramble the capitalized word in quotations to solve this riddle:

Where a sauce may "THICKEN": _ _ _ _ _ _ _

Unscrambling words of this length isn't usually very difficult (although I won't dare suggest that you'll never get stuck!). The answer to this riddle, by the way, is *kitchen*.

The difficulty increases along with the number of letters and words involved. For example, try to solve this one:

Where's a good place to see a "SCHOOL MASTER"?

_ _ _ _ _ _ _ _ _ _ _ _

The answer is *the classroom*.

✔ You solve several word scrambles similar to those I describe in the previous bullet, and you then take a second step. Certain characters in those words are circled, and by using only the circled letters, you solve one more scramble: You rearrange them to create a word or phrase that answers a clue given by the puzzle constructor.

In this step, you're likely dealing with quite a few characters, and you're often creating more than one word. As with the examples shown in the previous bullet, the puzzle constructor usually provides blanks that show how many words are in the solution and how many characters are in each.

✔ You look at a group of letters and try to create as many words as possible from them. You don't have to use every letter in every word you create. For example, if you're given eight letters, you can create words with three letters, four letters, and so on. The goal is to make as many words as possible, and the puzzle constructor may tell you how many words you're aiming for. The puzzle constructor may also set certain rules, such as "No two-letter words."

The strategies for approaching word scrambles are pretty straightforward:

✔ If you're working on a series of jumbled words, look at each one in turn to see whether any words jump out at you. You'll be amazed by how quickly you can solve some scrambles; our minds seem built for this type of task.

✔ When an answer doesn't jump out at you, try writing the letters in a different order. Don't worry about creating a word right away — just putting them in a new order may trigger that "aha!" moment you're looking for.

✔ If the "aha!" remains elusive, try grouping together letters in what seems to be a logical way. Consider how many vowels you have; if you have twice as many consonants as vowels, chances are the word begins with a consonant. Try putting together common groupings such as *ing, sh,* or *th.*

Keep rearranging letters as long as it takes to find what you're looking for. Eventually, you'll stumble onto a combination that makes sense.

✔ If you're playing the last type of scramble that I describe in the previous bulleted list, be sure to look for words that can be pulled directly from within the words you've already created. For example, if you've written down *player,* be sure to also write down *play, lay,* and *layer.* You can also write down *pay, per, year, reap,* and so on, but the point is to notice the words that are already spelled out, in order, within the longer words you've created — they're your easiest finds.

Relaxing with Word Searches

As with crossword puzzles, you were probably introduced to word searches early in life. Most people work them in elementary school to reinforce their spelling and vocabulary lessons.

In case you've never seen one before, a word search is simply a grid of letters — in a square or rectangular shape — that contains hidden words. Your goal is to find and circle the words, which may appear horizontally, vertically, or diagonally within the grid. Some words may be written backward. Some word searches are constructed around a central theme, which means all the words you're finding are related to one topic.

How do you know what words to look for? The puzzle constructor usually provides a list — that's the case in this book. You may encounter word searches that don't provide a word list, in which case the puzzle constructor tells you how many words you're looking for (and whether they all relate to a certain theme). Those searches are more challenging, of course.

The puzzle constructor may let you know that the word search contains a hidden message (related to the theme, if the puzzle has one), which you discover only after circling all the words. To find the message, you identify, in order, all the letters you *haven't* circled. The letters form words that spell out the secret message.

The thing I love about word searches is they're really low-stress. If a word list is provided, I guarantee you can complete the search — no matter how large the grid or how many words you're looking for. How often in life do you get the satisfaction of knowing you're going to get the right answers? That fact, in itself, makes working word searches fun. Plus, they're great for increasing your concentration and blocking out the world for a while.

Tackling the Crossword Grid

If you really love crossword puzzles and want to learn more about tips on solving them and even how they're made, I highly recommend checking out *Crossword Puzzle Challenges For Dummies* (Wiley). Right now, though, I'm going help you get started on the fun part of a crossword puzzle: Filling in the blanks! Where to begin? Here are my suggestions:

- ✔ Use a pencil rather than a pen. Some people will disagree with me, insisting that working in pen is the only way to go. But until you get truly comfortable at working crosswords, don't give yourself a reason to stress about mistakes!

- ✔ Read through the clues one by one and answer those that seem obvious. Even in the toughest puzzle, you're likely to find at least a handful of clues you can answer immediately.

- ✔ After you fill in the easy answers, go back and see whether any of the letters you've written down help you solve any of the other, less-obvious clues.

Take your time with this step, and don't get frustrated if answers don't jump to mind immediately. You're still getting familiar with the puzzle constructor's phrasing at this point. It's almost as if he or she has written clues in a dialect that's new to you; the more time you spend reading them, the better you'll be able to interpret what's being asked.

✔ If the crossword has a theme, try to determine whether every clue seems related to it. If not, see whether you can identify the clues that relate directly to it, and work on those answers.

✔ If you're willing to use outside resources, identify clues that fall into the "Trivia" category. They're often the easiest to solve by consulting a Web site or other resource.

✔ Look for clues written as plurals, and consider penciling in an S at the end of each grid entry. You may end up erasing some of them (because plurals can be formed in other ways, of course — consider *geese*), but that's why you're using a pencil!

✔ If you find yourself feeling stuck, step away from the puzzle and go back to it with fresh eyes later. You may want to work multiple puzzles at the same time for this reason. When you're stumped on one, start a new one. By doing so, you expose yourself to various styles of clue phrasing, you start to notice that certain words (especially short ones) appear in lots of crossword puzzles (even though the clues differ from puzzle to puzzle), and you build your confidence.

And don't forget: It can be fun to bring your family members or friends into the mix. If you're truly stumped, give a tough clue to someone else to chew on for a while.

Chapter 3

Fun with Numbers: Taking On Sudoku

In This Chapter

▶ Joining the phenomenon

▶ Grasping the basics

▶ Using more advanced techniques

Solving a Sudoku puzzle requires a different kind of mental workout than solving a crossword puzzle or a word scramble. The breadth of your vocabulary and depth of your factual knowledge are pretty much irrelevant here — logic and diligence are the keys to success.

In this chapter, I introduce basic strategies for working a Sudoku puzzle, before turning you loose in Part II.

Jumping into the Sudoku Craze

I assume you haven't been living in isolation for the past few years, so you're aware that Sudoku has gained the kind of popularity that Rubik's Cube had once upon a time. In describing it, many people use the word "addictive," so I suppose I should warn you that after you get started, you may find yourself spending many hours playing these puzzles.

What's the appeal? It may be the deceptive simplicity of the Sudoku grid or the fact that, at its most basic, Sudoku requires only that you know how to count to nine. You don't need to gather any resources before putting pencil to paper, and you aren't testing your recall of words and facts you learned many moons ago.

But, of course, solving a Sudoku puzzle isn't actually simple. In fact, it can be downright mystifying when you get into the toughest level of puzzles, which some puzzle constructors label *killer, extreme,* or *treacherous.* I include some of these puzzles in Part II to make absolutely certain you won't accuse me of taking it easy on you!

Although this chapter covers the basic strategies you can apply to solving any level of Sudoku puzzle, you may want to use more advanced strategies if you decide to tackle the treacherous breed. In that case, I recommend consulting another resource, such as *Extreme Sudoku For Dummies* (Wiley). You can also type "killer Sudoku," "advanced Sudoku," or some other variation into your favorite search engine and locate playing tips online.

By the way, do you know what *Sudoku* means? *Su* is the Japanese word for "number," and *doku* means something like "single." So the name roughly translates to *single number.* If you've never worked a Sudoku before, you'll find out in the next section why the name makes perfect sense.

Applying Strategies

I provide two layers of strategies in this section: very basic ones and slightly more advanced ones. As I mention in the previous section, lots of additional strategies exist, but they're applicable mostly to the truly diabolical puzzles, and I don't have enough room to cover them adequately here. If you find yourself outgrowing the approaches I suggest, you can easily locate other resources that can guide you to the next level of Sudoku mastery.

Getting started

Here's the least you need to know to get going with sudoku:

- The basic Sudoku puzzle is a 9-x-9 grid; it contains nine rows and nine columns, and it's divided into nine 3-x-3 grids or boxes. (Tougher puzzles may be 12-x-12 or 16-x-16 grids, but I don't include these sizes in this book. I *do* include some circular or *target* Sudokus, which I discuss at the end of the chapter.)

- Your job is to make sure that each row, column, and 3-x-3 box in the puzzle contains the numbers 1 through 9. If you do your job correctly, each of these numbers can appear only once in each row, column, and 3-x-3 box.

- Each puzzle has a unique solution; you can't solve it in more than one way.

✔ The puzzle constructor's task is to get you started with just a handful of numbers in the grid — enough so you have adequate information to solve the puzzle. The difficulty of each puzzle depends on how many numbers are provided and where they're placed.

✔ When you start a puzzle, your goal is to locate one or more blank cells for which you can identify only one number that works. In other words, you're looking for definite answers — spaces where the numbers provided for a certain row, column, and 3-x-3 box offer enough information that you can eliminate every possibility except one.

For example, you may find a space in a row that already contains the numbers 2, 5, and 6. The same space may fall in a column that contains 1, 4, and 9. And the 3-x-3 box that houses the space may already have the numbers 3 and 8 in it. When you combine all those clues, you realize that only the number 7 can go in that space. It's a definite answer — precisely what you're looking for to get started.

✔ After you fill in one or more definite answers, you need to go back and consider how those new pieces of information affect blank spaces you've already considered. Solving one number may be just the step needed to solve another in the same row, column, or 3-x-3 box. ("Aha! I knew that space had to be filled with either a 2 or a 7. Now that I've written 7 elsewhere in this row, my answer has to be 2.")

✔ At some point — sooner rather than later, if the puzzle is a tough one — you're going to run out of obvious answers. Your next step is to start filling in possible answers in each empty space — doing so can help you identify definite answers that have been hiding from you.

You must use pencil here — you could end up with six or more numbers in a single space! You may even want to make a copy of the puzzle you're working on so you can scratch all over it and write only the definite answers on the original puzzle.

But what do you do after you've identified a bunch of possibilities? What do all these tiny numbers mean, and how do they help you figure out which is correct?

This is the step of the puzzle where you have a choice to make: Apply strategies such as those I outline in the next section, or start making best guesses and see where each leads you.

I'm not here to dictate your approach; the goal is for you to enjoy the solving process, and only you can decide how that's going to happen. But if guesswork makes you nervous, keep in mind that you can eliminate it altogether if you're willing to learn and use advanced strategies.

For many people, much of the pleasure in solving Sudoku is found in discovering the logic strategies that produce a solution. If you'd prefer to discover those strategies for yourself, feel free to stop reading now and jump right into the puzzles in Part II.

As I mention in the previous section, I offer a suggested solving time for each Sudoku puzzle in Part II. These times are completely subjective because actual solving times vary according to your experience, skill, and many other factors, such as your environment or whether you're having a particularly good solving day. The times I suggest are set at a level that an expert solver would expect to achieve, so please don't be disheartened if you don't finish so quickly. Just let the time estimates add an element of competition to the fun of solving sudoku. And if you aren't the competitive sort, ignore those estimates altogether!

Advancing past the basics

The key to solving almost any Sudoku is discovering every possible number for each square. These options can be found simply by checking each square and asking the question "Will such-and-such a number go here?" while checking whether the number is also in the row, column, or 3x3 box in which the square resides. Using a pencil, you want to write the possible options in each empty square on the grid.

After you reach a point where all the obvious numbers have been solved, you have to search for options in a systematic way. When you can't prove which number should be in a square, you can often more easily prove what *can't* be there. By a process of elimination, you can reduce the options for a square until you're left with only one.

A basic discipline of Sudoku solving is recognizing option groupings. Spotting the relationship of a group of options in one square to another group in another square is fundamental to solving difficult Sudoku puzzles. If you want detailed information on putting grouping strategy to use, I highly recommend checking out *Extreme Sudoku For Dummies* (Wiley).

Sudoku is a puzzle that you solve with logic alone, so it follows that the schemes for solving should be examined in a logical way. Learning about pairs and triplets gives you a good grounding in Sudoku logic and enables you to understand the reasoning behind the more advanced strategies.

Taking Target Practice

If you start getting square eyes from doing regular Sudoku, I can offer some relief in the form of circular Sudoku, sometimes called *target* Sudoku. Think of the puzzle as a big pie cut into eight slices, each slice with four bites. Your goal is to place a number into each bite of pie so that every two adjacent slices contain all of the numbers from 1 to 8. Every ring also must contain all the numbers from 1 to 8.

Here's an important clue: Every other pie slice will contain the same four numbers. That has to be the case because otherwise, you'd have duplicates in some combination of two adjacent slices. However, the four numbers appear in different orders in the different slices because of the fact that each ring comes into play as well.

As with 9-x-9 grid Sudoku puzzles, you start a target Sudoku by trying to identify definite answers: those blank spaces that can have only one answer based on the numbers the puzzle constructor has provided. Target Sudokus are a nice change of pace from grid sudokus and may be a touch easier because you're dealing with fewer spaces to fill.

Part II

Getting a Complete Puzzle Workout

The 5th Wave   By Rich Tennant

IT WAS THE LAST TIME EMILY SERVED ALPHABET SOUP TO HER WORD PUZZLE PLAYING HUSBAND.

CEDE, CEIL, CEBUS, LICE, CUBES...

OBSESSIVE, FIXATED, FANATIC, COMPULSIVE...

In this part . . .

Okay, enough preparation — it's time for the fun stuff! Get your pencils ready, find a comfortable chair, get some scrap paper, and have fun working whichever type of puzzle you choose. You can start with a crossword, a word game, a sudoku grid, some riddles . . . whatever makes your gray matter happy and keeps you coming back for more.

Chapter 4

Puzzles

. . . .

. . . .

*P*uzzles are labeled by type and difficulty level. Levels are Easy, Tricky, Tough, and Treacherous, "Easy" being (of course) the easiest puzzles, and "Treacherous" being the most difficult puzzles. When you finish solving all these puzzles, please see Part III for the answers. Have fun!

Logic Puzzles

Put on your thinking cap to solve these logic puzzles! Each has just one answer. See Chapter 2 for tips on tackling logic puzzles.

Easy

Puzzle 1

How many times can a mathematician subtract ten from 100?

Puzzle 2

Decipher this clue: YYYMEN

Tricky

Puzzle 3

A woman gave birth to two boys on the same day, in the same year, within minutes of each other, yet they were not twins. How is this possible?

Puzzle 4

Add one line, and one line only, to make the following statement correct: $5 + 5 + 5 = 550$

Puzzle 5

Alexander is a great magician, skilled in many things. He weighs exactly 199 pounds and is about to cross a bridge with a strict weight limit of 200 pounds. The problem is he is carrying three pieces of gold, each weighing 8 ounces each. The gold puts him 8 ounces over the strict weight limit. What did Alexander do to cross the bridge safely with all three pieces of gold?

Tough

Puzzle 6

Two people stand on opposite corners of a handkerchief. They do not stretch or alter the handkerchief in any possible way. How can they both stand on the handkerchief simultaneously without having any possibility whatsoever of touching each other?

Puzzle 7

Under what circumstance could a person walk along a railroad track, discover an oncoming train, and have to run *toward* the train to avoid being struck?

Puzzle 8

Imagine this scenario. You have an extremely valuable item you need to send in the mail to an acquaintance. You have a special container that has the perfect amount of space for the item, but no extra space whatsoever. The container does, however, have a place for locks on the outside. You have locks and keys, but your acquaintance does not have keys to unlock any of your locks. How can you send the extremely valuable container using your lock, and have, eventually, your acquaintance be able to open the package?

Treacherous

Puzzle 9

In a remote country ruled by a brutal monarch, a man was sentenced to death. Feeling godly, the brutal monarch told the man he would allow one final statement. The monarch advised the man that if he lied in his final statement, he would be drowned, but if he told the truth in his final statement, he be shot by firing squad. The man thought, and made his final statement. Due to the statement, the monarch was forced to release the man unharmed. What could the man possibly have said?

Puzzle 10

There is an English word that is nine letters long that can form a new word each time one letter is removed. In fact, it can change to a new word every time a letter is removed until only one letter remains. What is the word, and what is the sequence of words formed by removing one letter at a time?

Riddles

Each riddle here has just one answer. Think hard, and see Chapter 2 for information on good ways to approach riddles.

Easy

Puzzle 11

What becomes larger the more you take away from it, and smaller the more you add to it?

Puzzle 12

What grows up at the same time it grows down?

Puzzle 13

What gets larger as it eats, but smaller as it drinks?

Tricky

Puzzle 14

What has a foot on either side and another foot in the middle?

Puzzle 15

Although it is always before you, what is it you can never see?

Puzzle 16

What is constantly coming but never actually arrives?

Puzzle 17

What goes up and down without actually moving?

Tough

Puzzle 18

What is impossible to hold for more than several minutes although it is lighter than a feather?

Puzzle 19

Girls have it but boys do not. It's in your windows but not your walls. It's in everyone's life but not in anyone's death. What is it?

Puzzle 20

There are two Ws in front of two other Ws. There are two Ws behind two other Ws. There are two Ws beside two other Ws. How many Ws are there in all?

Puzzle 21

Homonyms are words that are spelled differently but sound exactly the same. One pair of homonyms is unique in that although they are true homonyms, the two words are also exact opposites of each other. What are the two words?

Treacherous

Puzzle 22

You have a balance-type scale with two trays and seemingly nine identical coins, except that one of the coins is a fake. The weight of the fake coin is slightly less than the authentic coins. What is the easiest way to find the fake gold coin?

Puzzle 23

What word can be read left to right, right to left, and can be written forward, backward, or upside down?

Puzzle 24

What two English words have three consecutive repeated letters?

Puzzle 25

It is more powerful than God. The poorest of the poor have it. The richest of the rich need it.
If you eat it or drink it, you'll die. What is it?

Cryptograms

Here a phrase or sentence is *encrypted* — each letter is substituted with a different letter or character. To know what the sentence or phrase says, figure out each substitution. Hints are given for each puzzle. See Chapter 2 for more information on cryptograms, and keep scrap paper close by, in case you need it.

Easy

Puzzle 26

BJVAY JSN CYP FULBN BJVAYI FOCY QUV. ISULP JSN QUV IBPPK JBUSP.

Hint: E appears 5 times.

Puzzle 27

UP YIGPBXW QB RQXG FNQXJNFD. FNPR ZIR UPYQZP AQGOD IF IVR ZQZPVF.

Hint: E appears 6 times.

Puzzle 28

NOWY AJUSYSNN. AC AN COS ZWNC COLC LCCLFOSN ACNSUR CE COS GENC VZAUUALYC GSCLUN.

Hint: H appears 5 times.

Puzzle 29

QD Q OLKG SLBG ND VZ SULBLSOGB, VZ BGIMOLOQNY XQWW OLKG SLBG ND QOPGWD.

Hint: I appears 5 times.

Tricky

Puzzle 30

OA GOJ AFXZKRTFOAF OTF ZVNEPAYX KB YJTFA ZYL
WJPPZYL FOJGF XOZX OTF VAZFJY TF GAZS

Hint: H appears 7 times.

Puzzle 31

QCHPHKHN B ZHHV VBFH HMHNUBTBPY, B VBH RXQP
OPWBV WCH ZHHVBPY LGTTHT.

Hint: The letter B is not used at all.

Puzzle 32

FEIDF UVIE VSC JCDFJCAF. UVIE BJDFPXND BJKHF PD
SNWW ON UVIE VSC JCDFNPR VG DVBNVCN NWDND.

Hint: H appears just one time.

Puzzle 33

WAG MIER CGMCEG OAM ELTWGI WM QMWA TLHGT MP
S PSKLER ZVSXXGE SXG WAG IGFW HMMX IGLJAQMXT.

Hint: X appears one time.

Puzzle 34

GSS LBO DOGTLYKTS HOALYUOALH YA LBO ZNFSX
ZOYJB SOHH LBGA G HYAJSO SNPOSM GWLYNA.

Hint: I appears 6 times.

Puzzle 35

VKMDM'Q SEVKYSF YS VKM HYTTGM EZ VKM DEPT ORV XMGGEA QVDYUMQ PST TMPT PDHPTYGGEQ.

Hint: I appears 5 times.

Puzzle 36

VZO ROW YFKKXV LO MXGEAZOI UEVZXBV SCEYVEXK, KXC WFK MOCSOYVOI UEVZXBV VCEFGA.

Hint: THE appears only once.

Tough

Puzzle 37

IYUYUSYI, XWYL MWY DYRJTJV ZMIAMZ WEZ ZMAQQ WY ZWTXZ WEZ SRJVZECY MT WRGQ MWY XTIGC.

Hint: One word ends with O.

Puzzle 38

XHWZ QM KFXX CQKIG HUS SGFBI WHJOI RQGI MHFXJ-GIO DAHU XHWZ QM FUDIXXFLIUWI HUS HVFXFDT.

Hint: F appears 3 times.

Puzzle 39

QWHYWBW YI VD KVI, VKPW MZVK U IYEW, UHH EWE-QWDN VT IFW TUEYHX FUL QDWUJTUNI IVAWIFWD.

Hint: THE appears just one time.

Puzzle 40

CQ HLI XCPP MYTRN ULVT FCUT MDSVYTRCRB FDT SJ, HLI'PP MYTRN PTMM FCUT ZDLYYCRB XLLN.

Hint: G appears 2 times.

Puzzle 41

ZQA NXYOQTL DXOZ PKKALZPIUA ZX MXC KXDAO EYXD P ZQPVFESU PVC KQAAYESU QAPYZ.

Hint: EE appears one time.

Puzzle 42

ZNO GHRF PV UBGL HRF NPROX NHD BZD FKHTSHJLD. XPA JHR QOZ LBJLOF SX H JPT HRF DZARQ SX H SOO.

Hint: K appears 4 times.

Puzzle 43

YDGF L ZLF RGGR ODG DLFSYXQOQFE CF ODG YLNN, ODGXG QR MXCKLKNP L TDQNS QF ODG HLZQNP.

Hint: The letter U is not used at all.

Treacherous

Puzzle 44

LSOQJDCIZFG PCD JLSD YJJOQ MXF JDIG PACOCPFSO PCD NSSL FASE JLSD.

Hint: K appears just one time.

Puzzle 45

NRL'W QRZRGGRS SDCC IV IVQQVG QXEU EUH HVWQV-
GLEH HRO XEBV VBVG PURSU.

Hint: The letter C is not used at all.

Puzzle 46

JSNI HLTEXV QS ESH ASUG MYAW; HLG VDSWGE RSIQ,
HLG VLSH YIISR, HLG DYVH PTJG YEQ HLG EGXPGAHGQ
SDDSIHNETHZ.

Hint: W appears 2 times.

Puzzle 47

C ZCQDNNF BQJV VUDA ECXACQHICXURX SDQ ZOJS
AUR GRDXAX - ZCQDQYCDN VJOOCRX.

Hint: The letter P is not used at all.

Puzzle 48

YD AGTTJDY TD HNNHEZCGMMS QDUT ZXH RIYK DN
GMM JZT ADBHQT DN GEZJYV GYK QHGTDYJYV GT
NHGQ.

Hint: B appears just one time.

Puzzle 49

ZNKQYNM OG UPY FKRKFOUM US RYNHSNC RNSRYNAM
YQYD BPYD GFKNYT PKAH US TYKUP.

Hint: W appears just one time.

Puzzle 50

NHHNLBEQZBJ ZC OZCCAG WJ ONCB HANHMA WATX-
ECA ZB ZC GLACCAG ZQ NIALXMMC XQG MNNVC MZVA
PNLV.

Hint: The letter H is not used at all.

Word Scrambles

Unscramble the capitalized word(s) in quotations to solve the riddles. See Chapter 2 for more details on word scrambles.

Easy

Puzzle 51

What some feel "ELVIS" does? _ _ _ _ _

Puzzle 52

What some "ACTORS" hate to do? _ _ - _ _ _ _

Puzzle 53

What mishandling "ROSES" can lead to? _ _ _ _ _

Puzzle 54

How a "RESCUE" can make the saved person feel?

_ _ _ _ _ _

Tricky

Puzzle 55

Easy thing to do when one is "SILENT"? _ _ _ _ _ _

Puzzle 56

EASY not Tricky What "THE EYES" do? _ _ _ _
_ _ _

Puzzle 57

What "THE IRS" thinks your money is? _ _ _ _ _ _

Puzzle 58

What courtroom figures in "ROBES" are? _ _ _ _ _

Puzzle 59

Simple thing to do with a "STIPEND"? _ _ _ _ _ _ _

Puzzle 60

While a teacher may be "TEACHING," a student may be?
_ _ _ _ _ _ _ _

Puzzle 61

Where a sauce may "THICKEN" _ _ _ _ _ _ _

Tough

Puzzle 62

Option for those with "BAD CREDIT"? _ _ _ _ _
_ _ _ _

Puzzle 63

This occurs when one is "PAST DUE"? _ _ _ _ ' _ _

Puzzle 64

Where's a good place to see a "SCHOOL MASTER"? _ _ _
_ _ _ _ _ _ _ _ _

Puzzle 65

TREACHEROUS, not Tough What illegal auto "RACES CAN
RUIN"? _ _ _ _ _ _ _ _ _ _ _

Puzzle 66

What "THE DETECTIVES" Do? _ _ _ _ _ _
_ _ _ _ _ _ _

Puzzle 67

What's "TWELVE PLUS ONE"? _ _ _ _ _ _ _ _ _ _ _ _ _ _

Treacherous

Puzzle 68

What's "HOTTER IN DEGREES"? _ _ _ _ _ _ _ _ _ _ _ _ _ _

Puzzle 69

PAYMENT RECEIVED! _ _ _ _ _ _ _ _ _ _ _
_ _ _ _

Puzzle 70

Many people leave "SLOT MACHINES" with?
_ _ _ _ _ _ _ _ _ _'_ _

Puzzle 71

Some people consider them to be "LIES. LET'S RECOUNT"? _ _ _ _ _ _ _ _ _ _ _ _ _ _ _ _

Puzzle 72

What a "CURE FOR BALD MALES" may be?

_ _ _ _ _ _ _ _ _ _ _ _ _ _ _ _

Puzzle 73

Some consider it "CRAP BUILT ON LIES"

_ _ _ _ _ _ _ _ _ _ _ _ _ _ _

Puzzle 74

One in a group of "NOTIONS WE RARELY USE"?
_ _ _ _ _ _ _' _ _ _ _ _ _ _ _ _ _

Word Searches

Try to find as many words as you can in each puzzle. Chapter 2 contains more information on word searches.

Easy

```
Y M C W J E Z Q K O O H T A E M Q O E U V
K E E T M A N A G E M E N T P F I P A L M
I C V U F O X T U P U A X Q V O H T J L X
P N J N D I D T N A D N E T T A V S T E C
E A X L O V L U F L D H G D Z V T S T T O
G D O F E C M Z J D A V E P H A O M S A M
R I X Y M J V B R S J L R Y F H Q J I I M
A U I E K L L I S O I L I F S G L A F C A
H G H W S B M I B V O C E U H N N X J O N
C I W R X Q S H E A W R P W O R K E R S D
A I E F K T O R C N E P M M J Q A X Y S T
Q V G T A L G I T H O M Q U W P Q T Z A H
T Y Y N D L E R C R E S L A B O R E R B Z
I G T E A K B J T U I U E N U X C G B X Q
L R R D I A O K G D W D J Y H O W X D O L
D N A H D B Y A E F G Z G E T K G W J A X
L Z X I E J E K D F N B L E N Y O L U W L
E Z C T I L I O X F G P Y H J T S N K M A
Q Q U E L C G V N F E B F V E D A R M O C
W Z K O K Y X K Q R D E R I H M O J D W B
C L C K S Y Q P F R E E Y O L P M E S Q K
```

Puzzle 75

AIDE	FIST	MANUAL
ASSISTANT	GUIDANCE	MEATHOOK
ASSOCIATE	HAND	MITT
ATTENDANT	HANDYMAN	PALM
CHARGE	HELPER	SIDEKICK
COLLEAGUE	HIRED	STAFFER
COMMAND	HIREDHAND	SUPPORT
COMRADE	JOBHOLDER	WORKER
CONVEY	LABORER	
DELIVER	LIFT	
EMPLOYEE	MANAGEMENT	

Puzzle 76

ACCOST
ADDRESS
ALOHA
BELLOW
CLAMOR
COOEE
CURTSY
EXCLAIM
GREET
HAIL
HALLOO

HANDSHAKE
HELLO
HOLLER
HOMAGE
JUMPUPANDDOWN
MEET
OUTCRY
ROAR
SALUTATION
SALUTE
SCREAM

SHOUT
SIGNAL
SINGOUT
SMILEAT
SOOEY
TIPONESHAT
WELCOME
WINKAT
YELL

```
B Q F X H A I M N T K T A G R E A T G J V
Y Y U B Q Z E P O R T L Y H E G C M Y F B
T Q T M S A J J H T Q Y T I S N E M M I Y
I R D C S G C L C O L O S S A L G B W W M
S D O U K W P W I C M X C S S J C N L E O
N Y R T T H D P D M L P L C T R A M K I N
E E V U U N Q U A N T I T Y Q Y K Q D G S
D C O R P N K M U Q T K S T X K L U B H T
H W Y E U R D Z C K U Z I U M J D B Z T R
Z A W K W A R D F H O I M T B T H I C K O
U I Q M V E V T N E T X E A E S M U G L U
D I M E N S I O N F S J Q S G O T F G H S
H H W T O V R E T T A M X Z G N H A M E S
R P R O D I G I O U S H X C P P I O N I T
S M Y M E X O B E S E G N F F B L T Z C J
Y S D F M I J Z F V C E F W M M N E U B E
S L A T U F E C N E L U P R O C B Y M D S
Q L G M L O N N I G G I J R J U E U D F E
S G A J O Y F S X R H Z D Q Q G E N Q K X
J S B T V I J H U A C R Z O V H L S O J C
M R P R G N E W K L D G C I N A T I T Q J
```

Puzzle 77

AWKWARD
BULK
COLOSSAL
CORPULENCE
DENSITY
DIMENSION
EXTENT
GREAT
HEFT
HUGE
IMMENSITY

LARGE
MAGNITUDE
MAMMOTH
MASS
MATTER
MEASURE
MONSTROUS
OBESE
PORTLY
PRODIGIOUS
QUANTITY

ROTUND
SIZE
STOUT
SUBSTANCE
THICK
TITANIC
VOLUME
WEIGHT

```
O C E S S A T I O N C R O S S O U T P K F
T Z W I P L L A C E R N G I C B F C R E F
E P H O T J C O W Z S U J M I T N E N K O
V X T D X A M B D N A M R E T N U O C V Y
N S G K L L K T C A R T E R O W L J G I W
E Z Q K L A D E P K C A B A I C L J L T V
T D E Z B L W G B R L S W T Y P A G Y I P
A J M H D E T A C A V F L O H Z N E F A M
D S H X K M W P A N C W F S H C D D I T E
I T S Z D A W H P N G K F U N A V I L E O
L Q I R O Z I K C U Q Y C P V N O R L K K
A K L E I Q M Q P L H B X E Q C I R U V R
V R B V X J C R P N O B Q R N E D E N O V
N E A E D E E E J C M U R C J L V V P K E
I P T R A G L N P O Q Z Q E B P F O Z C R
N E S S M H A E C X K M Z D A D B W N O I
E A E R U N G X G S P J E U K L U V N Q
G L S V L L D E V G D M N J O U O H W U X
A D I S C H A R G E D D Q S G N A F A H C
T T D L S G I O M U X N T J E D F S F V Q
E U N I T N O C S I D N A R O K H U N I P
```

Puzzle 78

ANNUL
BACKPEDAL
BREAKOFF
CANCEL
CEASE
CESSATION
COUNTERMAND
CROSSOUT
DISCHARGE
DISCONTINUE
DISESTABLISH
INVALIDATE

NEGATE
NULLANDVOID
NULLIFY
OVERRIDE
QUASH
RECALL
RENEGE
RENOUNCE
REPEAL
RETRACT
REVERSE
STOP

SUPERCEDE
TAKEBACK
VACATE
VETO
VITIATE
VOID

```
L K W W T S L H J J E Y G I D L C I I Z Y
A Y V H S U T C E P S O R P A T A Q D P F
S H G C Z H O Z P E B M R J X F D E R E E
O J O E W N O I T P E C N O C X H O D F A
P X A M T Z Y I K M A L E D P X G F K H S
O L L E W A A N O I T A N I M R E T E D P
R B E H U G R D R N X I V M A F C I P E I
P U Q C F C D T K D X A T M J B R U C S R
C V J S L N R A S Z T K P S M E R C A I A
O G I J H O A M W C S K H R S P A E L R T
N D D O K I W B J Q A K E O O L R V C E I
T U P S T T U I H Q R J L S C J T I U E O
E E P Q H A P T D I S U E U E F E T L R N
M Z G Q R T A I S M T I L N N I I C A A T
P O E N K I P O B I M A J W I G P E T E B
L N G Y D G L N O O T L O F L U B J I G T
A Q F M G O A N X E B N P W T R K B O E U
T E J D F C N B R C E O E Z U I Q O N I Q
I G B P P Y D D E S I G N T O N Z G X K V
O W S I V E E T Q N I C L W N G S L X E O
N H E N N F P O T B U Q U G S I T L R I R
```

Puzzle 79

AMBITION	DRAWUPAPLAN	PROGRAM
ASPIRATION	FIGURING	PROJECT
CALCULATE	GOAL	PROPOSAL
CALCULATION	HOPE	PROSPECTUS
COGITATION	IDEA	PURPOSE
CONCEPTION	INTENT	RESOLUTION
CONTEMPLATION	MIND	SCHEME
DEAL	OBJECTIVE	STRATEGY
DESIGN	OUTLINE	
DESIRE	PLAN	
DETERMINATION	POINT	

Puzzle 80

ADDITION
ADVANCE
ASCENSION
ASCENT
BREAKTHROUGH
CATCHUP
CLIMB
CONTINUE
CREATION
DEVELOPMENT
DISCOVERY
ELEVATION

EXPANSION
FURTHERANCE
GAIN
GOAHEAD
GRADUATION
GROWTH
INCREASE
INNOVATION
INVENTION
LOSENOGROUND
MOUNTING
MOVEUP

PRODUCTION
PROGRESS
PROMOTION
REVIVAL
RISE
SCALING
SPREAD
STEPFORWARD
STRIDE
SWELL

```
E  D  O  C  W  I  X  M  C  P  E  B  Y  Q  R  U  Z  F  I  M  O
V  W  N  O  I  T  A  L  U  G  E  R  C  M  U  D  A  J  D  R  Z
I  S  K  P  T  J  V  Q  G  O  X  M  U  Q  L  E  F  I  D  T  M
J  X  W  C  P  U  I  D  D  V  P  J  M  S  E  C  X  E  R  X  B
H  S  O  D  U  X  N  L  M  V  O  Y  U  C  A  R  R  H  L  G  K
R  A  F  P  S  A  Y  C  W  P  G  M  E  X  S  E  H  I  S  R  M
A  L  I  L  M  A  N  D  A  T  E  M  U  H  L  E  M  Z  E  V  N
S  G  Q  M  X  J  D  I  K  S  I  U  B  P  O  P  K  T  X  F  W
Y  W  O  Q  I  N  S  T  R  U  C  T  I  O  N  M  R  C  K  J  B
E  C  A  U  A  J  O  U  O  J  N  C  E  M  B  A  R  G  O  X  O
R  O  S  L  M  E  D  I  T  X  N  I  H  T  H  Z  B  Y  L  X  Q
Q  L  L  T  F  T  N  G  T  I  J  D  F  C  A  R  C  A  X  L  I
M  I  G  E  A  O  P  A  R  I  I  J  B  W  A  T  S  S  O  U  N
B  W  U  P  L  T  Y  P  C  L  B  M  F  E  J  O  C  R  B  T  J
U  G  I  A  U  X  U  D  W  T  H  I  R  C  U  Y  T  I  X  X  U
K  I  D  F  M  M  K  T  O  A  M  J  H  C  N  N  X  D  D  S  N
I  R  E  D  R  N  V  E  E  B  L  E  F  O  O  S  Z  P  T  K  C
O  H  L  J  O  L  Y  W  D  W  V  Y  N  C  R  O  E  I  V  I  T
W  N  I  J  F  U  V  N  B  I  Q  A  B  T  W  P  Q  X  P  R  I
E  C  N  A  N  I  D  R  O  K  C  D  I  R  E  C  T  I  V  E  O
Q  D  E  S  R  E  S  T  R  I  C  T  I  O  N  E  K  E  H  C  N
```

Puzzle 81

BILL
BODYOFLAWS
BYLAW
CANON
CHARTER
CODE
COMMAND
CONTROL
DECREE
DICTATE

DICTUM
DIRECTIVE
EDICT
EMBARGO
ENACTMENT
FORMULA
GOLDENRULE
GUIDELINE
INJUNCTION
INSTRUCTION

MANDATE
MEASURE
ORDER
ORDINANCE
PRINCIPLE
PROHIBITION
REGULATION
RESTRICTION
RULE
STATUTE

```
H  S  I  F  L  E  S  N  U  N  O  C  J  E  V  C  K  J  W  D  W
U  N  S  T  I  N  T  I  N  G  V  V  T  O  G  D  T  N  V  A  P
Z  T  F  K  P  R  O  F  L  I  G  A  T  E  X  P  L  E  D  L  V
U  N  F  Q  X  K  X  Q  V  R  R  W  L  X  O  N  R  I  E  F  Y
F  E  X  M  R  A  T  V  Y  E  O  L  C  P  W  F  V  N  W  H  N
C  D  T  G  N  N  K  T  P  A  G  E  G  T  Z  B  I  V  S  M  S
S  I  N  H  V  M  N  M  G  P  U  X  Q  R  N  T  M  I  H  U  M
K  V  A  F  O  E  E  P  W  C  I  C  Y  C  U  E  V  U  M  O  S
O  O  G  X  L  T  L  R  U  G  S  E  S  D  U  A  L  P  L  U  T
Y  R  A  P  N  N  U  I  Z  N  F  S  E  E  L  S  T  U  O  M  W
L  P  V  I  S  A  F  N  H  I  F  S  E  U  F  U  F  I  P  P  O
C  M  A  L  K  D  I  C  A  R  F  G  F  L  O  E  P  P  S  O  R
L  I  R  A  S  N  T  E  I  E  M  I  O  U  T  O  G  S  S  X  N
A  T  T  G  U  U  N  L  V  D  T  C  S  S  C  F  E  W  P  A  A
R  S  X  I  Q  B  E  Y  M  N  U  D  A  X  T  L  I  A  E  W  T
E  T  E  D  R  A  L  P  U  A  L  W  A  Q  T  O  V  R  H  Y  E
B  E  C  O  E  A  P  O  I  U  I  N  A  I  G  K  U  Y  H  Z  V
I  R  A  R  N  Z  B  T  L  Q  R  M  M  V  R  C  K  I  B  T  Y
L  B  K  P  E  H  N  Y  N  S  P  I  L  E  I  Y  E  Q  E  A  F
Q  K  G  L  G  G  K  T  S  L  L  N  J  P  R  D  M  U  B  B  Y
M  A  H  I  V  A  Z  C  E  D  G  D  E  D  N  A  H  N  E  P  O
```

Puzzle 82

ABUNDANT	LAVISH	PRODIGAL
AMPLE	LIBERAL	PROFLIGATE
BOUNTIFUL	LIMITLESS	SQUANDERING
COPIOUS	MYRIAD	SUMPTUOUS
EPICUREAN	OPENHANDED	SYBARITIC
EXCESS	OPULENT	THRIFTLESS
EXCESSIVE	ORNATE	UNSELFISH
EXTRAVAGANT	PLENITUDE	UNSTINTING
GENEROUS	PLENTIFUL	WASTEFUL
IMPROVIDENT	PLENTY	WILD
INTEMPERATE	PRINCELY	

Tricky

```
K W S U N T B I B X V L Z A A D P K C T L I S
Y L G Y Z D T N A T I S E H A N Z B O N U S E
F F O K A E R B S C G C T W M F D I N A N M M
L H C N H S P A B C I F P U W V E D S V N I M
U A A T E K U C U U L L N V O L I F I R A N A
F S G L P D S O A G A Y N N A C R G D E Y D L
H M U Q T L M W I V N I W D B E R O E S E F E
C T A O N Q K H E T T O E C V H O A R B V U R
T C R Z T H O E M K U P O V Q S W X A O T L T
A E D B J I G E P X K A S S M A R T T W A R Y
W P E B O L C D M C P V C H K Q N B E E O J T
A S D D R U N I A E W D X E I Q O A H V V U H
H M U U A F I B L P B U T F Y M B U A I N D O
Y U D W H E N D T O V M P R U D E N T T H I U
C C A P P R E H E N S I V E Z O L E Q N G C G
Q R I Z H A E G R N W F E P I L O W C E I I H
E I Q H V C Q G K E R D I S C R E E T T Q O T
T C J B N W Y V A Z C E X L Z P I M I T Z U F
W C Y S A U E O V R S O C S K G Y L Y A B S U
N H T N R H U Z P L D V I N M V O E T Y W C L
D A V P Y Z S E L U M F X Y O P Y Q E A L E J
I R V J P Y K G K D J Q U B D C Y A P Z V A H
F Y A M U M F J Q K P V B L H Z R Y P X H H N
```

Puzzle 83

ALERT	CONCERNED	ONGUARD
APPREHENSIVE	CONSIDERATE	POLITIC
ATTENTIVE	DISCREET	PRUDENT
AWAKE	GUARDED	REGARDFUL
AWARE	HALT	SOLICITOUS
CANNY	HEED	THOUGHTFUL
CAREFUL	HESITANT	VIGILANT
CAUTIOUS	JUDICIOUS	WARY
CHARY	MINDFUL	WATCHFUL
CIRCUMSPECT	OBSERVANT	WORRIED

```
M Y T E V O W E C P U O Q S F J K F U M X P L
R U Z Y U G E J O H X I S Y T H G I E X Z P R
F G Q S N Z X S D G U Y D W P E X T S S R N U
D O X I N B Y I E W D C H I J A C B T Z G H H
M G L W J F C T V F H A K L J V P R O J E C T
T S L H T H R K I E G P R R V E E E B U X J X
O B Z T B I M O H J W N G T F W T R U P S X V
S F H H D N E S R E T T A C S M S O H N S G X
C I G O Q R E O F C Z G X G S W L E P O R P P
P K F T O S S O U T W B C N T H O W F G I Y V
O A M R E T T A P S G F U I Y I O N S T K W A
C F N G M J P H Q S H M B L P C G O C L P V C
Z J S L U W C M B S U D D F B N A H T X R C V
S S G D Y N I M P E R K D M P E I S S D J D J
X W Q T U L P V R R M A G U C C X L T G A M V
P L T A H O C O I S B U J F B G O Z R E M O B
C O L L M C O T S P O I Z S Y U X B R L S W I
Q H U W K D N U J R G A P X G J H P S O S X V
J L P U R T S P G I C R R H H N S S F G A A H
S Y A Y N T H E L N F H M A Z U M L A J E R K
J J T H R O W Z K K I G M Q E Z I L W D N K H
Z M A N U D S F E L S T N Y P R H G A P I Q V
H O C Q J O J A G E H A T A T Y L F T E L K H
```

Puzzle 84

CAST	HURL	SLOUGH
CATAPULT	JERK	SPATTER
CHUCK	LAUNCH	SPREAD
DART	LETFLY	SPRINKLE
DASH	PITCH	SPURT
EIGHTYSIX	PROJECT	STREW
EJECT	PROPEL	THROW
FLING	SCATTER	TOSSOUT
FLIRT	SEND	
GETRIDOF	SHOOT	
HEAVE	SLING	

```
G Y L V U A C N Z Z D L U E F S H P X Y H M V
L G V X G M I Q M I H N M Y T I R A H C Y Z E
Y T I U T A R G S V S L N S Z A C V S P T P I
A V Z W K W S D Z E V K H D I Z N H S E I E N
P T A B G U E B L T R O V A F U Q O S N N C O
J L G E L N T F I G D V T T V P R F D O G N I
J B E P V A I H R O T S I Q A B V T S I I E T
Y O C H M S E V U E E K R C E O R C L T N C U
T N Q Q H Z T C I U L W L S E E S Z J A E I B
I U V O F K E S Q G D I T I F P M X W L B F I
N S A H Q U Q E E R T O E F B D Q O G B G I R
A W H F R G B X P P W T O F E E Y B M O R N T
M I M U X F A C A Y X V V T T P R X U A A U N
U D N I K L A U G P W A R L A K C A D I N M O
H Z Z I M D F T A F T A C D R Q I W L B T N C
E Y Q B O C R G N A E N G E N E R O S I T Y K
O X S L C O N L V H N B E O J J S L K S T L F
J L E E X Z N K G J P R O S O X A M F F N Y C
O D O V T U Z I F Q J D U U E D L I L T B C F
I X U V W R B R N B L E S S N R W L F A L L B
Z L W S E E U Q Z P P B H P H T P I R V R L C
I O D E P G F O F K N R C R I Z Y D L H Q O J
A K S U Z P C C C O J P R E Z V X E R L T W D
```

Puzzle 85

AGAPE	CONTRIBUTION	HUMANITY
ALMS	COURTESY	KIND
GIVING	DOLE	LIBERALITY
ALTRUISM	DONATE	LOVE
BENIGNITY	DOUCEUR	MUNIFICENCE
BEQUEST	FAVOR	OBLATION
BESTOW	GENEROSITY	OFFER
BIGHEARTED	GIFT	PLUS
BLESS	GOODWILL	PRESENT
BONUS	GRANT	RELIEF
BOUNTY	GRATUITY	SERVICE
CHARITY	HELP	UNSELFISH

```
B D Q G K K O H A V C E V C C T E C K Z F U X
F O O Q O K G W B X F G Z I E Q J E L K Y Q M
Y M K K S U T T S B J Y T Y N X P A V R N K A
R R U F A T K C A S P S E H T I L B R X W L U
F N E L L R N M O M I R T H F U L E G H X U G
I I K E I Q I A V M E O T Y H P M U N A R D R
N Y N P H A Q Q I T C P W O N Y X J I P B J Z
B B Z G B C M T A R Q Z X L C U C S O P J S K
Y J N L O Q P L D E B O N A I R E F G Y U C D
Y L E W G O E K P O S I T I V E E U Y G F Q O
D S L P V Z D E I Z W L L V L U R N S O J U U
F F A O Z V Q S I X D B U O M Z F C A L S H L
N T C E J C Y U P R W E I J U E E O E U L A L
S J W E D Q Y H R I J A R W G Y R P K C U P A
U U R M S N Z A Y K R E X U L T A N T K F P I
O B N N A C A M R Y P I X I T M C H T Y E Y V
I I G N M X T E R I G S T B E A M L N Z E A I
R L U H Y O Y I E I J Z A S A I N Q A Z L S V
A A X B G I A I Q R H D R J N D Q D Y J G A N
L N O H G L V M N P F R I E N D L Y O Y M L O
I T T P R H W S L A I N E G V O B G U O N A C
H F J B G M D O A T R E J O I C E V B L G R S
L I G H T H E A R T E D Y Z E E R B D V K K G
```

Puzzle 86

AIRY
AMIABLE
BEAM
BLITHE
BREEZY
BUOYANT
CAREFREE
CHEERY
CONVIVIAL
DEBONAIR
EASYGOING
ELATE
EXULTANT

FREEANDEASY
FRIENDLY
GENIAL
GLEEFUL
GOODNATURED
HAPPYASALARK
HAPPYGOLUCKY
HILARIOUS
INGOODSPIRITS
JOLLY
JOVIAL
JOYFUL
JUBILANT

LAUGH
LIGHTHEARTED
MERRY
MIRTHFUL
OPTIMISTIC
POSITIVE
REJOICE
RIANT
SUNNY

```
F V F Z M F W T M P X U N Z T M N D I M Y T P
M I A L C O R P I H E Z H N N Z V U B F E I P
P C E D U E A P W U T V H Y E D U U S R S M S
N T Q E V T M B V Y R I W N V D S T C E R E P
J U G C P E T S U R F B R O L T S C K D E J R
A O D L W C R E H R G E D N R A G A U N P Q E
H E R A L D W T R B P R H E C D L L D A S W A
E V I R A E I Q I O N U W D L Q O I G E R F D
L I S E P D D S R S T M A I Z L S R O M E L S
X G P L V R F T P W E O P P I T N W S O T E C
U Y D H A P H L F E R R U T R T N C L R N N F
C I R C U L A T E B R M V I L C E X A D I W S
Q Q A V Z O I M C C K S B R J L Q V O S E O B
U L X J Q B E I Z W R U E J N V E U J A O N V
P E R Q A S W Z R E T T A C S L T G C X S K S
B J Y E Q M H S S E X Q J U E T L W J O B E P
U Y T Q W R M A C A H M P Z Q C Z A H C C K F
L E E I T C A F Q L Q G R R F O N Q E F N A R
Y B L A Z O N X N J U E H S I L B U P A U M I
A L L X W T E Y F Y N O I S E A B R O A D A S
P R O M U L G A T E K N H V E S R B X N Q P S
G F P U B L I C I Z E W O U T F Z O T T N W U
X N M L T P A Y K V W P E V E M A N A T E A E
```

Puzzle 87

ADVERTISE	GIVEOUT	REPORT
ANNOUNCE	HERALD	RUMOR
BESTREW	INTERSPERSE	SCATTER
BLAZON	ISSUE	SENDOUT
BROADCAST	MAKEKNOWN	SPREAD
BRUIT	MEANDER	STREW
CIRCULATE	NOISEABROAD	TELL
DECLARE	PLACARD	TRAVEL
DISPERSE	PROCLAIM	UTTER
DISTRIBUTE	PROMULGATE	VENT
EMANATE	PUBLICIZE	
EMIT	PUBLISH	

```
R Z J T C W G O A C Z B A U N I T E K G I S F
U K X S O K N U T C O Y F F F J B F N P D Y W
O U L N U P K T Q B K M D Q Q Q A L L M Y N X
F B M E P G E B W E G M P H L Q K G E H N T V
W W M Z L U S N N E G N U O N T N T M N T H G
S C Q O E B E L B M A R C S S L I D K X D E B
C P Y Q C U M I H E I A G I V E L C M K O S B
C T A I P Y E U I P K Y E J P L V I T C X I E
V O C I X I W S J G Y T W F H Y O L L A Q Z N
Y X R K R S W V J L V F R I N B U T X Y N E O
I O B R J U C O M P O U N D I M D F G J R N I
C E S E E C P J S E Y T C K P G Q I H I X C S
C O K X F L L T F H Y Z P T N P G X S Y R O U
O B I I C N A W Q C K X O V N K H J J L S M F
N N V U P P O T M A N G E I R E K J G Z Y M O
S X U T C P G C E T E M U L L I N T F R M I X
O S R G R I A J U T G T A U G K W U M R X X A
L S M J E O G R H A U E D T R N B I H O R D P
I B P S S M Y E T G M E R G E F I O D O M J Q
D I S T K C R J N N C O N N E C T M Z I R C A
A N D W H I O F T N E F Q P S J V T X J E V E
T D E I J I L R Z E V R R G Z M T R M A T C H
E V O N N C Y Z C Y A L E K O Y H M G X Q R B
```

Puzzle 88

ADMIX	COUPLE	PAIRUP
ALLOY	FUSION	PARTNER
ATTACH	INTERMIX	SCRAMBLE
BIND	JOIN	SYNTHESIZE
BLEND	JUMBLE	TWIN
COMBO	LEVIGATE	UNITE
COMMIX	LINK	YOKE
COMPOSE	LUMPTOGETHER	
COMPOUND	MATCH	
CONNECT	MATE	
CONSOLIDATE	MERGE	
CORRELATE	MINGLE	

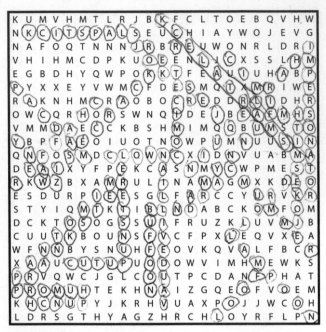

Puzzle 89

BUFFOON
CARD
CHAFFER
CLOWN
COMEDIAN
COMIC
CUTUP
DROLL
FOOL
FUNNYMAN

HARLEQUIN
HUMOR
IMPERSONATOR
JESTER
JOKER
JOKESMITH
LAMPOON
MADCAP
MIMIC
MUMMER

PANTOMIME
PRANKSTER
PUNCH
PUNSTER
SLAPSTICK
SMARTALECK
VAUDEVILLIAN
WISECRACKER
ZANY

```
N O K X T A G F B F W T T R A Z H Z L R A
U Q F T I B I H O R P Q K B E X N L G Z J
H S S A T S M Q G Y O R Z T W H E L I X E
H O X P D I B R O F M Y O A N U T N R N E
C Z B O V T Y M U R I S Z S Q Z T O L U D
U L D T W S Y Y W A T D X E C E W S M T U
H Z C E J D Z O F R E O O E R R H I H S L
Y S P V S E L A A N T C D D Q U I R H A C
F S A G M L L C Y T M U I R T C O B X H E
I G H U A T I E D D L C Z O L W H L E U R
L A W S Q Z L X P C T H U A O C O D Q B P
A W I H E C I C X X W T N U P B U P H L I
U D X E T A G E R G E S T X K N H T X A W
Q S K R U O N P H S I N A B P V Q Q B C A
S I I P U D W T P M U M T Z R X K O J K L
I V K O D O B R L D J H T C C T O Y I B T
D C I Z P E A U E U S H I L E Q R C G A U
H S Y B J T A B S F B D B H T J K O Z L O
S T Y H T S A J Q H B U R O I O E R P L J
U W X U T R C A L P H X O J U R C R O E C
E X C O M M U N I C A T E T Y O K Z D A D
```

Puzzle 90

BANISH	EXPEL	QUELL
BLACKBALL	FORBID	REJECT
DEBAR	INTERDICT	SEGREGATE
DENY	KICKOUT	SHUTOUT
DEPORT	OMIT	SMOTHER
DISALLOW	OSTRACIZE	SUBDUE
DISQUALIFY	OUTLAW	TABOO
EXCEPT	PRECLUDE	THROWOUT
EXCLUDE	PROHIBIT	VETO
EXCOMMUNICATE	PROSCRIBE	
EXILE	QUASH	

```
J  L  C  Q  O  R  K  E  H  P  K  R  H  H  S  I  V  A  L  E  V
K  K  T  P  S  A  T  Y  V  E  T  U  B  I  R  T  S  I  D  T  U
T  L  T  B  W  A  D  J  O  R  F  U  E  F  I  L  L  V  N  U  D
R  A  A  H  N  J  R  F  Z  J  E  T  S  A  N  Y  O  H  O  B  E
E  U  T  O  L  J  O  C  A  H  K  S  T  U  V  E  P  F  I  I  O
T  T  D  F  B  J  F  Y  O  Q  S  K  O  C  E  E  M  K  S  R  L
A  C  U  W  K  Q  F  A  I  O  Y  F  W  Q  S  R  T  D  I  T  Z
C  I  I  P  I  E  A  X  D  B  B  T  I  F  T  U  O  V  V  N  I
Q  V  H  A  R  A  T  U  H  M  M  J  W  H  J  S  E  W  O  O  D
I  Y  A  D  T  O  G  A  W  E  I  C  I  U  S  M  S  X  R  C  T
X  W  P  Y  X  I  V  G  D  K  T  N  J  L  L  I  E  W  P  Z  K
Z  P  P  U  R  U  I  E  A  O  J  I  I  E  W  P  N  D  Y  G  Q
P  I  O  D  P  V  Y  H  N  H  M  R  T  S  L  G  L  R  P  U  X
E  U  I  J  E  D  L  Q  P  D  Y  M  G  O  T  N  C  Q  U  B  E
D  Q  N  Y  N  A  P  H  R  R  E  Q  O  P  P  E  L  B  B  F  D
I  E  T  E  S  C  P  L  E  O  S  R  L  C  L  X  R  G  B  B  C
V  A  X  V  T  C  U  Q  S  E  E  T  M  E  C  N  D  R  V  N  A
O  N  N  R  O  O  S  F  E  F  R  B  O  Q  I  A  R  P  U  E  I
R  A  Q  U  R  R  X  P  N  A  I  S  R  C  D  E  A  A  Y  K  X
P  V  E  P  E  D  F  O  T  X  E  K  B  B  K  I  W  X  A  Z  R
J  I  Q  G  M  U  C  K  X  C  J  Y  T  U  O  L  A  E  D  Q  B
```

Puzzle 91

ACCOMMODATE	DISTRIBUTE	PROVENDER
ACCORD	DONATE	PROVIDE
ADMINISTER	EQUIP	PROVISION
AFFORD	FILL	PURVEY
APPOINT	FURNISH	SERVE
AWARD	GIRD	STOCK
BESTOW	GIVE	STORE
CATER	INVEST	SUPPLY
CONFER	LAVISH	VICTUAL
CONTRIBUTE	OUTFIT	
DEALOUT	PRESENT	

```
V  S  I  S  F  B  S  F  Q  A  D  S  S  T  R  A  G  S  J  Y  O
D  R  C  G  B  K  G  P  M  X  D  B  E  T  E  E  O  Y  F  B  D
T  W  O  B  R  O  R  Y  L  I  M  I  R  J  A  L  T  E  X  R  F
K  A  A  O  M  E  E  E  Z  A  U  Z  T  U  K  R  D  S  D  Q  A
D  J  G  C  R  S  G  E  Q  Q  G  U  H  D  T  N  T  G  E  K  P
G  E  Y  L  U  M  G  D  S  N  C  U  E  A  C  R  T  O  L  P  N
B  T  J  A  K  C  R  I  A  G  N  J  E  C  E  E  E  Q  W  H  E
S  A  C  D  N  X  D  I  G  B  P  Y  R  T  L  U  K  P  W  K  O
S  V  R  Z  T  E  O  Y  F  W  X  X  C  U  T  I  D  U  O  U  O
E  A  M  D  R  U  H  X  C  Z  G  X  W  A  T  H  J  V  H  Z  X
R  R  A  P  B  J  N  T  L  U  Y  K  I  T  E  A  O  O  J  X  X
T  G  N  A  T  R  M  J  N  Z  H  N  Q  E  N  R  H  R  G  E  C
S  G  E  V  C  H  A  F  E  E  S  D  R  V  P  A  A  E  P  F  E
I  A  A  M  A  D  D  E  N  T  M  G  U  F  Y  S  V  G  Q  N  B
D  V  E  S  N  E  C  N  I  R  S  R  E  F  D  S  G  N  R  D  D
C  E  N  W  W  H  P  G  U  O  H  N  O  R  W  J  R  A  X  B  N
H  J  D  X  E  M  A  Q  H  M  E  M  Q  T  U  B  G  P  O  K  E
O  V  M  C  Y  T  T  M  O  S  W  E  T  A  R  E  N  E  G  D  F
Y  X  T  M  E  E  C  Q  I  M  W  R  F  C  S  S  E  U  U  S  F
I  O  W  N  H  Y  A  A  X  V  I  X  G  C  Z  W  W  V  U  Q  O
R  W  I  N  F  U  R  I  A  T  E  F  F  E  C  T  E  Q  Z  K  T
```

Puzzle 92

ACTUATE	ENRAGE	NETTLE
AGGRAVATE	EXASPERATE	OFFEND
ANGER	GENERATE	OUTRAGE
BADGER	GOAD	PERTURB
CAUSE	HARASS	PESTER
CHAFE	HECTOR	PLAGUE
DEFY	INCENSE	POKERAISE
DISQUIET	INFURIATE	START
DISTRESS	INITIATE	TORMENT
DISTURB	INSTIGATE	PROVOKE
EFFECT	MADDEN	

```
C E T K N C F U L Q B Z I W D F L P M R Y
Y M R H P Q G Z O L X F Q G C U Y N Z S N
U W E I I R R S T A E K X M T S W A O N K
C R T K Z R U R E X P Y O Y Q S N E N X V
G S T C C C N X U G U C P B Q R E B B A J
Y U A L S T N C T G O R O L O N P T E K F
J P L A Q I K S L R N Y X G W O H F W R Q
K M C M Y E A G W A A I F T U A G Z O D E
J U L O I Z N L Y G N N L H V L R L A I Q
G R S R V B Z L R B B G K L L B I B T S E
H F H T O M K A I O J Q O C A C V F O T T
G S L N I Y O B A W L C T R R U S S I U F
K N E T U R B U L E N C E U O C Q K R R C
R B I L O C Y Z H W C T Z C R A L S T B M
B P S T C T H V O E Z E V E E M W D R A E
S L G G U U H L O E W K E N L W O W B N L
G S U F Y O F E T L Y C U O L W O I X C T
E H U S W E H N I B H A B I O K C L L E T
N P W L T C D S N B I R X S H K G I L T A
A C T U L E I G G A Q Y F E L Q E A X E R
G O Z X R J R Q X B Y C V W T U O W O L B
```

Puzzle 93

BABBLE	FROLIC	SCREECH
BAWL	FUSS	SHOUTING
BELLOW	HOLLER	SHRIEK
BLOWOUT	HOOTING	SQUALLING
BLUSTER	HOWL	STIR
BRATTLE	JABBER	TURBULENCE
BRAWL	NOISE	TURMOIL
CLAMOR	OUTCRY	UPROAR
CLANGOR	RACKET	WAIL
CLATTER	RIOT	YELL
CRYING	ROAR	
DISTURBANCE	RUMPUS	

```
P D P V T U W U Z Q R K S F S Y V E Y W G
F V F B E R S M I E D I W H W C T E P Z U
I U E E L C F Z N R H W C E D S B S W E P
B J U V B E L T C B N N G Y T P J V J O
R Y N W A R B U L Q A I S J A R C I Y E W
O V I O M S P G U T S F O I K O S Q A D E
U M T N E T O P S F W E L L K N I T I Z R
S U B R O A D T I C E D I G E G N R G D F
D S L T J L V E V U I U D T O H O O Y D U
B C H E C W Y C E S U T X I P N Z T Q E L
T U O T S A X C S C J E E S L M F N A G R
N L E N X R O D Y L Q W T L G E L B F G C
Y A N J W T T P R Q Y U N N H H Y F C U M
L R Q H Y T H G I M R V I A C T Z M C R Y
Q G T B A T Y V W D E P M N E J A H I N D
N Z O Y V X J U Y S P K R U M L U F H B E
E O E N C C A S G A O A H P Z S U I D K Y
G J H T H E W Y R B F O L P K U K C A L O
Q H E P T H Z T P P I P T Y Z J Z U R X D
H C N U A T S X Z H G U O T P R V U R E U
N A F A A A D G P P B I W I X X B J M U H
```

Puzzle 94

ABLE	INCLUSIVE	STAUNCH
ATHLETIC	IRON	STOUT
BRAWNY	MIGHTY	STRAPPING
BROAD	MUSCULAR	STRONG
BURLY	POTENT	STURDY
EXTENSIVE	POWERFUL	THEWY
FIBROUS	RUGGED	TOUGH
FIRM	SINEWY	WELLKNIT
HEFTY	SOLID	WIDE
HERCULEAN	STALWART	WIRY
HUSKY	STANCH	

```
W G R D R D S Q Y Y W Y Z E B Z O G I I C
B K A D I J T E L O I V A R T L U I T R H
O A Y S F E G F R N R E P A T V N A D C U
P I C K L E B S I G N A L F H F L V X T S
P Y G E E A Z O P R Y V I E R L L I G H T
Z Y Y G K G M U L D H L V A O U F Z T C L
R Y W V X T A P P G A A R W F X F T E C A
I F R E Z U L G X M T E M S L S N E L A S
L N Y A C R B C E X D P M B B R E W P N A
L O E R N N U N B L U B A A D D J A M D T
U R R E Q I T L T V R N A F M O E A A L J
M G U I Z N M Y L S A N Z C L O Y X L E J
I C T L H D J U E N R E T N A L A M P A D
N G X O F I P W L B A O I V T F L V M Q V
A A I S L C L V A C U U M T U B E M G X U
N S F A D A F H V U D B R O V X P G Y L Z
T J S G H T G L X T U L E O L D E N Q Z W
B E A R Q O A F A N Y C H A N D E L I E R
J T G K M R S R I R F H H D C D I G V D L
H C R O T C I R T C E L E Y G O N T Q M D
Z W A L L W A S H E R A F R E O N T U B E
```

Puzzle 95

BEACON	GASLAMP	RIFLE
BULB	GASOLIER	SIGNAL
CANDLE	GLOBE	TAILLIGHT
CHANDELIER	ILLUMINANT	TALLOW
ELECTRICTORCH	INFRARED	TAPER
FILAMENT	LAMPAD	TUBE
FLARE	LAMPLET	TURNINDICATOR
FLOOD	LANTERN	ULTRAVIOLET
FREONTUBE	LIGHT	VACUUMTUBE
GASFIXTURE	LUMINARY	WALLWASHER
GASJET	PICKLE	

```
X E P X V E J T U E Q W E V A L S N E A U
S U T A M Q V R R T N R J S I A Z D K I T
R Q M A D H I O C A A I U R N D Z E L P G
Q P K E U H Y A L Z N Y H V K Z K J C M K
E R U L G T R P S H V S M R D U E F K Z S
Y W I D X T A G N W N E P E A T A T N D W
B E W I T C H F S O N N L O A L B U N S F
E V I A C T M Z N I T I A V R T L R N V P
R Z T N A H C N E I G I I L Z T V N V N A
A W A T R N F K W H W T Z S J E E O X R P
N J B N R X J G T Z P Q E E B E M N W A V
S G U T Y Q Q N Y A R D X S Q Z D E S A R
X R O M A N E N C D U B O P E I Y S Q E J
D G X N W M Q L G C Y D J N T R Z H R Z E
A R R I A V T I F R F I R J A E N E Q I H
W P V N Y A W C X A I A C E N M X A U L D
D J N F Y N L S A O P X T C I S Q D X A A
W K O L M Y V I R T C O R H C E X O A T Z
S Z V A C P V J U R C M R A S M F Y P N Z
N C O M L R R R U W S H L R A V I S H A L
J N P E B M E I T Z I C K M F E W T H T E
```

Puzzle 96

ATTRACT	ENCHANT	MESMERIZE
BECHARM	ENRAPTURE	RAVISH
BEWITCH	ENSLAVE	SEDUCE
CAPTIVATE	ENTHRALL	SNARE
CARRYAWAY	FASCINATE	TANTALIZE
CATCH	HYPNOTIZE	TRANSPORT
CHARM	INFATUATE	TURNONESHEAD
DAZZLE	INFLAME	VAMP
DELIGHT	LOVE	
ENAMOR	LURE	

Tough

```
M D N A E Z B A L M O E P I U U T W B I Y
X R O O I K A N L J B C F X A E C Y L A T
E V L J Y N I E E C L W A E W Z A D G S Y
V E T I Q A J O T K I F D R J I X N P P X
O S R N M S L P X T G Z S O D R E I C T G
E N M C A P E B C N A L P C M O L O T P C
A K U C E R O U C T T E B T F H G J G N W
K T A Q B D R S K M E P R A F T P N H D K
P P N M H T I A E M Z M K J L U J E L W L
L Y H I S E J V W U L O F L S A T V R Y L
N T D N O A A L H S P C I U U Q H E L B E
E U I S L P S M L I O O U V M K D K I T E
G D M E E X P Y C F Z F N P M R D N A R F
R R E R F G B A Z G P S X E O Z B N I A D
A F G N O P U T C I L F N I N U G U C R N
H E B I R C S E R P M I O U F I Q L I I A
C G B R C F Z N L K J A J F S E V V J R M
F R Y G E V W A G U O K O E R E W U Y D E
E R U J D A C C O H R O D L E T A T C I D
A S S I G N K T L B N O U U F K A D W X E
U Y C T C E R I D H V G D N A M M O C S Z
```

Puzzle 97

ADJURE
APPOINT
ASSIGN
AUTHORIZE
CHARGE
COMMAND
COMPEL
DECREE
DEMAND
DESIGNATE
DICTATE

DIRECT
ENACT
ENJOIN
EXACT
FORCE
GIVEORDERS
IMPOSEUPON
INFLICTUPON
INSTRUCT
LAYON
MAKE

OBLIGATE
ORDER
PRESCRIBE
REQUIRE
RULE
SUBPOENA
SUMMON
TELL
WARRANT

```
G N T G G E N I L T U O A D O N G G P M Z
K N O I N Q I B L U Z J M E N L L C A C U
G S I I N I G O U J H L Z X O N U V G I F
N R K C T N K S Y S T E M O T D A P U C I
I D R E H C D C G D E V M U Z D N T U N G
T P E H L J U S A L U P V V U H E Z U E U
N S H L W E G R X B P K T A O P A S P R R
U B C Y F M T L T A E I F U O N X A I Q E
O T Y H S G D O M S Y D S E S W H E A G M
M E J K E I G R N R N I U I T S Y B N Q N
O M Z T R M Q L W X N O U T S A B I P U S
L P D U U D E U Y G J I C F I S T E H I T
K E D Y O C M W E Y U D L A U I A S S A R
B R Y I T F D D Y C R X B T E B T H C P U
Q A M G N P X Z N K E V D S M L O A C A C
T M O E O L B I Z Q D M W B A F O V D A T
P E T H C M O O D Z R C C O K B U I L D U
U N A X U Y S B D W O A R D E Y R D O C R
H T N W E L A Q Q Q B S T Y D G S U M Z E
F R A M E V L C B I O E Q G S T M N B T B
I O Y S D I C D I S P O S I T I O N F I P
```

Puzzle 98

ANATOMY	FIGURE	SETTING
ATTITUDE	FRAME	SHAPE
BACKING	HOUSING	SKELETON
BODY	MAKE	STATE
BORDER	MOLD	STRUCTURE
BUILD	MOOD	SYSTEM
CASE	MOUNTING	TEMPERAMENT
CHASSIS	NATURE	CONSTRUCTION
CONTOUR	OUTLINE	HULL
DESIGN	PHYSIQUE	
DISPOSITION	SCHEME	

```
R T X M U D U W W H S U L B R K U S G B R
E B T W M I N N G B F S V R U O S H Y C C
K G D S P A R K L E G L E A M J L M E G V
C R E J O P J X V A Z R W N Z Q Y O L A U
I E T C Y U L E K G M V A R T R K I C J T
L D A I F E R V O R M P R D E H M H I O E
F L M S N F I R E W P M M T I M G P O C U
O O I J X G R O G O L S T U E A Y I N H N
K M N G N L L T K L G I H R X T N E R S O
H S A Y H B Y E F G L Z B S I D C C H B I
G K Q B W T A K P G X L H S J S R I E F T
G V Z L C S F N W V O I N G E Y M K J J A
I E V W V L K G T O N E V B T M X J A A I
D E Z I U F L A M E T W U S E O T S U G D
K H J S V A O L W N F R C R B I Y U J H A
E M H D E I U I I Y L V B Q N Q B A K N R
I J R W K C D Q G Y F E K P U I W U P S W
C D W M L N F N K B X U Z E Q C Z J R W C
E S S S E N H S E R F M D A A Y A K W N P
Y U J Y O W O O B S B P R S E G U A C A A
C L K H Y I Y H V X S R U G J T E Z C W T
```

Puzzle 99

ANIMATED	FLUSH	RADIANCE
BLOOM	FRESHNESS	RADIATION
BLUSH	GLEAM	RUBESCENCE
BRIGHTNESS	GLIMMER	SHIMMER
BURN	GLITTER	SHINE
COLOR	GLOW	SMOLDER
FERVOR	GUSTO	SPARKLE
FEVER	HEAT	TINGLE
FIRE	INTENSITY	VIVIDNESS
FLAME	LAMP	WARMTH
FLICKER	LIGHT	

```
C B K N A Z H G B Y U T Y R T G U I D E L
N E C L V W U D F U D H B W E H P C M Y X
R I D N A M M O C T Y I O U H H L F O T T
E U T N A D N E T T A K R N I A S C V I D
T S L R K L V T N J E L A E C R O U N F D
T L T B W F C I J Y F U O M C U E C Q R Q
A T B G W U Y T S W K D A R N T V E E O E
P N J Q D T F O X O L P B S T F P H T L Y
N X Z N F W V S V Y R U E O Y N P M D S S
K B O G U D V J C N T L C H Z E O N E A D
D C Y H G U B C Y L O E B P H T A C L C H
R G P Q D A R L E R L C G S G H K T E C E
Q U Q O I L T R I P L E D O M G R O S O J
Z Z L O G J E E M A R S H A L T F L L M N
M G P E A G U A K T R O C S F F A I S P D
L O S J U I X D M E W A N L A A A P S A C
N C N L I E B Z N U E L P U M C Y D Z N C
C E A I R O T N E M F P C T P H O W E Y I
W T A M T G Q L C K Z N E T A E D Z Y R J
E S U I T O I A W D Y Z W R O R Z N M Y N
O K C F W Z R T I M B G A K H J K A L T G
```

Puzzle 100

ACCOMPANY
ADVISOR
ATTENDANT
BUTLER
COMMAND
CONDUCT
CONTROL
CONVOY
COUNSELOR
DIRECT

ESCORT
EXAMPLE
GATEKEEPER
GUIDE
HANDLE
LEADER
MARSHAL
MENTOR
MODEL
MONITOR

PATTERN
PILOT
REGULATE
RULE
SHEPHERD
STEER
TEACHER
USHER

```
D A O L P Q D X F V Q B T B D W P M B J X
B P Y G G J J G P Y C E O L A I O F F U B
P Q R Y D B T F D V N L Y U Z A G L E A M
L U T V S S E N T H G I R B Z J L X G H R
E U M N E S V E K Y A D I X L K K E G S B
N D C I J V U C C P R E M M I H S F K I R
E A Q E C S Z E R N A M C Z N K I X Q L I
G H H E N E U C Z T A R B M G N B O O O L
E E O N W T X N N V A H W J E J P R S P L
C V K C E G L A Z E P P N S T X M G U D I
U A M C T J I G J E F O S E C C R G X Y A
V H J C N D G E F N P E E R J A E Z V R N
I S S O A Y C L L E V Y Z Q H W S F E U C
L R O R L E X E N A C V I E Q K H T R R E
H B K R I S X I X U A Y B Q E C S H I E B
G C N E T P F R E T S U L S F J I T V R P
Z V K C U E S U P W R G L O S S N O N A N
C O H T R N W H L N E H W Q C S R O Q L E
L F W P I Y Z V I N R K M B X P A M G G E
L D V T P L U S F N H F Q T M L V S X L H
A F M M X Y H J J J V E U D I J F Z E Z B S
```

Puzzle 101

AGLEAM	GLARE	POLISH
BRIGHTNESS	GLAZE	PUMICE
BRILLIANCE	GLEAM	RADIANT
BUFF	GLOSS	REFINE
BURNISH	GLOW	RUTILANT
CORRECT	IMPROVE	SHEEN
DAZZLING	IRRADIANT	SHIMMER
ELEGANCE	LUCENT	SHINE
ENHANCE	LUSTER	SMOOTH
FINESSE	PERFECT	VARNISH

```
G L T N F Z S M T P J Q V J L Z S C J Y D
F Z V K C W H G V F F F O W O H S P F E W
F Q S U O P M O P V X N Q N S G A J X T A
M C A X G C E U A M I A J U J R J V A G P
W G H D D T E I R R T I C W A B F W I Q X
J C Z L A Y N T T D E T B D S V L B F W T
I N O L Q G R R R N E G E R M C K M F E V
J N F N L Z E U H E A H G E D L M Y T M Y
G N V O C Z F M K R T G T A A F T I C T B
I T R I D E J P U U X S O T W U K F H Y X
Z Y I J B S I E R H F G U R A S D G F K O
H Y K C O C U T S S Q A M L R E U U W Y D
S M V M J G S R E T S I O R B A B R E Y A
B B F K L C K L K M O L T E H R U V G O V
K P U D E F F U P V A U N T A H W P V T A
G H C R B P B S Z O F D S G J O G T H R R
R H V U R E M B L A Z O N A W T P G F T B
D F L A U N T F L S H A U P O A Y R S J R
R Q I W S A O I T J O N E X U I E A O F K
A S F O H C U M E K A M H G E R O M Y U W
E D H T D Y N M B E A R Z W L B K E M B D
```

Puzzle 102

ARROGANT	HAUGHTY	SHOWOFF
BEATTHEDRUM	HOTAIR	SKITE
BLUSTER	INFLATE	STRUT
BOAST	MAKEMUCHOF	SWAGGER
BRAG	PARADE	TALKBIG
BRAVADO	POMPOUS	TRUMPET
COCKY	PROUD	VAINGLORY
CONCEIT	PUFFEDUP	VAUNT
EMBLAZON	ROISTER	
FLAUNT	SELFPRAISE	

```
R C E G N E L L A H C B X E V W W I I F Y D M
P A U B O E U T U X Y O D T J I Z U J N W T L
Z B B T E X B B N Y P U M E K Q H B K O C C A
S E K A T S P E E W S T R P T T U P A I O L V
V R A W R H T O E E H M G M E R I O P T N A I
A J U O Y V R C N M Y I E O A T A X F N F S R
X T Y L T W O O H P A Y D C Y P I C H E L H R
S R H O L V N V A R T G K S B Z I T M T I V O
L R U L A O L E Y T D Z P X S I N Y I N C N P
E E X K E Q G U D N X K N N B A B L E O T U Y
L T A N K T X H O I O C T N J P U H F C N R O
A N O D C F I I P J S S W N H G E F I T Q F U
U U C A X Q T C M F T R R T E P G F R U C I I
R O Y V H I M D E R F A E G Z M U D T R E F T
E C A R S J F O U V Y O T H R Y E O S K I O G
A N T O S Z S G Z X E R T Q T Y Q G W T U M H
V E P Y Q I G E U M U N Q T I O V W A R N X V
G P O E I L H A G C O N T E S T C H N G P F W
O P Q K E Y N T V I H W S E E S Y A V V N Q C
C X P P K Y N D S G Z Y N M F B M S V J Q E R
E R X N S J F O N L E T S M G E O K T H G I F
R H C T A M C G F X G V E F N G E H U N M Z A
I N M K W C G A R E D N E T N O C A G S R Y N
```

Puzzle 103

ATHLETICEVENT	CUTTHROAT	OPPOSITION
BOUT	DOGEATDOG	OTHERSIDE
CHALLENGE	ENCOUNTER	RACE
CLASH	ENGAGEMENT	RETRACE
COMPETE	FIGHT	RIVAL
COMPETITION	GAME	STRIFE
CONFLICT	INFIGHTING	STRUGGLE
CONTENDER	MATCH	SWEEPSTAKES
CONTENTION	MEET	TOURNAMENT
CONTEST	ONEONONE	

```
N  A  U  K  Q  P  T  N  O  J  S  E  P  T  J  A  I  O  H  X  M  B  K
G  I  Q  D  U  A  S  J  C  F  D  X  L  I  T  K  H  U  B  L  O  C  K
R  P  A  T  F  I  S  G  O  B  O  O  N  Y  E  J  E  M  V  W  M  W  A
A  S  E  G  Q  A  Z  S  X  O  A  R  D  Q  T  Z  K  R  R  M  F  H  R
A  S  J  Z  W  R  S  W  E  T  M  D  M  G  A  S  T  C  R  E  A  T  E
F  B  K  E  L  T  H  H  E  M  R  X  X  A  E  R  U  T  C  U  R  T  S
S  G  U  E  N  B  G  I  I  E  D  J  B  F  T  Y  J  F  O  T  E  R  H
U  F  P  E  V  R  I  Z  W  O  V  L  D  I  Y  Z  W  Q  K  J  T  X  E
O  H  V  K  T  F  A  U  A  Q  N  V  E  S  O  P  M  O  C  V  A  D  R
B  N  D  L  A  P  A  Z  A  H  T  W  H  R  S  I  B  B  U  I  L  D  U
I  M  K  J  W  U  R  B  J  P  E  N  L  O  N  M  Z  W  L  Y  U  O  T
M  Z  O  X  M  T  P  O  R  T  O  W  T  Q  B  H  T  G  H  E  M  S  P
H  C  P  R  S  T  Q  B  D  I  M  E  X  C  P  I  Y  C  I  L  R  M  L
P  I  F  H  F  O  P  J  G  U  C  N  B  M  U  I  L  U  A  O  O  E  U
C  L  J  X  W  G  C  Q  E  A  C  A  M  D  R  R  Q  N  Z  L  F  K  C
L  C  K  Z  P  E  G  N  C  V  Q  E  T  A  C  P  T  E  D  J  I  A  S
A  P  A  T  E  T  L  S  Z  X  Y  D  G  E  P  A  H  S  V  A  X  M  F
Y  C  T  S  D  H  J  Y  D  J  Y  K  E  B  W  S  A  I  N  E  T  X  E
O  X  N  Y  T  E  S  N  S  U  S  C  Z  L  W  K  O  A  N  O  R  F  R
U  A  Z  Y  A  R  E  R  U  T  C  A  F  U  N  A  M  R  V  R  C  O  E
T  S  T  U  O  R  E  M  M  A  H  S  B  W  A  Y  M  G  Y  S  B  R  C
N  G  I  S  E  D  G  S  I  H  Y  D  C  T  T  I  O  L  D  Q  Q  G  T
R  S  U  B  E  M  A  R  F  S  D  S  E  S  I  V  E  D  K  P  D  E  W
```

Puzzle 104

ASSEMBLE	FASHION	MOLD
BLOCK	FORGE	PRODUCE
BUILD	FORMAT	PUTTOGETHER
CAST	FORMULATE	RAISE
COMPOSE	FRAME	SCULPTURE
CONSTRUCT	FROM	SETUP
CREATE	HAMMEROUT	SHAPE
DESIGN	INVENT	STRUCTURE
DEVISE	LAYOUT	STYLE
ERECT	MAKE	
FABRICATE	MANUFACTURE	

```
L  E  G  A  M  M  I  R  C  S  E  C  O  N  F  L  I  C  T  E  W  N  V
O  D  Y  S  F  C  A  C  L  T  C  G  M  H  U  Q  S  M  N  O  O  D  A
R  D  U  H  C  O  A  X  X  L  A  C  A  D  R  O  P  C  H  H  V  B  R
B  E  Q  B  F  I  H  N  I  U  R  K  T  W  F  V  O  E  T  U  A  O  U
L  R  Z  S  I  T  P  A  I  D  N  L  C  J  M  U  A  A  L  T  U  G  L
F  B  F  C  Z  S  R  M  T  Z  I  W  H  K  N  C  R  L  T  N  P  Y  C
Y  Y  F  M  Z  T  X  O  Y  N  Y  Z  O  T  Y  A  W  L  D  P  N  I  R
X  U  F  S  L  E  C  K  S  L  I  E  E  D  M  R  E  O  R  N  C  B  K
D  N  O  F  T  E  F  E  M  N  O  R  R  W  W  E  L  G  J  O  L  T  M
H  J  N  M  U  P  U  T  T  T  Z  G  P  K  N  O  S  A  L  I  M  L  W
H  A  U  Z  O  L  S  D  A  S  G  G  L  S  A  E  H  R  V  T  W  A  H
D  S  R  P  B  E  R  E  G  A  T  T  A  L  N  C  T  S  S  I  U  K  X
E  N  P  M  T  C  H  X  J  B  H  A  M  G  E  W  X  N  U  T  R  W  W
Z  F  Z  N  E  H  Z  O  C  P  T  X  A  T  L  N  U  H  T  E  G  N  J
F  D  O  E  R  A  U  S  Z  U  A  G  N  U  G  X  M  W  P  P  V  C  F
Q  C  F  Z  C  S  N  K  U  W  E  M  A  G  G  Y  I  J  H  M  V  O  B
Q  E  Y  Y  T  E  N  A  F  M  D  E  P  O  U  P  T  P  E  O  W  C  M
V  E  J  N  V  D  M  H  E  P  N  K  L  F  R  J  M  E  M  C  L  D  R
S  R  B  P  D  W  X  N  S  S  E  R  S  W  T  Y  T  D  Q  C  F  G  X
Y  E  N  R  U  O  T  M  G  A  D  W  C  A  S  M  I  W  Z  R  R  Y  A
T  M  R  R  H  X  H  Z  Y  V  D  B  R  R  L  A  J  G  L  B  H  O  B
M  U  G  Z  C  I  H  W  J  I  U  S  Y  K  S  O  B  T  N  S  G  C  G
B  O  S  T  R  Z  D  G  I  T  S  K  G  T  G  V  I  V  V  K  B  Q  Z
```

Puzzle 105

BATTLE	GAME	RUNOFF
BOUT	HEAT	SCRIMMAGE
COMPETITION	JOUST	SHOWDOWN
CONFLICT	MARATHON	SPRINT
CONTENTION	MATCH	STEEPLECHASE
CONTEST	MEET	STRUGGLE
DASH	OLYMPICS	SUDDENDEATH
DERBY	RACE	TOURNAMENT
DUEL	REGATTA	TOURNEY
ENCOUNTER	RIVALRY	TRAIL
ENGAGEMENT	ROUND	TUGOFWAR

```
N B H N U J C U A E X T Q A Y T N A R R A W F
O G S M C I T B B D R Z Z T B I P U J R M E U
I U L C V L S L A G E A N J K N G P R X S Z W
T N A N E V O C C J G E J F X R I A I I X U V
A B D O C H B P F D K U D D O T N U M S N K E
G T O I O F R X M I R P A K M G T O T X K W I
I A F T M E I V O T W X L R E F R A G W P K L
L B B C M N S I J F D R Q M A P K G E W I N Z
B W M A I T S G R P N U E K W N T Z Y A M O K
O W V S T E H B U P O N A U H U T X A Y A I H
I R S N M N J V L Y T U B L E N K E T R T T H
E U N A E T O Z M M Q Z T P A D C N E J A N S
O E V R N E C N B N F P G M T E A I P P D E Q
T B P T T X Y O T I E H F C Q R A D T B R V B
N O V A K U N C R A R G I M A S G E A M O N T
E D I B G D A U E G L R D U J T K A Y M C O F
M W R Z W R A C A R E E G N C A L L I A N C E
E O X O T K E K T A P N A Y E N Q U I U O J E
L Y O N W X P E Y B W I G S H D M C X A C G U
T Q O D E A L K M V K U M M E I I T C V D W W
T C A P A K Q I F E L C C Q Y N Y G O E O N R
E D N I B X F R U T N E D N I G J Y L L V O S
S F L L W K R E T R U T P R R N T P L Q G V J
```

Puzzle 106

AGREEMENT	CONVENTION	PACT
ALLIANCE	COVENANT	PLEDGE
ARRANGEMENT	DEAL	PROMISE
BARGAIN	DEED	SETTLEMENT
BIND	ENTENTE	TRANSACTION
BOND	GUARANTEE	TREATY
COMMITMENT	GUARANTY	UNDERSTANDING
COMPACT	INDENTURE	WARRANTY
CONCORDAT	LEASE	WORD
CONTRACT	OBLIGATION	

```
T F A R D K C G G H S J S A E A J E M I L O H
M F E U U U N V B K E E S U R F R T S Y O D M
W B N N A L P P P K J B U O T A L X A D C C I
E E R E L L I B G K C Q T H F C Q S P I O I A
M I P I E L F Q T U Q A Q L P U E N I L T M H
E X L N L D O S R S B D A R E F G P O Q O E G
Z F U U C R I R U S F A A P W S R I S N R Z O
H V S H S L I U N O C D T J M O O C E O P M O
Y G L W K C W B G V N G W T G S A C T V R W Y
X I P C U D X E H E W A S R I O K V A G R P Z
F L E L L T W E L S P L A T W N Y O L G E Z T
L H U U I K B A N P K M K C S Q G P S X T M X
C M V J D O C K E T H Z F G Q M G O G T S N S
L F I R A T D S Y N O P S I S E F X R J O C S
D M A O J A G E N D A K I L N G W D G D R E C
Q O S A A S W J L D O B M I A E W E R D E N H
O W E U E E Y G X I C H T S J B A N A A S R E
E U A P T W Y L S C R Q F T Y Y P X M K C M D
K A T J C Q F R L L F J W I B W N B E P X U U
B J D L R S Z J X A O H W N M S L T R Y Z Y L
M O A A I U X E F G B B M G V J C Q W S A Z E
G N O L S N Y Y H E U U E O T H J F Z Q X A H
O C I K F X E H B E W L S R H T M R U Q L Z T
```

Puzzle 107

AGENDA	FARE	PROTOCOL
BATTINGORDER	GUIDE	ROLL
BILL	LINEUP	ROSTER
BOOK	LIST	ROTA
CALENDAR	LISTING	SCHEDULE
CARD	MENU	SCROLL
CHECKLIST	OUTLINE	SKETCH
CURRICULUM	PLAN	SLATE
DOCKET	PROGRAM	SYLLABUS
DRAFT	PROSPECTUS	SYNOPSIS

```
X I P K O O R C A N X P R P Z T D X L R O W Y
F M K K U I W K S C U P B X Y U R P B U P L C
V K G I A R M E D R O B B E R D I S U Z X X E
A N U U M S S O Q P M R D R O S B R N K D N R
I T S C H W H O B X F E Q O H O L D U P M A N
R E P F U T O A Q S V K G S J O I G O Z A G B
O D O W K J P L C R T A T S T J A N F E K I W
U G C M C B L K G Z G E B E E M J E R U Q L M
G C U L P R I T P D A R R R K V S F Z G L O Z
H S L M M G F J Y L H B V G C G I R M T S O S
N B A N D I T Z E Q O W F S O S A L U B I H T
E R X C B A E R C J O A B N P O T N D K U P G
C T Q V Y C R K A Q D L R A K C H M G O R C O
K F S G H F D W S Q L R E R C F O Y L S E J V
L M U G G E R N D K U E S T I F A N Q U T R E
M H D R P Z J E D G M E S S P C E F V C T E A
S O C R E D N E F F O T A E P E R L A I P F R
Q I N Q M M Y B P W H E P O E U C I O P C P J
R A L G R U B Q F I E K S X G O M L M N Z T P
Q W I F E Q M C E O W C E N B J H T O I Q D Z
W G U W V L S F N Q Q A R C I O L O J Q N F L
D E S P E R A D O J W R T S A N G P X I V A J
Z P G D N L R J N S J N U F M K X M O S R V L
```

Puzzle 108

ARMEDROBBER	GANGSTER	OFFENDER
BANDIT	GOON	PICKPOCKET
BURGLAR	ROUGHNECK	RACKETEER
CONVICT	HOLDUPMAN	REPEATOFFENDER
CRIMINAL	HOODLUM	SHOPLIFTER
CROOK	HOOLIGAN	STEALER
CULPRIT	JAILBIRD	THIEF
DESPERADO	LAWBREAKER	THUG
EVILDOER	MOBSTER	TRANSGRESSOR
FELON	MUGGER	TRESPASSER

```
Y P Y U E R Y W A E D E L K L M O E M O A V Q
E J D L A B L Z L E T L I R G U H S L D S E N
K H N D P Z Y B T I R B S C P N L G S P M L A
D R X C C H A C W F L I Q E U E M H T B T E D
I Y T M R L E I D L P S F D Y N X B E J U C M
X W L S I L P M A U E I Q I V C A P X Z N T I
N Y O A E R J O B D W V Y W I L C G O K I I T
X V V Y R F T L I T M Y U E G O Q D R S V V T
P A F J X E I W P L A I N T O S E E A C E E E
U R G F E C N N P H C E A A A E K R P E R D D
N N D R H O D E A R Z G B T B D E A P Z S W A
R E F B I L A B G M V A B S V N F H A J A A W
E Y P T Z L E D X C J R P F Q Z Z S R C L G H
S R A O B E R K E L B I S S E C C A E O H T K
T N E R C C P X U E T A V I R P T O N P Q A N
R K J Y N T S L E G N E R J K M R C T K L C N
I W C T A I E S U O I V B O K B X O T I J T A
C N K E T V D Q B E S E E W C O S M X D I X G
T A D Y I E I O V K M Q Z R D N T M S L S L D
E K W T O T W D A B Y R A T N U L O V B X B Z
D E O I N D X H V C K N O W N L G N R O C V V
F D V X A N D L C O M M U N A L U Y J S H W O
R X P C L K R I W L Y I K S U N C W B P R M N
```

Puzzle 109

ACCESSIBLE	FREETOALL	PUBLIC
ADMITTED	GENERAL	SHARED
APPARENT	KNOWN	STATEWIDE
AVAILABLE	MANIFEST	UNENCLOSED
BALD	NAKED	UNIVERSAL
COLLECTIVE	NATIONAL	UNRESTRICTED
COMMON	NATIONWIDE	VISIBLE
COMMUNAL	NOTPRIVATE	VOLUNTARY
ELECTED	OBVIOUS	WIDESPREAD
ELECTIVE	OPEN	
EXPOSED	PLAINTOSEE	

```
E S J C X S S Q R X I U U U E P I M M A K E W
T C H G N E N S P I A T B J W Y S H L K Q T J
X U Π W G I C M C O A Y C V S Π Π L A Π S Π Π
A M P O E I M D U C T J D A K S F D D E R R W
C H V R F I X H K L O P S U X U A R C H E S S
M E A E T A T I S S E C E N Z E E R W V Q E J
C Γ C O N S T R A I N M T O P K Ľ M A Π U L A
I S Q U E E Z E I K H B A U V O J I T H I T S
E V I R D A K C Q E M C G B C E L K E L R S H
T W J P V N D X C Q Q O I B B U X X D G E U T
A H W Q R G I T S N T M T D P O T T A W V H T
N P R X L O O C H X H P S O Z L G Z U S Z K P
M N P E N R V I Q O Y E N E F O F P S W G H I
D Y C L A D Q O L Q N L I M D D I S R K E A R
I N Q S Y T W V K D M M Q D T Z M M E H H G C
N Z I I M P E L E E E S U A C U E N Π C X N S
Y Z O B E B R N U G U O V E V G C P P R W G N
Z Y O Q V X G E R K I Z U E R O P A U Y E J O
Y X Q F D L T L S W Y L L U B V K T B L K S C
D D K W A M Q O W S N F B K J R S U G G B G S
I J Q Y K V F E R K U B J O P D X E G S L H O
G U X W H C P M K T Z R K P Z Y A D R A F T V
U W D W N N R Q V J E C E Z O D A O R L I A R
```

Puzzle 110

APPLYPRESSURE	EXTORT	OBLIGE
BIND	FORCE	PERSUADE
BULLY	HARASS	PRESS
CAUSE	HECTOR	PREVAILUPON
COERCE	HUSTLE	PROVOKE
COMPEL	IMPEL	RAILROAD
CONSCRIPT	IMPRESS	REQUIRE
CONSTRAIN	INDUCE	SQUEEZE
DRAFT	INSTIGATE	THREATEN
DRIVE	MAKE	URGE
EXACT	NECESSITATE	

Treacherous

```
Y D Z S G O E Z T W U W T Z G C C U T H P R Q
Y F I T A R L O L E G A L I Z E A D N V W V S
F U I D A O B D E L E G A T E P Y Z A A M B Z
T I F T U O A E T A T I C A P A C F R L M R E
F E H D R L N B M S X K I R H Q D N R I M B T
V L F E V E E O E W O M O M L O O R A D Q Q U
D T L P E H C V C C C V T N P R H C W A C M T
W J W U N X N G O P E U F O T R G L E T I X I
O B P T T I J M E Y S A X J U I Z N H E C M T
Q K F E R A M B Z T N E M U C O D S T L R D S
E J V R U I Y F I L A U Q I W O I J S N F M N
S C Z D S R L I C E N S E E W L U A E M V H O
I U O S T K W S W X R U Z T B A N Z M N B Y C
H I I N X Y G I M R N Y R A D C W P E E D P T
C O L G F C G C E T M K T T T R V Y Z Z E U I
N G U B I I R T E S P S I I I W Z P I I L I E
A G D W Z Z R Z N Q E B O L G I E Q L R T O E
R V S U Q A T M W O U N W I J R A A A O I F W
F T T R H S D R Z U I I P C Q U S E M H T G Y
X C A C C R E D I T V Q P A X S C L R T N H R
N K B Y S T R I S K C F X F I Q S H O U E E O
E E Y S F U I Z Y W Z N V S T O F P F A H W I
O Y A Q Q P O Q F S N A T F V X O I N M S D Z
```

Puzzle 111

ACCREDIT	DEPUTE	FRANCHISE
APPROVE	DOCUMENT	INVEST
ASSIST	ENABLE	LEGALIZE
AUTHORIZE	ENDOW	LICENSE
CAPACITATE	ENDUE	OUTFIT
CERTIFY	ENTITLE	QUALIFY
CHARTER	ENTRUST	RATIFY
COMMISSION	EQUIP	SANCTION
CONFIRM	ESTABLISH	VALIDATE
CONSTITUTE	FACILITATE	WARRANT
DELEGATE	FORMALIZE	

```
K X T Q E L E I R U Y O D I C Y S I N A X H Y
B O Z R V C Y G U L P R B I Y G O C A S G X E
P P U Y J O U U E B J I L Q N W G V I R I P E
C P U Z J H K I H L X E Y I Y S X H D A V Z C
K T Y B L I R D X I G A E F G I G T R P Y Z N
S L G T Z B I A U N H B A K S J V Q A H Y D B
G M O F A V E N A I Q V F B A O O B U A I I Y
W N L G I T Z C N O V G S Q N I C G G E F E E
Z I O N I S N E C C J R Z Z G H Q P Y L O H Y
P E E M I C H A F I M A S N E B C C J R B B B
Z V H R Q J W P I B Q T F R L H X G X N S Y U
M E T S E Z A F G D D L U A O I Q N H P L H W
I I H B Z D X Z V Y A B E I L I G H T N A K Y
H L K Y K Y R T M G I R R O O O S I E M R M B
P E A A U P H O G M E S T F G O S V W E F A E
A B Y R M Z L L D H T Y C D Y A A I Y S S X A
R B U N C R F X T N I Q V N L E N D Z S K M U
E J M Z Y H R E D R O T S E H G I H F E A S T
S J Y Q T D A M B B M C O Z E B W F F N I D I
K A M N T P M N F E R M E D B L T A O G G W F
L H J O Q N X H G D K W O S Q A W R S E Q O U
I H Y Q E Y H X V E Z U F H J Z E Y O R P T L
E V O L X V K E U R L I Z C E L E S T I A L R
```

Puzzle 112

ANGELIC	ETHEREAL	MICHAELMAS
ANGELOLOGY	FEAST	PURE
ARCHANGEL	GABRIEL	RADIANT
BEAUTIFUL	GUARDIAN	RAPHAEL
BEINGS	GUIDANCE	SECONDORDER
BELIEVEIN	HEAVENLY	SERAPHIM
CELESTIAL	HIGHESTORDER	THEOLOGY
CHERUBIM	LIGHT	URIEL
CHOIRS	LOVE	WINGED
DIVINE	MESSENGER	

```
D P H A T N E U L F F A Y F I H D T C C U O R
N B J L K A T V T A T J S M V K E Z E R R E G
M M C Q A E K T A Q C M M D N I T H C A X S C
M F D E K C O T S L L E W I H C E B H C S T T
H E S P I I H U E Q A X Y E M B A W E E N M C
P X L H N Y C C J S M H F J P T D S L L W C J
J T T P N G R C U X T W H G T W S M A N L Z C
E R U A Q E I R R M V D G L L I O R Q I O S O
L A M W L C A T A I S O E W V T E X H M U C M
B V B N T B O N V E C F X E T B Q M Y O Z K P
I A U D L N H V L L W H U O I S D T E K P R E
T G M E F S J B O U T S B L P K N T M S L R T
S A P N M U D X N U U B Y I L A N P B S E Y I
U N E B R P P A G O I H L L D U W T T G N Y T
A T R W K J L Q R K T L U N O J X M A R T A I
H X D Q B I N E G L I R U B X S S G O E Y V O
X C B U R F M N A N A B Z V U C I O C I R E N
E V N U C U A E G N A L W Y J V K R E D D G G
N U I N N R W O F M M S G Y Q M B Z O P E R I
I I L B Z R V D U E P H S X H Z C S F H Q A F
W O B T M E K C T Y L O Z H U T I Y Q F O L I
N P L X R Z K P K F E Y S O G M S O Q K W Q C
X D G C O N F L I C T G B D E C D X U W C R T
```

Puzzle 113

ABOUNDING	GREAT	PACKED
ABUNDANT	HUGE	PLENTEOUS
AFFLUENT	IMMEASURABLE	PLENTIFUL
AMPLE	INEXHAUSTIBLE	PLENTY
BOTTOMLESS	LARGE	RICH
BOUNTEOUS	LIBERAL	SPILLINGOVER
BOUNTIFUL	MANY	THICK
BUMPER	MUCH	UNMEASURED
EXCESSIVE	NUMEROUS	WEALTHY
EXTRAVAGANT	OVERABUNDANT	WELLSTOCKED
FULL	OVERFLOWING	

```
E V T V E C L M X H T B R Y E E A P F S J S S
Z H N J N X O C Z X J K T L T L E B Z L Z X B
O P E Y R P U O R G M Z V G E D H L U K M E Y
U X K N T T W R V S S K A E K W Y P D X P G U
B V S I X W C D A M E K V L C P O U C N M S A
O L C N U U W K Z E K Y O M I T E T I T U R D
U N L A H E R D N Z Y Z U F H B U N C H L B K
Q S L M X Y Z K C L P N O I T C E L L O C I G
U B X A P R J G E Y D M I O V R F E W K E N B
E K V E K N O T W F E T M H Y F J A Z Z I V J
T P E O B A N D J L S V Y H K B S V A R A J A
F Q K U Y T F A C O W S N I O H Q W E Z S S B
Q T Q D U I Z X W C G B U O P N S H P C R D P
O F R C F G Y X A K Q W R R C I T O H J X G G
F L G B U F S Q Y A O Q P U T A T O A U Y D A
D T E I D D O A A L I O G G G F O O U P G E B
Z B Z U W I P B M L B T P X T L X Y Q R V A E
Q E A B O D Y R P G H M Z R N B G P S O T S V
N L J T R Q A F X R A G E P J C G H R X I O Y
P I C B C W E I O E V I H S O L E D I J K R Z
U P A R S H I N G R O V E Y S A V G U R W S J
H L G T D C G R R I L C O M P A N Y W P A C K
E Z N U M B E R R E T S U L C J D J Y O I T L
```

Puzzle 114

ASSEMBLY
BALE
BAND
BATCH
BEVY
BODY
BOUQUET
BUNCH
BUNDLE
CLUMP
CLUSTER

COLLECTION
COMPANY
CONVEY
CROWD
DROVE
FLOCK
GATHERING
GROUP
GROVE
HEAP
HERD

HIVE
KNOT
NUMBER
PACK
PILE
POSY
SCHOOL
SWARM
THICKET
THRONG
TRUSS

```
Y G X L W N P Z G C M F D J G X W V H O D Q K
S Y I H P D M N Y O N E I D F U X G K R T Y M
K M E O H O L G O G S B P Z D H R V I K D S E
S A J L I P S N B P G I P N F V I Z J G Y E G
M E I S V Y L A I D T O B I O F Z C L F N D B
F T T J L E H L O N H F F A R L K M L S P Q D
X S F U S S C J U C G Y X T Y K Z S D Q V P V
S D T S N E F R G C N U E W B B Z O V K T J Z
M I E R U C S B O A U M R L K Z I M Y G W D K
O V O Q N H L E L S D Q O N O Z W B Z C R W V
F D X Y E C M E G P E G R D I A G E A E G T W
H M Q M D L X R A T M M M X D U Y R A P V P A
U Y Y F A O O B N R L R I Z Y V O R O A B K B
G T L D E U Q W X T C A D S G I Y D S D U A F
X O E H L D S P E P A H R X T O A P D G D N S
R U B C L Y S Y Y R L U A I R Y X A X S Y Q Y
U R I Q C C W Z W W I C V A P O R O U S Y G Q
Z W S O Y O A C U N G N P U P K X Y L M G R D
J O M K D H G A B T I D G M E Y V N O U H R W
T C R A K U F T K K N C A N L A H O M U I D H
Y U H T S A C R E V O D E S E R L M M P P X L
M S D J Y J S X R S U D F H B G J I P Z U C E
P V T L X G P F P X S S W I L U D Y Y F P J E
```

Puzzle 115

CALIGINOUS	GRAY	MURKY
CLOUDY	HAZY	OBSCURE
DAMP	HEAVY	OVERCAST
DARKENED	HUMID	SHADOWY
DREARY	LEADEN	SOMBER
DRIPPY	LOWERING	STARLESS
DRIZZLY	MISTY	STEAMY
ECLIPSED	MOIST	SUNLESS
FOGGY	MOONLESS	UNCLEAR
GLOOMY	MUGGY	VAPOROUS

```
R Q M X T J N F W E R E S H I A B S F V R F J
F K W T L N W M I H K C A T C H N P K W G F K
P J E M Z Z S U W A U T M P W A T B C O H Z R
Q U N O P U N E T S A F T T G L Z D L I H E U
I G D K A P P R E H E N S I O N P L C S N V C
K R M N G K L F M A Q S P J C E G V K S G U D
O M C A R E T A A H I C C P N Z Y M N O R G N
O F O D L O H Y A L G Y T J C P N A M A K D Y
H C R V D W A N A V M Y S A Q U R E M S N H G
J L O X H J G S S J X C Y L I E Y R K Z U S X
I U F F F O S M F G C R E T J J C S G I S R E
R T E P N M S F T D E R Y H M G T P C D A S I
S C P T E D F J V V D D M T N R S Z A N V S S
N H O P R Q B Y M C E S C H F A I P S A L C W
A F R I U O G T M C I O Z L E S Q Z T T E E K
T I G L T R R K A Z O G B P I P R I P L U F P
C O J C P E A R C H F G O L K N I E E P S D C
H S N K A A B D V X H U B Y K V G R M Y J C L
J P E Q C M W Z G K N H B E A A T A G F L R I
E E P I E V T H N C C L F D Z M L F G E W P N
Z A K D Z O H G E N E L U M S C U W N A A E C
R S E E P E Q O D U X O M U P L D C D Y L W H
D B E K X F N V M R P P C J J S H R B S C O K
```

Puzzle 116

APPREHENSION	CLIP	HANGONTO
CAPTURE	CLUTCH	HOOK
CARE	EMBRACE	LAYHOLDOF
CATCH	ENSNARE	MAKEAGRABAT
CLAMP	FASTENUPON	POUNCEON
CLASP	GRAB	SEIZE
CLAW	GRASP	SNAG
CLENCH	GRIP	SNATCH
CLINCH	GRIPE	TAKE
CLING	GROPEFOR	

```
M J F R U F O A B Y L E V O L S P W F J P S C
D B E K E N M C B J Y H G A J L M I E O V L S
P A Y C A G M V A E J N S H N X D T C S R W A
X X E D I W W E O E I S B M S U I L G J O E D
S A L M C N Y U X L R R U G W L G O X L A W C
H G E G O P V Q A J I K O O O C O V X S A N O
Q O G F I P U E C G D G E P E D D D I V I N E
U N A Y V I P I H K W Y U K L C Y Q M O T Y T
B F N H S P N T W H X S S O I H A U N N L S U
E O T I A L E G O Y B N O H T L B V W F U U Q
A G T E M Y P L F X W K I L A H Y T R N F I V
U E Z B E G E G G N I S A E L P N D W U T T G
T T G D U S K H W N O E Z D W A E E A U C A R
I J N M O O V A G U H T L W I K I L Z L E B A
F O T M M Q D R S Z V J Q D B W V I Y L P L C
U Y E N J V V E M G T J A J L I K C R M S E E
L A C F S Y D H C H A R M I N G G A D L E S F
U V K O E P H C E E E V I T C A R T T A R M U
X G A H E B R W G B N K O R W X R E V R O V L
Y E K G M F T E X W N T V O G R I U S D W J Y
P N X U L W L S T R T Y U S E T X H E R O R P
H S D T Y Y W T F T I E L Y W V I S T F V T O
M C O I V W W M K Z Y R S H I P T Y F I N E Z
```

Puzzle 117

AGREEABLE	ELEGANT	PLEASING
APPEALING	EXQUISITE	POLITE
ATTRACTIVE	FINE	PRETTY
BEAUTIFUL	GOODLOOKING	RADIANT
BECOMING	GRACEFUL	RESPECTFUL
BRIGHTEYED	HANDSOME	ROSY
CHARMING	HEALTHY	SEEMLY
CURVACEOUS	LADYLIKE	SHAPELY
DECENT	LOVELY	SUITABLE
DELICATE	MODEST	WHOLESOME
DIVINE	NICE	

```
G N I D I B A P E T E R N A L F Q K D I Z I C
K X I E R E L D H Y O A O M I Z T K Z T N M L
U X R T D B M O B T R E C U R R E N T M H P A
Y P R O B J L A Y S O L I D E N T I C A L S C
Q Z E V N Y T Z S A V X F A M A O K I B S E I
K G V E E D E X I F L S P D M B T H M P S R D
B M E D C D V K Y T Z X S F L T N Z T L N I O
X F R N O X A F H R Y C I T A M E T S Y S O H
R V S Q N M R C T E G O Q N R S W O M R U U T
J V I Y S M N A R S O H X J N R A Y J R N S E
K L B Y T U B Y O O N C F B E F M C D R I Q M
V Q L L A E Y E W L X M E R K V L E D A Y H Y
X E E T N N M R T U B Z I Z O X U A Z D E F E
Y Y S U T D R E S T S M N C R N F S V P Y T O
E B S M F U C G U E M S N J B L H E S E V S S
Q Y S G C R H U R U V Z E L N Y T L F R H W R
E U E W P I W L T P C F S L U A I E V M A N M
T R L A P N O A H O J M V T G J A S N A B I M
U H D A K G B R J M I Z R O A N F S Y N I T O
U X N K N L T R V E T V H I A B A X E E T P E
A V E O E I H J H C W Q I T F O L H Y N U D C
T L Q M I E E A H A D Q R K O F E E C T A M Q
H D N R A C I W C F U J T N E U Q E R F L F X
```

Puzzle 118

ABIDING	FIXED	RESOLUTE
CEASELESS	FREQUENT	SAME
CHANGLESS	HABITUAL	SERIOUS
CONSTANT	IDENTICAL	SOLID
DEVOTED	IMMUTABLE	STABLE
ENDLESS	IRREVERSIBLE	STAUNCH
ENDURING	LOYAL	STEADY
ETERNAL	METHODICAL	SYSTEMATIC
FAITHFUL	PERMANENT	TRUSTWORTHY
FAST	RECURRENT	UNBROKEN
FIRM	REGULAR	

```
D A Y F J H V T A P S M H T X Y K C J I U W W
H J Y D Z C P I C G R R H Z R G N I R U D N E
A H P Y A N A S A I N E T E R N A L M X E G S
N S H Y Y U Z T F Z L I T A N B Y Q N P O J Y
L A Y O L A O E H C U H D T P D W N Z R Y U H
Q E Z R C T W A S S R R W I E U L Z Y B V N W
N I W S Q S B D U H Y X A U B C C E Q P M B E
T E P I G I N Y O F A S O L O A G N S E L R X
N Y K Y T K T D I Z R D T V U S X F Q S A O J
E D I U L P X T R O E E K E S G R M C Q C K T
R V A W U R A T E C T D Z T M E E G P A I E T
R L C I D O R Y S U Z N K X Q A K R T E D N C
U M S P E A P E L M I U A U T K T B S W O M H
C T L T T T F F I X E D E T Q N T I V Z H B W
E Y M G O S J G E M W N O R S F E D C C T D V
R F Z U V U C T I O T K X H N N G N O R E K Y
Y V V Y L E A G M Q S C S T H X X O H A G M S W
S L H S D Y H T R O W T S U R T N C Y M L V J
O R E S O L U T E P T E L B I S R E V E R R I
L C D C R T Z V E M S U G Y A K U S L G F E K
I R T Z U P S Q H L A D F W F F Z A V V F W P
D E L B A T U M M I F S T U I N Z K T C I K R
D R L U F H T I A F L W F J X X D F Q Z W M S
```

Puzzle 119

ATTEND	LOOKAT	SCAN
BROOD	MEDITATE	SCRUTINIZE
CEREBRATE	MIND	SPECULATE
CONSIDER	MULLOVER	STUDY
CONTEMPLATE	NOTE	SURMISE
DELIBERATE	OBSERVE	SURVEY
DWELLON	PEER	VIEW
EXAMINE	PONDER	WATCH
GAZEAT	REFLECT	WEIGH
HEED	REVIEW	WITNESS
INSPECT	REVOLVE	

```
Q X X C N G V K Y H N F B D F F V T J T E T E
O D N A M M O C O T Q T E R H U X H M P J C R
Q L A V X Y T I R O I I T U A D S W A Y L F E D
R C C V D H K N S G U R T Y R A N N Y V S R O
E Q Q K B T L H O O X D A M U C W F E O W I M
I I M F Y B M O H X T C U D N O C Z H U H D I
G W G C A B W S O E X L E N I L P I S I D A N
N D K I A B H P L T K C H O R C N H A W M E A
O Z P K X L H T D A L X I S G K V Y E P G L T
V G M U D J L Z I L V O C D E V Q L L K C V E
E Y K L M G L T N U V B J I F I N Q C G Y A Q
R C R Y D G L R H G C W X B D K C B U F M K S
E Z O E Z M O R R E G L G P D N A H R E P P U
E C W N G E K L E R S F J R D G E D W B L C P
S T N D T I V K W I M H Y Y W Z J P Z R U L E
R K B E I R M A O W E Y O N H N A V B K S M R
E J G Y U C O E P B C S L T M L R N D S L H V
V G O R S L T L N H H H D M S U A T E H G Z I
O O O S H S F A Y T N X A B B J F N C C D P S
U K O V M A I N T A I N O R D E R O L V N E E
Z B Q Y E M A N I E O X X Y G A G Z R A K J A
G O M P M R E G A N A M A R H E I D Z Q Y X I
C H O I D K N F V U X Z W N G G H U O O N I G
```

Puzzle 120

AUTHORITY	DOMINATE	OVERSEE
BOSS	GOVERN	POWER
CALLTHESHOTS	HARNESS	REGIMENT
CHARGE	HOLDIN	REGULATE
COMMAND	INFLUENCE	REIGNOVER
CONDUCT	LEAD	RULE
CONTROL	LEASH	SUPERVISE
DICTATE	MAINTAINORDER	SWAY
DIRECT	MANAGE	TYRANNY
DISCIPLINE	ORDER	UPPERHAND

```
P  K  J  S  Z  I  Y  Z  X  T  U  M  R  X  E  N  S  F  T  Q  Q  V  E
C  R  K  F  Y  F  S  O  K  M  N  H  F  P  I  V  C  S  S  J  M  Q  H
E  R  Y  A  C  D  M  O  B  E  B  D  M  A  E  T  O  L  U  X  R  U  S
E  S  O  L  C  H  A  Y  P  E  E  O  L  L  U  O  A  C  J  A  W  N  S
E  T  U  L  O  S  B  A  O  X  N  P  X  E  R  U  T  V  E  O  A  C  W
J  P  A  J  V  D  T  L  I  P  D  T  F  S  T  F  E  L  T  D  P  Q  X
B  T  P  O  R  R  K  M  N  L  I  O  Z  C  E  R  C  C  D  K  E  D  K
C  T  K  I  T  E  L  L  T  I  N  O  A  P  A  A  N  T  U  I  R  K  Z
X  P  W  U  T  Y  T  L  E  C  G  F  J  C  O  I  S  H  G  Y  F  T  C
B  B  L  Z  Q  E  U  T  D  I  V  S  I  N  T  O  T  G  E  W  E  G  P
A  N  E  Y  F  I  X  E  D  T  T  O  P  S  P  E  C  I  F  I  C  B  N
Y  L  M  G  N  I  R  R  E  N  U  H  I  F  T  C  I  R  T  S  T  G  N
Y  L  S  U  O  I  V  B  O  S  U  D  W  A  L  T  I  Y  H  F  F  T  W
G  Y  L  K  E  T  I  N  I  F  E  D  H  I  T  V  B  S  E  Z  W  A  H
E  Z  S  Q  C  M  R  T  M  E  M  V  U  T  E  C  J  X  N  Y  Q  V  O
S  W  S  K  F  D  V  U  T  K  F  J  J  H  C  W  A  K  A  W  C  R  K
I  S  E  K  R  V  S  A  T  I  L  E  D  F  C  E  T  X  X  L  I  O  N
C  S  R  W  C  Z  R  G  P  G  M  Z  J  U  I  F  R  T  E  J  A  H  D
E  K  P  K  X  U  K  F  R  W  K  T  U  L  O  Q  R  R  P  O  S  K  D
R  B  X  D  C  O  R  L  Y  D  F  A  H  P  G  D  G  Z  O  E  F  R  Y
P  T  E  C  P  D  C  X  Z  X  Y  H  L  X  C  N  K  L  E  C  E  Z  F
G  K  A  Q  X  S  U  I  D  S  Q  G  O  X  Z  Z  A  S  T  A  J  J  A
P  A  E  L  B  A  K  A  T  S  I  M  N  U  D  K  G  T  L  S  V  U  M
```

Puzzle 121

ABSOLUTE	FACTUAL	RIGHT
ACCURATE	FAITHFUL	SPECIFIC
CLEAR	FIXED	STRICT
CLOSE	JUST	TRUE
CORRECT	OBVIOUS	UNBENDING
DEFINITE	PERFECT	UNERRING
DISTINCT	PLAIN	UNMISTAKABLE
EXACT	POINTED	VERACIOUS
EXPLICIT	PRECISE	
EXPRESS	REAL	

```
E R A D D S U W T U E Z E K C N M V R B E A M
H Z S I Y F H X W Z S Y S Q B B A A R A S L N
V S V E S S E I I S U O E G R O G I V G I I O G
V I V C S Y X S N I O O Q E W F L S E L A O I
V U Q Z O S Z Y K I J B P Q P L M R G O J N S
B X W E L V U T L I N U T P I E M L G W M C H
B P L Z G I V N I E S G I A S O E U K R T X I
C J V A D V A S N O Q Q N N M M W S D E X T L
N S X L Z D P X G Y B T E I A K C T G B A S U
H H Z B L A M B E N T T R L F F I R U B A Z C
O O A A A Q F Q X F N E F Z P L Q O K R J A E
N T A S P L E N D I D A D A A N W U C F T Z N
N S N S K L T G E A N N F K K I J S O R C I T
T D I L U U O L R I Z Q M W A L T C I C V U U
Q Z D J C C Z D I Z K Z Y Q A L I G H T R H F
T O D W R I Z W F P K R L H R U G K T I I U M
N Z E K F D K G A I C Q W E D M U O C J L X F
E K I B D S Q S F E A E W N X I H H O G L W Z
Z N K G Q O N M Z V R Y Z T Z N V L E W L A X
Z L L V W J T C G N U N L P W A J N D G X S N
O F K V Q X O X L O R E M B I T T Q M S E G H
Z K Y K Y P H D L T Q S U H R E P Y C N L A G
M B I H I L G J H L Y X X J H Q F R V M P Z N
```

Puzzle 122

ABLAZE	GLOSSY	MAGNIFICENT
AFIRE	GORGEOUS	RADIANT
AFLAME	ILLUMINATE	RICH
AGLOW	INTENSE	SHINING
ALIGHT	IRRADIANT	SHINY
BEAM	LAMBENT	SPLENDID
BRIGHT	LUCENT	SUNNY
BRILLIANT	LUCID	SUPERB
DAZZLE	LUMINOUS	TWINKLING
FULGENT	LUSTROUS	VIVID

```
F P U Y T T N E E T A L U D O M Z H E S Y K E
L L Q L W N C I M B H C A A P H H S S T C O M
L M D J C M E U Z O O G I Q L B S H A C Y C K
A N E T O O Y T R N D N D M T I I W E D C K V
F M O Z I O Y U F B R V E I I C N J R E J N N
D C Z I X Q X W R O N W P D Z V I R C T I S E
X E H P S H T E V L S Q N K A P M Z E H P N T
H Q P E M N W W E L X A S W N E I S D A Q C H
W V L K C O E S K H Q O T O N E D O W N U U G
T W Z A L K S T I K M I L D E N Z U N T I S I
I N J L N E A F B T G N H P H Q X G L Q E H L
S Y U S N U X B W R L S S G R O S O I L T I P
P W K L E C U D E R B E R Q T E T A R E D O M
H S U H B W C O U T G Q O L P M N J L A P N W
Q Y P Q O F K C K A A E V E I L E R D Q G M R
Y F I L L O M L U N Q I P K S R B J L O O S E
X A L E N F H S E S E W V S N O X E H S L B J
E E S O Y Z S K E N V I E E I X N D L I V D P
M V M V E A C C W J U Z T A L O T I C A I H C
W L L W S A L W L A D S R H K L D H Q L G F Q
C R I X L S R L N L A C H T G E A F J C X B H
M E I S F V T T A H M G W E B J N C Z R F W E
G Q K R E L A X C P P I C T A Z S D G Q A Y Q
```

Puzzle 123

ALLAY	DULL	QUIET
ALLEVIATE	EASEUP	REDUCE
ASSUAGE	HUSH	RELAX
BLUNT	LESSEN	RELIEVE
CHASTEN	LIGHTEN	SLACKEN
CHECK	LOOSE	SLAKE
CURB	LOWER	SOFTEN
CUSHION	MELLOW	TENSION
DAMP	MILDEN	TONEDOWN
DEADEN	MODERATE	WEAKEN
DECREASE	MODULATE	
DIMINISH	MOLLIFY	

```
S  Z  P  T  V  I  T  D  R  Z  N  D  U  W  M  T  Y  U  R  D  Y  D  Y
F  H  X  Q  H  R  E  S  Q  V  I  Z  O  H  N  R  G  I  P  Y  N  Z  K
E  O  R  J  A  Q  Z  C  O  K  M  M  Q  Z  O  C  U  Z  U  Y  F  R  Y
R  R  N  T  X  H  E  D  Q  N  C  Z  O  E  E  W  V  K  D  J  X  W  K
L  N  S  Z  C  A  Z  T  G  K  K  I  H  S  E  B  U  E  I  X  N  X  X
M  O  N  W  Z  U  N  B  D  N  X  T  U  A  K  V  O  T  G  G  N  V  T
H  I  S  K  C  H  P  Q  R  U  I  I  W  Y  K  O  R  V  X  I  Y  C  Z
A  N  W  L  V  N  K  H  T  I  N  T  P  X  J  F  E  O  U  T  O  Z  G
N  I  G  I  R  O  K  H  N  F  N  A  F  Y  X  W  H  N  S  N  B  S  L
F  P  Y  V  Y  A  C  G  E  K  G  G  O  A  C  J  Z  V  S  F  W  E  W
R  O  T  J  U  D  N  R  M  I  H  D  I  T  R  J  Q  I  F  B  V  T  E
F  U  D  V  N  G  E  D  G  L  D  C  P  N  K  D  D  R  F  S  D  R  T
Y  W  R  V  G  N  G  Z  D  C  O  E  C  E  G  E  P  V  F  F  P  M  A
B  K  H  C  C  B  W  V  U  N  V  G  A  T  R  F  A  J  H  O  X  U  L
E  I  U  E  H  D  M  E  J  J  N  B  H  A  P  S  O  V  G  O  V  D  U
L  M  T  O  G  C  S  E  O  I  I  O  I  B  O  E  U  R  V  S  N  L  T
I  J  A  O  C  I  C  J  D  E  U  I  Q  W  K  N  C  A  T  I  O  B  S
E  U  U  X  M  T  O  D  N  G  O  B  N  T  T  M  R  N  S  H  E  H  O
F  Q  U  R  U  K  U  K  H  N  P  X  W  W  S  Q  J  K  O  I  O  W  P
S  K  U  R  A  B  Z  T  L  J  R  X  A  V  K  L  P  S  V  C  O  K  D
Z  S  E  Z  P  X  H  I  Z  V  I  V  D  M  R  A  V  H  Y  Y  C  N  T
G  T  W  H  C  N  U  A  L  R  M  Q  H  Y  P  O  T  H  E  S  I  S  Y
P  K  C  E  M  K  C  K  T  H  E  Q  Q  T  L  X  Q  H  K  U  G  I  G
```

Puzzle 124

ABSTRACTION	DAWN	ORIGIN
APPREHENSION	DRAFTING	PERSUASION
BELIEF	HYPOTHESIS	POSTULATE
BRINGINGFORTH	IDEA	PRESUMPTION
BUDDING	INCEPTION	PRIME
CONCEPT	INFERENCE	START
CONCLUSION	JUDGMENT	SURMISE
CONJECTURE	LAUNCH	THEORY
CONSIDERATION	NOTION	THOUGHT
CONVICTION	OPINION	VIEW

Crossword Puzzles

Answer each question based on the number of boxes allotted for a given answer entry. For tips on brushing up on your crossword puzzles skills, please see Chapter 2.

Easy

Across

1. Karim of the Khans, e.g.
4. Where to make waves?
9. Barber chair attachment
14. Grier of "Jackie Brown"
15. Freshman cadet
16. Ho opener
17. It's right under your nose
18. Vegetable spreads
19. Calliope kin
20. Small rural community
23. Variety of sheep
24. Spanish article
25. Setting for many jokes
28. Sired
29. Berth position, perhaps
32. Former Venetian chief magistrate
33. Boredom
35. Showed amazement or pleasure
36. It cuts both ways
40. Make oneself heard
41. More demure
42. Bold and sassy
43. At right angles to the length of a ship
45. "Coming of Age in Samoa" author
49. Japanese capital
50. Vinegar partner

51. TV type
53. Shot from beyond the arc
56. Beethoven wrote one
59. Maid preceder
60. PC key
61. Melchior, for one
62. Bathtub part
63. Status of an unresolved contest, perhaps
64. Preference
65. Some beans
66. Teacup handle

Down

1. Self-assurance
2. Certain dive
3. Unit named for a French physicist
4. Part of a place setting
5. Complete, as an athlete
6. Van Cleef and Grant, for two
7. Woodwind instrument
8. Hershey competitor
9. TV Guide listings
10. Cousin of a gull
11. Unprestigious publication
12. Fertility clinic needs
13. Sword vanquisher, figuratively
21. Go underground

22. It's needed for a stroke
25. Atomic physicist Niels
26. Elderly
27. Type of meat or pepper
30. Certain diminutive dog
31. Jigsaw part
32. Hotel employee, perhaps
34. It's not gross
35. IOU component
36. Pilgrim's pronoun
37. Threadbare
38. 1950 film noir thriller
39. Formal meetings
40. Bug someone, e.g.
43. Broadcast
44. Uses a certain kitchen appliance
46. Grand property
47. Famous aviator Earhart
48. Fast freshwater fish
50. Chicago airport
52. They may be put on homes
53. Race pace, perhaps
54. Continental currency
55. Evangelist's suggestion
56. Mel of the 500 home run club
57. Whistle part, perhaps
58. Printing measures

Puzzle 125

Across

1. Spanish munchies
6. Vegetable or tomato, e.g.
10. Industry magnate
14. Come up
15. Lhasa ___
16. Memorable Robinson role
17. Patty of "Peanuts"
19. Some queens, e.g.
20. 67.5 degrees, to mariners
21. Unspecified amount
22. Italian bowling game
24. Spanky and the gang
26. Company car, e.g.
27. Screech, for one
28. Varieties of nuts
32. Super Bowl V winners
35. Pick the pick of the litter, e.g.
36. Prefix follower
37. Item of finality in the paper, briefly
38. Insanely
39. It may be delivered at a nightclub
40. Noted clown
41. Assocs.
42. Deejay Casey
43. Epitome of thinness
45. Pen name
46. Mama of pop music
47. Word in a Captain and Tennille title

51. Token room?
54. Drops the ball
55. Pie-mode link
56. Bird in a crazy simile
57. Hard-to-pronounce word
60. Vended
61. Jai ___
62. Famous Butler
63. Sanction
64. Icarus appendage
65. Lee and Teasdale

Down

1. Give a point to
2. Rock concert venue, sometimes
3. Plumber's concerns
4. Viper
5. Boards with ups and downs
6. "Dynasty" actress
7. Sheriff Taylor's boy
8. Mil. branch
9. Personal trainer's target
10. Jim-dandy
11. Vitamin additive, sometimes
12. Opener on Broadway?
13. Gift for a diva, perhaps
18. Great thing to be on
23. Royal symbol
25. Circus confection

26. They may be hard to swallow
28. Falsify, in a way
29. Aussie hoppers, briefly
30. It's a drag
31. Goblet feature
32. Ballplayer Ty
33. Shawm follower
34. Maugham's "___ of Lambeth"
35. Reiner and Perkins
38. Saskatchewan city
42. Mugs
44. Launch site
45. Duel personality?
47. Character in gangster film spoofs
48. Suburbanite, on some autumn days
49. Prince Valiant's wife
50. Some pastries
51. Furthermore
52. Fischer's castle
53. A caffeine source
54. McGregor of "Trainspotting"
58. He stung like a bee
59. "So, there you are!"

Puzzle 126

Across

1. Certain superior's title
6. 41st on a noted list
10. Old foolish person
14. Flintstone's boss
15. Victor over Connors, 1975
16. Opulent
17. Nest up high
18. Boilermaker part
19. Miss Kett of old comics
20. It counts votes
23. They may be ringing
24. Army outfit
25. Browned in butter (Var.)
29. "Yuck!"
31. Semicircular recess
32. They take sides
38. You may vote in it
41. Vote checkers
42. Second highest in a family of instruments
43. Govt. health watchdog
44. Picture puzzle
46. Follow
50. Love, Spanish style
52. Cause of some confusion in 2000
59. Anthropoids
60. "It must have been something ___"
61. 24 sheets
62. 500 sheets
63. Type of matter
64. Word before city or workings
65. Dried and withered
66. Blood and guts, e.g.
67. First U.S.-born saint

Down

1. Posthaste, briefly
2. ___ cheese dressing (Var.)
3. Storm start
4. Relating to the ear
5. Subdued chuckle
6. Storybook elephant
7. Kind of manual
8. Jettison
9. Mainz mister
10. Limpid
11. Go one better than
12. Prefix with arthritis
13. "Amadeus" choreographer
21. Bounder
22. Set of values
25. Spice rack member
26. The very top
27. Md. institution
28. Abound
29. WWW addresses
30. Co. that merged to become Verizon
32. Petition
33. ___ Lingus (Irish airline)
34. Hunting target, perhaps
35. Is unwell
36. "___ creature was stirring ..."
37. Kind of leopard or goose
39. Tin soldier's prop
40. Common connection
44. Paragon of patience
45. Basra natives
46. Aspen lifts
47. 100 paise
48. Shed ___ (show sympathy or sadness)
49. Informal response to "Who's there?"
50. It may have a cross to bear
51. "I don't believe you!"
53. Diana of "The Avengers"
54. Casino game
55. Crescent-shaped figure
56. It may get the brush-off
57. Popular cookie
58. Cousin of a

Puzzle 127

Across

1. Some mantel pieces
6. Holiday helper
9. "___ not amused"
14. Prefix for mural or venous
15. Opening for a maid?
16. Baseball Hall-of-Famer Monte
17. Trace, as of hope
18. What a kid may say
19. Broadway luminaries?
20. Dessert choice, perhaps
23. Pertaining to the eyes
24. Used a backhoe, e.g.
25. Liveliness
26. Online initials
29. Passover breads
34. Rainy day amusement, perhaps
37. Soup du jour, sometimes
40. ___ Lanka
41. Star observer
42. Author of inspirational stories for boys
45. Annika Sorenstam's homeland
46. Where to find good schools?
47. "No ___" (sign in certain restaurants)
50. They assist MDs
52. Long, slender sword
55. Befuddle
60. Currency in 40 Across

61. Intention
62. Member of a Jamaican religion
63. Disburdened
64. Reggae relative
65. Highest stages
66. Dude, to a Brit
67. Certain layer
68. Timothy who took many trips

Down

1. Type of circus
2. Prepare to remove an ice skate
3. Increase, as the pace
4. Follow the leader
5. American or Western follower
6. Thompson of "Howards End"
7. Bissextile year
8. Charlatan
9. Anemometer
10. Part of a palindrome
11. Shakespeare's river
12. Pug's place
13. Running's three
21. Rugged cliff
22. Hauler's destination, sometimes
27. ___ buco
28. "___ Theme" ("Doctor Zhivago" tune)
30. Former Russian ruler

31. Sound asleep?
32. Cheer for a bullfighter
33. Rev.'s oration
34. Family name in "The Grapes of Wrath"
35. Help mediate a conflict
36. ___ E. Coyote
37. Expressions of understanding
38. This very moment
39. Intense outrage
43. Words with uncertain terms
44. Distinctive clothing
47. Foreboding atmosphere
48. Irish hunting dog, for one
49. Type of spoon
51. Kind of hit
53. Ear-related
54. Word with mat or kick
55. Twofold
56. ___ facto
57. Use a search engine
58. Human-powered vehicle
59. Arabian monarchy
60. Fighter at Vicksburg, briefly

Puzzle 128

Across

1. Bestial hideaway
5. Letter before epsilon
10. Frank's daughter
14. Lot of rows to hoe?
15. Lunchbox cookies
16. Mild expletive
17. Chinese restaurant offering
19. ___ mater
20. Range of vision
21. Secret store
22. Preamble
23. Heroic narrative
24. Baseball league
25. Basic commodity
28. Northwestern U.S. capital
30. Kind of premiere
31. Well-defined prevailing wind
35. Start for lock or knock
36. Earthenware jars
37. Two pounds, plus
38. Surpassing everything
40. Spanish title of respect
41. Some siblings
42. Show for critics
43. Union of old
46. Long stoles
47. Films with casts of thousands
48. One of the world's religions
50. Gift for a malihini
53. Computer insert
54. Tense tennis situation
56. Charge for a hand delivery?
57. Blow away
58. Tuftlike mass
59. Orderly and systematic
60. Condition of many fences
61. Porgy and bass

Down

1. Be without
2. Need liniment
3. Word with Age or cross
4. Business solicitor, for short
5. Senility
6. Susan's soap role
7. Poland's Walesa
8. Strong puff
9. Burro
10. Extremely sad films
11. Dome-shaped structure
12. Title giver
13. Sixth president
18. Heat to the boiling point
22. Tense choice?
23. Type of ballot
24. Pageant contestant
25. Absorbent stick
26. Musical sound
27. They may be fine
28. Ducks and most people have them
29. Viva voce
31. Comic King
32. One from Hanover
33. Balm ingredient, perhaps
34. Even. opposite
36. "Wanna make something ___?"
39. Is indebted
40. Disney dog
42. Taken to the cleaners
43. Enclosed automobile
44. State one's belief
45. Western scene, e.g.
46. Five-alarmer, e.g.
48. "___ La Douce"
49. When it's saved it's taken
50. 1953 Caron role
51. He lived for 905 years
52. Yen
54. Help at the checkout counter
55. Switch setting

Puzzle 129

Across

1. Place for a pat
5. It can hold its wine
9. Lamp complement
14. A malarial fever
15. Lotion base, perhaps
16. Runs sweetly
17. Scene under the big top
20. Frogs-to-be
21. "C'mon, move it!"
22. "Help ___ the way!"
23. Survey
24. Upper chamber
27. Former Russian sovereigns
29. Send off, as broadcast waves
33. For everyone to hear
35. Prepares for planting
37. "Right you ___!"
38. You may bring it to a picnic
42. Procrastinator's shopping day, perhaps
43. More than a handful
44. Semiconductor giant
45. State of inactivity
47. Clowns around
50. "Voila!"
51. "... pretty maids all in ___"
53. "Nope"
55. Type of tea
58. Voodoo deity
62. Small orchestra
64. Flap-door shelter
65. Micronesian island group (Var.)
66. Side by side?
67. Pokes along
68. Pharaoh's serpents
69. Battleship color

Down

1. Sheet of matted cotton
2. Turkish general (Var.)
3. Edible flower head, as of cauliflower
4. Parent's words of warning or encouragement
5. Where lemons are picked?
6. Extraterrestrials
7. Mama's boys
8. It can hold its beer
9. Pitchman's delivery
10. Speed madly along
11. Circle pieces
12. Word with miracle or wonder
13. Old gas brand
18. Dawn goddess
19. One side of a store sign
23. Faculty title (Abbr.)
24. Holography tool
25. Kind of oil or branch
26. Some carnivores
28. Shouts on a deck
30. Sea ray
31. Vexed
32. Inventor Nikola
34. It can hold its water
36. Start of several Indian place names
39. Urge with sweet talk
40. Was privy to
41. Like a done deal
46. Put on the back burner
48. Gap plugs, etc.
49. Small, crude dwellings
52. Rants go-with
54. Tiny Tim's prop, briefly
55. Start of millions of addresses
56. Washstand pitcher
57. Vehicle at an auction, perhaps
58. Some military addresses
59. "Tootsie" actress
60. Draft-eligible
61. June 6th of 1944
63. Harper Valley grp.

Puzzle 130

Across

1. Beanery sign
5. Pin or cup, e.g.
10. Persuade
14. Restaurant choice
15. Like organza or chiffon, e.g.
16. Architect Saarinen
17. Country established in 1948
19. Despot of old
20. Word of agreement
21. Bootlicking
22. Courage
24. "Tom Thumb" composer
25. Seven-time AL batting champ
26. Maturation process (Var.)
29. Secondhand products
32. Sun block
33. "61 in '61" slugger Roger
34. Kind of tide or cord
35. Vacuum feature
36. Malaccas
37. CCLI x VI
38. Low or high tail
39. Cookout implements
40. "Yankee Doodle Dandy" songwriter
41. Prehistoric time
43. Criminals

44. Misguided act
45. Whiskey ingredient
46. Imago of a grub
48. St. Peter's station
49. Rookery sound
52. Put aboard
53. Where a diet originated
56. Manual reader
57. Social system
58. Andy Taylor's TV son
59. Nights, poetically
60. Heavens
61. Bump on a log

Down

1. Europe's highest volcano
2. Naval hail
3. Waste allowance
4. Command to a guest
5. Kind of price
6. Unbroken
7. Hawk's home (Var.)
8. Riddle-me-___
9. Cast (with "personae")
10. Seat for two or more
11. Wagonmaster's cry
12. Central Asian sea
13. Time long past
18. Tuneful Lena
23. Writes "hiar" for "hair," e.g.
24. Second hand?
25. Largest asteroid

26. They were once hot stuff
27. Author's author
28. James Dean film
29. Vocal limits
30. Backless sofa
31. Kissing game turns
33. Squalid
36. Grow together
37. Shed hair
39. Break the news
40. Show-biz biggie
42. Observant people, say
43. Word with Time or figure
45. Photo finish
46. "Rhapsody in ___"
47. "___ on down the road"
48. Show love excessively
49. Mob boss
50. Etcher's purchase
51. Sound of a child on a swing
54. Feedbox grain
55. Longish time span

Puzzle 131

Across

1. Stimulates
6. One way to hide a present
10. Church section, perhaps
14. Honor a loan
15. Rodentlike mammal
16. Give two thumbs up
17. Conversation opener
19. Recipe qtys.
20. Rational
21. Insignificant speck
22. Plaint for Billie Joe
23. Bart's grandpa
24. 19th in a Greek series
26. Monopoly quartet (Abbr.)
28. Much-loathed emperor
30. Obtains with effort
32. Friend abroad
33. Pie-mode connector
36. Table protector
38. Cottonmouth
41. Type of vinegar
42. Seventh Greek letter
43. Add'l phone line
44. State or city in India
46. Instinctive motive
50. Transcript stat.
51. Tokyo, once
52. Whipped cream unit
55. It merged with Time Warner
56. Part of U.S.A.

58. First name in boxing
60. Second word in a fairy tale
61. Cafeteria feature, perhaps
63. Repair
64. Actor Penn
65. Immigration Museum island
66. They may be liberal
67. Bubkes
68. Frozen raindrops

Down

1. Where "Don Quixote" was conceived
2. Become more distant
3. Show's first number
4. Applies with a cotton swab, e.g.
5. Part of the Fertile Crescent
6. Pequod, for one
7. Not leave leaves
8. Something I can't use, but you can
9. Word with diem or capita
10. Vocal range
11. Deli order
12. Seinfeld's comic book hero
13. Actors Asner and Harris
18. Wane
21. Capital on the Gulf of Oman

24. Soft end of the Mohs scale
25. With celerity
27. Command to a pet
29. Mare fare
31. Miocene, for one
34. Beginning of a cassette tape
35. Partner of dangerous
37. Levi's uncle
38. Aluminum foil alternative
39. Rock concert site chronicled in "Gimme Shelter"
40. "Venus de ___"
41. Ask, in an undignified way
45. Lizard in a Tennessee Williams title
47. Walk or talk aimlessly
48. Certain hockey player
49. Firstborn
53. Electrical resistance unit
54. Famous film motel
57. These might be split
58. "Coming of Age in Samoa" author
59. Anchor store locale
60. Thurman of "Batman & Robin"
61. Taxpayer's ID
62. Mad Hatter's drink

Puzzle 132

Across

1. Noted Washington
6. It's east of the Urals
10. Trident-shaped letters
14. It may be present in undercooked meat
15. Like some memories
16. "Alas!"
17. Burton who played Kunta Kinte
18. It may have fallen on a foot
19. Matter to go to court over
20. Idiom for a multitude of ongoing projects
23. Type of part
24. Flat payment?
25. Idiom for the noblest members of society
31. It has its own Web site
32. Indicator of age
33. Were in the present
34. Bar Mitzvah dance
35. Fix
36. 1957 Nabokov title
37. Tolkien flesh-eater
38. Fizzles out
40. Forms metal, in a way
42. Idiom for no longer able to function
45. Prexy's associate
46. Publisher who transformed Vogue

47. Idiom for an impracticable dream
53. A famous Fitzgerald
54. Problem of pubescence
55. Pontificate
56. One of 10 leapers in a song
57. Mrs. Dithers
58. Remove the groceries, e.g.
59. Eyelid flare-up
60. Blyton the writer
61. Former Russian sovereigns

Down

1. Where cuts might be treated with salt
2. One finishing off the cake
3. De ___ (from the beginning)
4. Five-time Emmy award-winning actor
5. Shaggy like the stereotypical caveman
6. Avidly supporting
7. Start doing laundry
8. Part of a foot
9. Sticks (to)
10. Green stuff on copper
11. Type of missile
12. Hungarian political figure Nagy
13. "Game, ___, match"
21. "Take ___ leave it!"

22. Features of some fancy bathtubs
25. Fern's beginning
26. U.S. Army's helicopter assault division
27. Tear down verbally
28. Participate without the lyrics
29. Judge, e.g.
30. Their teeth are rare
31. Sporting footwear
35. Whirlpool feature
36. Seamstresses' guides
38. Intentionally lay off the fats and sweets
39. Ensconced
40. Flatten a fly
41. Road erosion after a rain, e.g.
43. Infamous marquis
44. Three trios
47. Coagulate
48. Supply-and-demand subj.
49. Cross inscription
50. Rhyme scheme
51. ___-TASS
52. Size category for shirts, briefly
53. Overhead trains

Puzzle 133

Across

1. "___ to leap tall buildings ..."
5. Some playing cards
9. Base and boot, e.g.
14. Sword fight, e.g.
15. Issued a command
16. It's larger than Lincoln
17. Like some tests
18. Canal completed in 1825
19. Singer Newman
20. Sailor's delight?
23. "... we fear ___ evil" (Burns)
24. Turncoat
25. Windshield accessories
28. Beachgoer's goal, perhaps
30. Good thing to jump for
32. Chinese chairman
33. Minor interruption
35. Blokes
37. Unwanted possession
40. Word with tacks or knuckles
41. Defense mechanism
42. Ache
43. Get-up-and-go
44. Executor's concern
48. Ingratiate
51. Step into character, e.g.
52. Brine-cured delicacy
53. Arguer's state?
57. Ermine in the summer
59. Statistics, facts and such
60. 1984 Olympics no show
61. It's created in a snap
62. Arabian ruler
63. Comic vignette
64. Joins the team?
65. It's usually smaller than a denomination
66. ___ pareil

Down

1. Embellishes
2. Article of furniture
3. Oppressively sluggish
4. Some extensions
5. State of limbo
6. Lapidary's measure
7. Fix errata, e.g.
8. Detected
9. Cardigan or Pembroke
10. Nurses in the Orient
11. One type of talk
12. Master's follower
13. Articulate
21. Some snakes of southeastern Asia
22. It could be poison
26. Mesmerized
27. ABBA hit
29. What you may now hear?
30. Minty drink
31. Hiding nothing
34. Surrender
35. Pure-minded
36. Come to a standstill
37. Brown bird
38. Manual
39. Meeting overhead, perhaps
40. When doubled, a remark to Birdie
43. Start for school
45. Kodiak locale
46. Warning bell
47. Puts forth effort
49. Lift up emotionally
50. Latter-day chariots
51. Web site, perhaps
54. Roman calendar notation
55. Anthroponym
56. Tizzy
57. Operative
58. Even if, informally

Puzzle 134

Across

1. Narrative of heroic exploits

5. Shout of encouragement from the bleachers

10. Way around London, perhaps

14. "I've Got ___ in Kalamazoo"

15. In what way?

16. Costa ___

17. Does the expected amount of work

20. Mariner

21. Music fan's purchase, perhaps

22. Homages that may be urned?

23. Writer Morrison

24. Irritates

27. Airline ticket word, sometimes

28. All ___ (attentive)

32. Loan shark's offense

33. Ray of the tropics

35. Writer Scott-Heron

36. Turns a whisper into a shout

39. Word heard at the Westminster Kennel Club

40. Apportioned (with "out")

41. Remained still while running

42. First family's residence

44. They can get burned in PCs

45. Cake tiers

46. They were once completely nuts

48. Kids connect them

49. Wind-tunnel sound

52. Puts an end to

56. Waits in anticipation, in a way

58. Initial victim

59. Some British change

60. Forearm bone

61. It's sometimes struck

62. Got up

63. Sound of an angry exit

Down

1. Gullible ones

2. Chills and fever

3. Festive affair

4. Position for playing horsey

5. Daily duties

6. Cutting edge creators

7. Pouring vessel

8. Man of Steel monogram

9. Dinghies

10. Ed Norton's wife

11. Arranges the outcome

12. Feel sore

13. "The Simpsons" creator Groening

18. Visibly woeful

19. One billion years, in geology

23. With prongs

24. Prize money

25. "Why? Because ___ so!"

26. Considerably

27. Turbine features

29. Spry

30. Chef's gadget

31. Vehicles with runners

33. Shapes and forms

34. Fly guy

37. Teen dances

38. Penelope's husband

43. Lo mein ingredient

45. Tossed, as a grenade

47. Sure-footed work animal

48. John Travolta danced to it

49. Sound of a hard smack

50. Bindlestiff, e.g.

51. Spanish cheers

52. Lotto cousin

53. Corridor

54. Italian volcano

55. Put-on

57. Circus performer's insurance?

S	A	G	A	■	C	H	E	E	R	■	T	R	A	M
A	G	A	L	■	H	O	W	S	O	■	R	I	C	A
P	U	L	L	S	O	N	E	S	W	E	I	G	H	T
S	E	A	F	A	R	E	R	■	B	O	X	S	E	T
■	■	O	D	E	S	■	T	O	N	I	■	■	■	■
P	I	U	E	S	■	V	I	A	■	C	A	R	S	
U	S	U	R	Y	■	M	A	N	T	A	■	G	I	L
R	A	I	S	E	O	N	E	S	V	O	I	C	E	
S	I	T	■	D	O	L	E	S	■	I	D	L	E	D
E	D	E	N	N	■	C	D	S	■	L	A	Y	E	R
■	O	A	K	S	■	P	O	T	S	■				
W	H	O	O	S	H	■	K	I	B	O	S	H	E	S
H	O	L	D	S	O	N	E	S	B	R	E	A	T	H
A	B	E	L	■	P	E	N	C	E	■	U	L	N	A
P	O	S	E	■	S	T	O	O	D	■	S	L	A	M

Puzzle 135

Across

1. Supergirl's City
5. Balloon
10. Places for pickles
14. Prefix meaning "skin"
15. Shoptalk
16. Words signifying trouble ahead
17. Quickly, quickly
18. Remove a tube top?
19. Joan Sutherland or Judi Dench, e.g.
20. Nobel Peace Prize winner of 1979
23. Have great faith in
24. Grinned from ear to ear
28. Word with Gatos or Altos
29. Really big singer?
32. "___ Sexy" (Right Said Fred tune)
35. Asian peninsula
36. "Well, ___-di-dah"
37. Sounds of pleasure
38. Al Capp's Pansy Yokum
39. Old-time wraparound
40. X-ray supplement
41. Fertile soils
42. Extend a subscription
43. House owner in a Martin Lawrence comedy
45. Lacking brightness
46. Term of respect in colonial India
47. Apollo's twin sister
51. Term of endearment
55. RE:

58. Cheese type
59. Run, but go nowhere
60. Fourth rock from the sun
61. It's for good measure
62. League constituent
63. Capital of Samoa
64. Like a flophouse
65. Sweet potato cousins

Down

1. Sixth U.S. president
2. Plant new crops
3. Frame of bars
4. Belly button
5. Some dust jacket paragraphs
6. Like a dryer's trap, typically
7. Start of many Grimm tales
8. Gelling agent
9. Lift one's spirits?
10. Like the laws of kosher food
11. "Now I get it!"
12. CD follower
13. That boat
21. Ending for switch or buck
22. Overwhelm with humor
25. Bird of prey's weapon
26. Application
27. "Balderdash!"
29. "___ Mia!"
30. Poor contributions?

31. What 5 can represent
32. Frost's feet?
33. Natalie Wood portrayal
34. Chicken portion
35. Title of respect
38. Maternal palindrome
39. Fearlessness
41. The gray wolf
42. "Educating ___" (Caine film)
44. Brunch beverage, perhaps
45. "Once upon a midnight ___ ..."
47. Threw in
48. Euripedes tragedy
49. Sunni religion
50. Poppy supporters
52. Leaders in baseball, briefly
53. Pouty look
54. Season to be jolly
55. GPs' grp.
56. Vermont harvest
57. Prefix for pod

Puzzle 136

Across

1. Home run hitter's gait
5. It's full of roots
10. Film terrier
14. Mister, abroad
15. Verboten
16. Impediment to smooth sailing
17. "Nay!" sayer
18. Town in Maine
19. Deal with it
20. Tree in need of comfort?
23. Silly Putty container
24. Opposite of paleo
25. "This is only ___"
28. Distributed the cards
30. Alluring skirt feature
33. Syndicate head
34. Formal speech
37. Reject one's betrothed
38. Celebratory lifting device?
41. Growth period
42. Sharply reduced, as a price
43. Mannequin part
44. Kind of loaf
45. Knock over a joint
49. Fred's sister and dance partner
51. Shoe designation for spindly feet
53. Baden-Baden or Aix-les-bains, e.g.
54. Stream of run-on sentences?
59. Roentgen discovery
61. Luckless fellow
62. Certain woodwind
63. Facilitate
64. State one's case
65. Indonesian island
66. Some have white tails
67. Davis of "Death on the Nile"
68. Prefix for while

Down

1. Prepared for cooking, in a way
2. Not do as promised
3. Former president of Nicaragua
4. Stumble
5. Biblical weapon
6. Loadmaster's concern
7. Take ___ (acknowledge applause)
8. Burt's ex
9. Merge resources
10. Fancy tie
11. Stranded, in a way
12. Water outlet
13. Topic of many a lie
21. Emcee's job
22. Back muscle, to a bodybuilder
26. Cobbler's concern
27. Smithereens maker
29. Impend
30. Egyptian peninsula
31. Fireplace fodder
32. Type of worm
35. Chevet
36. Cash drawer
37. An overworked horse
38. Solemn promise
39. Runner's goal in baseball
40. Addict's program
41. Bleating sound
44. Rookie socialite
46. Line on the weather report
47. Thread holders
48. Start of an Eagles hit title
50. Wedding cake feature
51. Concerning
52. Correspond, grammatically
55. Film monster of 1958 and 1988
56. Slow running pace
57. Start of a guess
58. Garb for the bench
59. Crossed out
60. "Norma ___" (Sally Field film)

Puzzle 137

Across

1. Driver's decision point
5. What some film scripts are written on
9. Hawkins of Dogpatch
14. Chemical element
15. Folklore component
16. Even a bit
17. Building projection
18. ___ impasse
19. Devotional ceremonies
20. Hopscotch, for one
23. Engaged in a diatribe
24. The Moor of Venice
27. Pulver's rank (Abbr.)
28. It's yet to come
31. Small charge carrier
32. Rope maker's fiber
33. Strategy board game
35. Director's order
39. Stereotypical fussbudgets
40. Great thing to be on
41. Part of science class
42. One may follow a lead
44. J.F.K. abbr.
47. Show the ropes
50. You need a cracker to eat it
52. Bad luck, to some
55. Kind of furniture
57. Word with act or gear
58. Common transport
59. Bouquet
60. It's right on a Spanish map
61. Land of the leprechauns
62. Where Alice worked
63. Animal that may be "XING"
64. Camera attachment

Down

1. French carriage
2. Foundling
3. Some pine extracts
4. Got on one's knees
5. Carmichael classic
6. Canape topper, perhaps
7. Panache
8. Blacklist
9. Wife of Abraham
10. "Once upon ___"
11. Pacific divider
12. Mob follower?
13. South African golfer
21. Flies in the face of
22. Former communications corp.
25. Trent or Ronnie
26. Ending of most odds
29. Eastern way
30. Half of the forearm bones
32. Command to a guest
33. Word before "One Two Three" in a film title
34. Subj. for immigrants, perhaps
35. College courtyard
36. Open, in a way
37. Capote, on Broadway
38. Bad thing to be in
39. Draft pick?
42. Sault ___ Marie
43. Stared salaciously
44. Plenary
45. Do a nighttime parental chore
46. Plato's hometown
48. Clock feature
49. Like a loud waterfall
51. Identify
53. Seine tributary
54. Short entry
55. Knee guard
56. Shipping nickname

Puzzle 138

Across

1. Shoe type
4. State since 1948
10. Aletsch Glacier locale
14. "The greatest!"
15. Unlikely to fall over
16. Secular
17. Bar supply, perhaps
18. Lunar lander, e.g.
19. Not for here
20. Lentil, e.g.
22. Words with everywhere
24. Castle features, perhaps
26. Comedic Bean
27. Semilunar valve neighbor
29. Greek letter
31. Recent USNA grad
32. Words sung by the Beatles with me
37. It comes to a head
38. Zorba portrayer
39. Maligned hopper
43. Words with toil and trouble
46. Cavity-filler's grp.
49. Insult, slangily
50. "Golden Boy" playwright
51. Slow, in music
53. Like some eyebrows
56. Words with pumpkin eater
59. A shiny fabric

62. Writer Kingsley
63. Pleasant smells
65. Long fish
66. Dollar value
67. Something to bash at a bash, perhaps
68. Scottish negative
69. Start for date?
70. Made a bird noise
71. Everyday article

Down

1. They may be applied in baseball
2. "I cannot tell ___"
3. Needle dropper
4. Ideal suffix
5. "Uncle Tom's Cabin" author
6. Kind of gun
7. Borders on
8. Femme's pronoun
9. Lecherous look
10. Sacrificial spot, perhaps
11. Taoism founder
12. Dove's city cousin
13. Views with contempt
21. Senile one
23. Romances
25. "It ___ a Very Good Year"
27. Police radio alert, briefly
28. Bullring "bravo!"

29. Russo of "In the Line of Fire"
30. Kind of puppet
33. Prefix for lateral or distant
34. Places for pints
35. "___ Darlin'" (jazz standard)
36. Piano student's assignments
40. Dutifully compliant
41. Keyboard key
42. ___ Moines, Iowa
44. Polecat's trademark
45. Sound of amazement
46. Wool producer
47. Evil spirit (Var.)
48. Manet or Monet, e.g.
52. "Beau ___"
53. Square things
54. Amend, as an atlas section
55. Shipping box
57. Theatrical producer Joseph
58. Lake, city or canal
60. One of Jacob's wives
61. Swiss painter Paul
64. Melancholy

Puzzle 139

Across

1. Egyptian cobras
5. Fashionable
9. San Antonio tourist stop
14. Lacey on "Cagney & Lacey"
15. Word with mark or slinger
16. Character assassination
17. ___ Bator (capital of Mongolia)
18. Spicy Spanish stew
19. Unsavory character
20. I vow to ...
23. Jerry's cartoon foe
24. Discovery at Sutter's Mill
25. Slip up
26. Computer of film
28. Wolf's warning
30. Vampire slayer
32. Of a previous time
33. Sundial numeral
35. Barbarian
36. Emulating a sleepyhead
37. I vow to ...
42. What a siren does
43. It's for the course?
44. Keen longing
45. Canton of William Tell
46. Wearing less
48. Type of fire
52. Clansman's topper
53. Mountain climber's challenge
54. Mentally quick
56. What wasting food is, according to moms
57. I vow to ...
61. It's full of holes
62. Bear of a constellation
63. Part of a futhark
64. Facilitator
65. Fish feature
66. Italian volcano
67. A password provides it
68. "... not always what they ___"
69. Beyond recharging

Down

1. Grown people
2. Miss Kitty's place of employment
3. Type of TV
4. Year's last word
5. Mormon Tabernacle, for one
6. Bisects
7. Man in the Irish Sea?
8. French toppers
9. Appeal
10. Zodiac animal
11. One of the United Arab Emirates
12. Communiques
13. Toreador's acclaim
21. Sheet of print
22. Island group off Scotland
27. Mother of mine?
29. Become prominent
31. Consoling word
34. Pierce with a point
36. Adolescent's bane
37. Flood, as a market
38. Pertaining to both sides of the Urals
39. Most toned
40. Parental purchase for a rock concert?
41. Right-hand page
46. Torte vendor
47. Grapple, to Li'l Abner
49. Very perceptive
50. Reddish-brown pigment, when burnt
51. Group of nine
55. One of a biblical 150
58. End of a walkie-talkie transmission
59. Great Lakes name
60. Ginger's partner
61. "Didn't I tell you?"

Puzzle 140

Across

1. Org. kin
5. Road scholar's book?
10. Methane's lack
14. Start of a Langston Hughes title
15. Where Kent went for a change?
16. Temp's pad
17. "Heaven Can Wait" actress Cannon
18. Impaneled one
19. Commiserator's word
20. Two times?
23. Miniver, for one
24. Princess's annoyance, in fable
25. Lassie, for one
29. Roman goddess
31. Type of tray
34. Situated between poles
35. Quaintly attractive
36. Percussion instrument
37. Three times?
40. You're tense on this
41. Wealthy
42. Language for the masses?
43. Part of WYSIWYG
44. First word in a Melville title
45. Map's table
46. Kind of pill or rally

47. Water temperature gauge, sometimes
48. Four times?
57. Sinister
58. Rustic abode
59. The life of Riley
60. Monthly expense, for many
61. When penitents convene?
62. National League stadium
63. Mine finds
64. One who avoids others
65. Bulgarian's neighbor

Down

1. Adjutant
2. Mythological river
3. Cleansing bar
4. "___ Nanette"
5. Renounce formally
6. Guided trips
7. Traditional knowledge
8. It's a little matter
9. Shell fragments
10. Cornhusker State hub
11. Sandwich shop
12. Muscat locale
13. Table wine
21. Dimple maker
22. Company exec.
25. Wear for Batman and Robin

26. Word with zinc or nitrous
27. Feudal superior
28. "Arsenic and Old ___"
29. Titillating
30. Mormon base
31. More than peeved
32. Aromatic seed
33. Correct text
35. Where baby sleeps
36. Word with race or queen
38. Caribbean climate
39. Baseball card manufacturer
44. Singer Torme
45. Car given as a temporary replacement
46. Trapper's collection
47. Lightweight cord
48. Cold reading
49. Word with throw or turn
50. Midmorning
51. Int'l org. formed in 1949
52. Deep black
53. Nuisance
54. Hawaiian island
55. Consumer
56. Shipbuilding wood

Puzzle 141

Across

1. Pilgrimage site
6. Whale of a movie
10. Sibilant sound
14. Part of an ice cream cone
15. Gaseous element
16. Against
17. Upscale abode
18. Type of wood
19. Gin flavoring
20. Idle gossip, e.g.
23. Poetic form
25. Vessel edge
26. Virtuoso
27. Barrel cleaner
29. Bring to ruin
32. "The Conspiracy Against Childhood" author Le Shan
33. What this is
34. Proboscises
36. Technologically advanced
41. Computer neophyte
42. Catches in the act
44. Muppet name
47. Nudnik
48. Unjust accusation
50. Lower in public estimation

52. Part of some college courses
53. Victorian, for one
54. One with good judgment
59. Jam ingredient
60. Vulgarian
61. Heavy and then some
64. Mini-nuisance
65. Protracted
66. Violin bow application
67. Abridge, e.g.
68. Low female singing voice
69. Gets the better of

Down

1. Advanced sci. degree
2. Author Umberto
3. Court violation
4. Musical wrap-up
5. One of Rocky's rivals
6. Winner's position
7. Shipwreck cause, sometimes
8. Word with rain or sport
9. Looped cross
10. "___ la vista"
11. Under Cupid's spell
12. Put away
13. An earth color

21. Young goat
22. Act passionately
23. Fun food for Fido
24. Diurnal periods
28. Speckled reddishbrown
29. Not worthy
30. It can be flat
31. Self-deprecating utterance
34. Boo-hoos
35. Even wood
37. Home on the range?
38. Sheepcote matriarch
39. Scarcity
40. Ski resort fixture
43. Health farm
44. Uncivilized
45. Be plentiful
46. Rum concoction
48. Sheepish response
49. Incorporate
51. "Rob Roy" author
52. Relinquish one's hold
55. Large earthenware jar
56. April honoree
57. Litter's smallest
58. High-pitched instrument
62. Host's invitation
63. Printers' widths

Puzzle 142

Across

1. Roman calendar notation
5. Some exams
9. Cuddly bear
14. Shout heard on a city street
15. Bushy coif
16. Belching flames, e.g.
17. Hemingway's posthumous "The Garden of ___"
18. Cassoulet or haricot, e.g.
19. Phrase homonym
20. Bobby Darin classic
23. Move a gig
24. Send back to a lower court
28. Cutting-edge
32. Run without rushing
34. Born
35. Prefix meaning sun
36. Nicholson film
38. Black in verse
39. Degree requirement, sometimes
40. Partiality
41. Annual event since 1967
43. Spectrum
44. General-turned politician
45. Fumbler's word
46. "Ship of Fools" author
47. Noted TV street
49. Predicament
50. Clotheshorse
57. Perform like Alfalfa
60. "Puppy Love" singer
61. Not suitable for farming, in a way
62. Chaos
63. Goblet feature
64. Demeanor
65. Relative on mother's side
66. "Que ___ es?" (Spanish 101 question)
67. Pound the poet

Down

1. Docket entry
2. Anti-art art movement
3. Corporate VIP
4. Swim alternative
5. Strut showily
6. Before partner
7. Arduous voyage
8. Like scattered seed
9. Party dress material
10. Violinist Zimbalist
11. Day in Granada
12. Type of dock
13. Permissive reply
21. Hurly-burly
22. They may be in the fire
25. Consecrate with oil
26. Type of music
27. Slower mentally
28. Degree requirement, sometimes
29. Express disapproval
30. Eschews nuptial formalities
31. Mudville number
32. Responds to heat, in a way
33. Lunar valley
36. Type of circle
37. It'll give you a lift
39. Orchestra tuners
42. Type of novel
43. Cakewalk
46. Summer hat
48. In progress
49. It can be wild
51. Chop into small pieces
52. Very much a fan of
53. Certain brocaded fabric
54. London Bridge loc.
55. Ticket info, perhaps
56. Poet St. Vincent Millay
57. Ernesto Guevara de la Serna
58. Was published
59. Macrogametes

Puzzle 143

Tricky

Across

1. Jeanne d'Arc's title (Abbr.)
4. Lightweight hat
10. Bausch's partner
14. ___ in Charles
15. Excessively orna-mented
16. Revered one
17. Flop opposite
18. No real consolation
20. Nails down just right
22. Type of guide
23. Chancel
24. Biblical dead place
26. A wife of Charlie Chaplin
28. Holiday helper
30. Bad luck
33. Move emotionally
34. Samples
35. Pluck eyebrow hairs, e.g.
37. Proof of ownership
40. Engaged in repartee
41. Cuban ballerina Alicia
42. Harbor of Hawaii
43. Clothing store department

44. West Coast football pro
49. Desktop devices
50. Type of American
51. Make a sound in the night?
52. "Who Framed Roger Rabbit" character
54. "Wasn't me!"
57. Feta source
58. Assume responsibility in another's absence
61. "Spring ahead" letters
62. Words in a popular palindrome
63. Mount Hood locale
64. Count Tolstoy
65. To be, in old Rome
66. Tough boss to work for
67. Directional suffix

Down

1. A division into factions
2. Chinese exercises
3. Lauder and Chandler
4. Gomer Pyle's rank
5. Oodles
6. ___ contendere
7. Burdensome
8. One millionth of a meter
9. Ruckus
10. Jacket opener?
11. Dashboard display

12. Emulate Aesop
13. Eatery order, perhaps
19. Postgrad deg.
21. Lessens in force
25. Large-eyed primate
27. Take-home amount
29. Mister Rogers
31. Swindle
32. Vietnamese New Year
33. "The Twilight Zone" creator
36. Admonishes
37. Use it to change levels
38. Qualified voters
39. Allays sorrow
40. Part of a musical gig
42. Mistake-catcher
45. Mean as a snake
46. Ribbon of pasta
47. It clears the boards
48. Gymnast Mary Lou
50. Picnic intruder
53. "Garfield" dog
55. Roman raiment
56. Curling tool
58. Half a bray
59. Stolen
60. Blaster's need

Puzzle 144

Across

1. Places for coats
5. Songdom's pistol packer
9. "Achilles and the Tortoise" subject Mark
14. Algerian port
15. Poetic pronoun
16. Carrot-top creator
17. Doris Day comedy
20. "Bye," somewhere
21. Posted
22. Great lack
24. Green sage of film
25. Short trip
28. Subj. for immigrants, perhaps
29. Apply with a swab
31. North American capital
33. Word in a Christmas carol title
36. Ship's frame
37. One way to be in love
41. Chicken style
42. Petty officer
43. Assert without proof
46. Don'ts partner
47. Sculptor's leaf, perhaps
50. Rocky's greetings
51. Easy-to-grow houseplant
54. Tristram Shandy creator
56. Pulled vehicle
58. Argentine first lady
59. Richard Dreyfuss comedy
63. Walking ___ (elated)
64. Abound
65. German's neighbor
66. "The Divine Miss M"
67. Bit of progress
68. Got a load of

Down

1. Scented hair ointment
2. Wears down
3. Crocodile kin
4. Unwelcome look
5. Music channel
6. Polite interrupter
7. Snakelike tropical swimmer
8. Sound on the air
9. Thug's message
10. Merge metals
11. "Wheel of Fortune" buy, perhaps
12. Keeper's charge
13. Faultfinder
18. Surpassed
19. Tough-guy actor Ray
23. Angelic ring
25. Transport, as freight
26. They fly by night
27. Sidekick
30. Group of people, animals or things
32. And so
33. Use a piggy bank
34. Maiden name intro
35. Walked heavily
37. Hawaiian city
38. Snakelike fishes
39. Some medical grps.
40. Day for bonnets
41. Bandleader Kyser
44. In abundance
45. Ht.
47. Sergeant with badge 714
48. Chant
49. Made to mesh
52. "Golden Boy" playwright
53. White-plumed bird, often
55. Sidestep
56. State of irritation
57. Fencing blade
59. Type of scene
60. Bottom of some scales
61. Meal starter?
62. It helps pump up the volume

Puzzle 145

Across

1. Chronological brinks
5. "Home Alone" kid
10. Chesapeake Bay catch, often
14. Feeling for the unfortunate
15. Don't exist
16. Tramp
17. Three-time US Open champ Lendl
18. High-count fabric
20. Enormous
22. Agglomerate
23. Versifier
24. Asian phrase of insight
26. Melted-cheese dish
30. Graduates, briefly
33. Prefix meaning "sun"
34. Shakespeare title starter
35. Orchestra's place, sometimes
36. Epochs
37. Came at from all sides
39. Hepcat talk
40. Fire preceder?
41. Starstruck trio?
42. More steamed
43. Hyson, e.g.
44. Part of the woodwind family
47. Tout's concerns

48. Element found in none
49. Utter boredom
52. One way to ride a horse
56. 3M innovation
59. Caspian feeder
60. 1855 Tennyson work
61. Entertainer Cheech
62. Currency in Pisa
63. Cube maker Rubik
64. Brief indulgence
65. After the bell

Down

1. Of majestic proportions
2. In ___ (occurring naturally)
3. Substitute for the unnamed
4. Summary
5. Old German emperor
6. Literary errors
7. Sign of secrecy
8. Ones with the power
9. Ultimate, degreewise
10. Material for khakis
11. Part of The San Francisco Treat
12. Act as an accessory
13. Sacrum or parietal
19. Commits a deadly sin
21. London area
24. Qualified

25. Weapon handle
26. Bearded growth
27. Mysteriously spooky
28. Andes creature
29. Cooking herb
30. Richard's first veep
31. Missouri, Arkansas or Connecticut, e.g.
32. Uncompromising
37. Chicago or Boston, e.g.
38. They run only when broken
39. Typical English person
41. Combat doc
42. Nursery rhyme domicile
45. Where to find baked blackbirds
46. Unflustered
47. Surpass
49. Salinger dedicatee
50. State south of Va.
51. Subject, usually
52. Roseanne's maiden name
53. Callas solo
54. Dessert display place
55. Swiss painter, 1879–1940
57. Pinafore lead-in
58. Spigot

Puzzle 146

Across

1. Everyone has one
4. Valuable violin, for short
9. Parasitic pests
13. Basra locale
15. Place to see pro hoops
16. ___ about (approximately)
17. Bank sign (Part 1)
20. Computer letters
21. Before surgery
22. Button on a camcorder
23. Improvises chords, e.g.
25. Words with "care" or "mind"
27. Bank sign (Part 2)
32. Venerates
33. Camera angle, for short
34. Cry of shock
38. Easter prefix
39. Road atlas abbr., perhaps
41. Contractor's figure
43. Wonderment
44. Memorable writer Bombeck
46. Infamous Amin
48. Portuguese capital
50. Bank sign (Part 3)
53. Studies into the wee hours
56. Louisiana stream
57. Cash chaser?
58. The last thing a gambler loses?
61. Acts the worrywart
65. Bank sign (Part 4)
68. "We try harder" company
69. Villain's visage
70. Diary capacity, typically
71. Feel dizzy
72. "___ Gabler" (Ibsen play)
73. Sounds of hesitation

Down

1. Distance in a Stephen King title
2. Beehive State city
3. First name in spydom
4. Mineo of moviedom
5. Excessively, in music
6. Gets on one's high horse?
7. Last Stuart monarch
8. "The Banana Boat Song" word
9. Baseball legend Gehrig
10. Opening remarks
11. "Suzanne" composer Leonard
12. On twos, rather than fours
14. Gear for Robin Hood
18. "Buffy the Vampire ___"
19. Andy Taylor's son
24. Occult figure
26. J.F.K.'s predecessor
27. Locks in a stable?
28. Olfactory stimulant
29. Group standard
30. San Francisco hill
31. In a wicked manner
35. Kotter of classic TV
36. Camp Lejeune truant
37. Prevent from scoring, e.g.
40. Japanese capital, once
42. Become extinct, e.g.
45. You can bank on it
47. Drenched
49. Having rugged physical strength
51. ___ buco (veal dish)
52. Stroked playfully or lovingly
53. Proud papa's handout, perhaps
54. Christopher of "Noises Off!"
55. Band leader Shaw
59. Lullaby word
60. "The Last Days of Pompeii" heroine
62. Extra-wide sneaker width
63. Construction piece
64. Orch. section
66. Fashion designer's monogram
67. "Are you a man ___ mouse?"

Puzzle 147

Across

1. Nascar sponsor
4. Repairman's stock
9. North Dakota city
14. Geological time span
15. Difficult to miss
16. Name on a famous war plane
17. Land in the Thames, e.g
18. "Goodbye"
20. Makes less tense
22. Again from the top
23. Check copy
24. Garner
26. What babies do eventually
30. Crave
32. Do-say connection
34. Colorful Vietnam city?
35. "Goodbye"
39. Beach-house support
42. Muscle car of song
43. Places to go around in circles
44. "Goodbye"
47. In the manner of
48. Bob Hope's WWII gp.
49. Venerated mementos
53. Endanger
56. Polish name ending
58. Enticement
59. The bulk

61. Offensively malodorous
63. "Goodbye"
67. Nancy Drew's beau
68. Makin, for one
69. They're rich in chips
70. Blood-pressure raiser
71. "Winner" in an infamous headline
72. No longer current
73. Positive thinker's word

Down

1. Hermetic
2. Vacuum tube type
3. Academese, e.g.
4. Attitudinize
5. Retribution seeker
6. Actress Witherspoon
7. Determine judicially
8. Greek covered path
9. Donnybrook
10. Bowled over
11. Word with so or interested
12. Center of the Grand Opry
13. Petroleum residue
19. Deal with a snarl
21. Muffle
25. Results of getting needled?
27. At that point

28. First name in wrestling legends
29. Stork's supper, sometimes
31. Pro ___ (proportionately)
33. Booted, e.g.
36. Freudian interests
37. Fish-eating sea bird
38. Brandishes
39. Spurious imitation
40. Fish story
41. Dr. Pavlov
45. Hospitality recipient
46. They hit in Baltimore
50. Unexpectedly appropriate
51. Brownie, for one
52. Home of Saab
54. Plentiful
55. Demurely
57. Gentle cycle items
60. Mechanism trigger
62. Spot of land
63. Owned at one time
64. Had a helping
65. Gunshot sound
66. Santa's trailer

Puzzle 148

Across

1. Musical phrase mark
5. "___ got a ticket to ride"
9. Noted fur trader
14. Sound quality
15. Like a sourball
16. Porter's beer
17. Opera about an Ethiopian slave girl
18. Inter ___ (among others)
19. "King Kong" star
20. "Before the Next Teardrop Falls" singer
23. Units of length, in physics
24. Apportions
28. Under favorable circumstances
32. Swap words
35. Oddsmaker's last words?
36. Quiz choice, perhaps
37. Biker's mount
38. Not just any
39. Oceanic eagle
40. Untold centuries
42. Property encumbrances
44. ___ buco (Italian dish)
45. Negotiate
48. Blew a gasket
49. The Entertainer
53. Calf-length slacks

57. Avoid cancellation
60. Not virtual
61. What you can take from me?
62. Sports center
63. "Young Frankenstein" character
64. 15th-century maritime name
65. Trivial
66. No layabout
67. Faculty boss

Down

1. Supply with workers
2. Valley of the chateaux
3. Word with wear or stand
4. Allow in again
5. Diligently pursues or resides
6. Football game segment
7. Weird-sounding lake
8. First name in slapstick comedy
9. Too
10. Like a moonless sky
11. Nursery moppet
12. Caught stealing
13. AAA offerings
21. Confused noise
22. Miami-___ (Florida county)
25. Frightful giants

26. Calendar col. heading
27. Shorthand pro
29. Successfully crashed the gate
30. Was audibly impressed
31. Without a break
32. Masticates
33. Fracas
34. One of Nixon's vices?
41. Biblical reptile
42. Cheryl or Alan
43. Worldly, not spiritual
44. Veteran
46. Elbowroom
47. D.D.E. beat him twice
50. Rally to even the score again
51. One of a Chekhov trio
52. Poli-sci buff's cable station
54. Sun-baked
55. He "jaws" at night
56. Doctor's interruption
57. Grammy category
58. Prior to, to Prior
59. Place to surf without a board

Puzzle 149

Across

1. List type
5. Where the Gurkha reigned
10. Broken-down horse
14. Oil cartel letters
15. Stand up and speak
16. Verdi's "D'amor sull'ali rosee," e.g.
17. Suckling spot
18. Where some of the talk is bull?
20. Book slips?
22. Mascara's target
23. Some paper rectangles
24. Distress calls
26. Feudal fellow
28. They may have a crush on you
30. Cowboys' ropes
34. Moises or Felipe of baseball
38. World Series workers
40. Unusual objet d'art
41. 1950 Billy Wilder movie
44. Big name in chips
45. Woody Guthrie's son
46. Focus group?
47. Greek marketplaces
49. Some boxing outcomes
51. Uses a tuffet
53. TV legend Red
58. Rose-rose linkup

61. Phrase of denial
63. Home of the descendants of Ishmael
64. Novel set on the Monterey coast
67. Like some records
68. Bart's teacher
69. Silents star Bow
70. "Dedicated to the ___ Love" (Shirelles song)
71. Called, in poker
72. Steel-driving man
73. Part of Doris Day's theme song

Down

1. Pillar of American Indian society?
2. Handel's "Lotario," e.g.
3. Term of affection
4. Group of eight
5. Characteristic of an impossible situation
6. Unforgettable time
7. Get wearisome
8. Mythical Titan
9. One of two evils
10. Cream container
11. Vicinity
12. "They ___ With Their Boots On" (1941 film)
13. Has vittles
19. Not just again

21. Liquor bill
25. Brazilian dance
27. 20th-century French painter
29. Football, for one
31. Highchair feature
32. Billion suffix
33. Lays down the lawn
34. Polo explored it
35. Respiratory organ
36. Not deceived by
37. Product requirements
39. Makes a pouty face
42. "Seinfeld" friend
43. Avert one's eyes
48. Larry of "F Troop"
50. Sun. message
52. Savoir faire
54. Largest city of Nigeria
55. Steakhouse order
56. Crude transportation?
57. Gymnast Comaneci
58. Completes a cupcake
59. Marquis de ___
60. Frank with a diary
62. Today's Persia
65. Bert Bobbsey's twin
66. Hockey great Bobby

Puzzle 150

Across

1. It comes in cakes or bars
5. Sends junk e-mail to
10. Villa d'___ (Italian landmark)
14. Clergy member, somewhere
15. Palindromic belief
16. Ostrich cousin
17. Moving picture?
19. Castle waterway
20. Come forth
21. Intentionally kept concealed, as a motive
23. Family tree word
24. "So what ___ is new?"
26. Deficiency
27. Vinegar holders
29. Swarms, as with life
32. Cosmo of early TV
35. Easy mark
37. Larry's tormentor
38. Spread out
40. Take into custody
43. Step into character
44. Grumpy companion?
46. "The Last of the Mohicans" author
47. Capital of Morocco
50. Remove a file, in a way
52. Item of finality in the paper, briefly
54. Endeavour acronym
55. Yield to gravity
58. Puts in an unsuitable role
60. Aristotle, to Alexander the Great
62. Walloping wind
63. "Gunsmoke" or "Wagon Train," e.g.
65. Congregational cry
66. Disc jockey's cue
67. Remains after dinner?
68. "Sesame Street" name
69. Certain fisherman
70. Lowest level of high tide

Down

1. Jammed with the band
2. Heavy to the max
3. Lower in public estimation
4. Tacna's country
5. French holy woman, for short
6. Read with great care
7. Short stockings
8. Swim contest
9. Toss about
10. Fur-bearing animal
11. Movie genre, slangily
12. Dotted-line command
13. Have a repast
18. Expressed derision
22. Word in a supposed Cagney quote
25. Drew in
27. Bookkeeper
28. Marsupial pocket, e.g.
30. Glutton's request
31. Clairvoyant
32. Slope conveyance
33. Bottlenose relative
34. Hardly fine literature
36. Treasure map distances, sometimes
39. Assent gesture
41. Word with skin or chip
42. Certain limb's end
45. Certain time zone
48. Heading on a roll book
49. Recurrent twitch
51. Famous pet
53. Lake on the California-Nevada border
55. Cubic meter
56. Main artery
57. Seize upon
58. Lansbury or Ball role
59. Unit of loudness
61. Well briefed about
62. Shoot the breeze
64. Answer incorrectly, for example

Puzzle 151

Across

1. Pack down firmly
5. Mast attachment
10. Crazy way to run
14. Orchestra pitch setter
15. Up in arms
16. Denmark native
17. Superabundance
18. Insincere promise
20. 6-3, e.g., in tennis
21. Circus structure
22. Macho types
23. Ghostly verb
25. "The Last Emperor" actress Joan
27. Consecrate
29. Cinephiles go to them
33. The Velvet Fog
34. High school dances
35. Big, fat mouth
36. They sometimes get the ax
37. Ruckuses
38. Jacob's son
39. Smart-whip connectors
40. Utilizes a spatula
41. Champion of dance
42. They're on the lookout
44. Absolutely useless
45. Opposite "yippee!"
46. Low grade?
47. Pallid
50. Japanese aborigine
51. Pen tip
54. Pearly-gray fur
57. Relinquish
58. Orange coat
59. Ring-shaped reef
60. "... against ___ of troubles"
61. They can be made to meet
62. Skein components
63. Peter the Great, e.g.

Down

1. Glad rags
2. Having the right stuff
3. Harmonica, e.g.
4. Dog or gerbil, perhaps
5. Word in a Christmas carol title
6. Computer command
7. Absorbed
8. "___ alive!"
9. It's only one until you cross it
10. Pre-Christmas period
11. Hurt severely
12. Some years back
13. Intellectually acute
19. Ostrich relatives
21. Melody
24. Draws a bead on
25. Pork portions
26. Mini features
27. First cervical vertebra
28. Gallows sight
29. Lint catchers, e.g.
30. One who sees firsthand
31. "Bolero" composer
32. Part of a steeple
34. Carries on, as a trade
37. Emulate a butterfly
38. Builder's units
40. It was spent on the Riviera once
41. Spiritual teacher
43. Fashion shifts
44. Epilogue or coda, e.g.
46. Occupies completely
47. Measurement in a Caldwell title
48. Tibia locale
49. Forest forager
50. Medicinal lily from Africa
52. Mental inspiration
53. Unwilling fairy tale host
55. Crone
56. Suffix meaning "resident"
57. Grimalkin, for one

Puzzle 152

Across

1. Some artists' studios
6. "The Flim-___ Man" (1967 movie)
10. Some exemptions
14. Alaskan native
15. River, cit,y or state
16. Took an elevator, e.g.
17. Historic Alabama city
18. Setting for three kings, perhaps
20. Paint-mixing boards
22. Note header
23. Not fixed
24. Some post office machines
28. Out like a light
30. Watergate conspirator
31. Loamy soil deposit
32. "___ to the Church on Time"
33. Important letters for Els
34. Cutlass, for one
35. Ore used as a cleansing agent
36. Organ part
37. The Bard's witch
38. Dweebish
39. Settle an account
40. Some synthetic fabrics
42. Four score
43. Tranquilizes
44. Pool-owner's problem
45. Cardinals' cap abbr., in baseball
46. It might be x-rayed

49. Result of flying the coop?
53. Adjutants
54. Traditional knowledge
55. Golden rule preposition
56. Bits of news
57. Look with malicious intent
58. Dispose of, informally
59. Kingdom of Croesus

Down

1. Cindy Brady feature
2. Prime draft classification
3. With complete status
4. Eternal
5. Pigeon perches, sometimes
6. Played a flute in a march, e.g.
7. Reed and Grant
8. Hole-punching gadget
9. Spike Lee film
10. Charlotte, Emily or Anne
11. Last word of the golden rule
12. Bradley and Sullivan
13. Part of WYSIWYG
19. Mass of humanity
21. Start to fall
24. Thai dish
25. Foolish
26. Spicy French stew
27. Word with "make it"

28. Greetings on some islands
29. Console
30. Range rovers
32. Injures with a horn
35. Mild stimulant from a palm tree
36. Wisdom
38. Smartly dressed
39. Braid relative
41. King's employee
42. Inventor Whitney
44. They create carbon monoxide
46. Former fleet
47. Trucking rig
48. Pisan pronoun
49. Building addition, sometimes
50. A Stooge
51. Opposite of post-
52. Former Roxy Music member

Puzzle 153

Across

1. Stallone role
6. Sanction misdeeds
10. Remove holes
14. One way to set a clock
15. Shady route
16. Skin-cream ingredient, perhaps
17. 1956 crime drama (with "The")
20. Hardly exciting
21. Former British prime minister Wilson
22. Protective shelter
25. Temperamental star
28. Source for a movie, often
29. On the fence
33. Had been
34. Ritchie Valens classic
35. Means to a diagnosis
37. 1959 comedy with Anna Neagle (with "The")
43. Glance over
44. "The Pink Panther" director Edwards
46. Day-after-Christmas event
50. Social protocols
53. Arkin and Alda
55. Like contented bugs
56. Braying beast
57. Bean or noodle
59. Violist's clef, perhaps
62. 1989 war film
68. Garner
69. Pride sound
70. It connects levels
71. To be, to Brutus
72. Superficially cultured
73. Land on the Sea of Japan

Down

1. Vied for office
2. "Eureka!"
3. Debussy's "La ___"
4. Shakespeare, for one
5. Olfactory property
6. Means of exoneration
7. Embargo
8. Chang's twin
9. It follows Georgia in higher education
10. Monkey Trial attorney
11. Recess or small room
12. Word with derby or coaster
13. Compass part
18. African ravine
19. Actor Holm
22. Pot top
23. Organic compound
24. U.S. poet Millay
26. Niacin, for one
27. Roman greetings
30. It's sometimes bitter
31. Low-lying islands
32. Title for a U.S. atty.
36. Toothpaste container
38. Truman's successor, popularly
39. Isn't off one's rocker?
40. Short elevation
41. Pro ___ (in proportion)
42. Barely makes do (with "out")
45. Feminine suffix
46. River formed by the Congaree and Wateree
47. Oahu greetings
48. Some brews
49. Wankel or diesel
51. Stone pit
52. Homely fruit?
54. Recruit's sentence ender, perhaps
58. Nick Charles' wife
60. To-do list item, perhaps
61. Having knowledge of
63. Neither fish ___ fowl
64. Create knotted lace
65. Predatory fish
66. Canard
67. Division of history

Puzzle 154

Across

1. Exasperated
6. Pond life
10. Nile reptiles
14. Preminger suspense classic
15. It needs room to grow
16. Low-level smuggler
17. Candied item
19. It's on tap in Mexico
20. It may be bitter or loose
21. The Gramophone Company Ltd., later
22. Turns from side to side
24. Cushion site
26. Barbarians
27. Acropolis locale
30. Straighten out, as an iron bar
32. Like some jokes
33. Professional charges
34. Hearty pub offering
37. Why you may give a darn?
38. Send to another doctor
40. Sarah McLachlan hit song
41. Greek letter
42. Certain Pueblo Indian
43. Computer programmer, e.g.
44. West of country
46. Settle a debt
47. Luke's father
48. Lorelei's river
50. Cartel leader
52. Env. extra
53. Period of note
56. Cuzco people
57. White House area
60. Prom attendee
61. Weather-beaten
62. Human herbivore
63. Gets it all wrong
64. J.F.K. sights, once
65. Plant swelling problem

Down

1. Mass in Arctic waters
2. Rake in
3. Twosome
4. Vase with a footed base
5. Where many a story starts
6. Chilled meat dish
7. "To Kill a Mockingbird" author
8. "___ Louise!"
9. Seat-of-the-pants talker
10. South American river
11. Gold digger's target
12. Name-drops a product
13. Global seven
18. Some grounded birds
23. Hits the road
24. Formally surrender
25. More thin-skinned
27. Throb
28. Horseback ride
29. Luau entertainer, maybe
31. Formerly known as
35. In ___ of
36. Tombstone tamer
38. Some tax shelters
39. Prefix with center or cycle
40. Top-of-the-line
42. Start of a Web site address
43. Like some lenses
45. They may be vital
46. "Turandot" role
47. Mel works here
49. Obeys
50. Toy with a tail
51. Yuletide quaffs
53. Chisel feature
54. Do boring work?
55. "Black Beauty" author Sewell
58. Matched parts or part of a match
59. Type of meat

Puzzle 155

Across

1. Monk's hood
5. Frat alternative
9. Charlotte Corday's victim
14. "What ___ mindreader?"
15. Small toiletry case
16. River past Grenoble
17. Essence
20. What have you, briefly
21. Jelly brand used for fuel
22. Corrodes
23. Ship of fuels
25. Nautical flag
27. Coach and teacher in one
29. Armor plate that protects the chest (Var.)
31. Any of three English rivers
32. Sure-footed
33. Common pronoun
36. Essence
40. Unit of time
41. Started a poker pot
42. Hourly wage, e.g.
43. Used a firehouse pole
44. Christie detective
46. Golf ball material
50. Maximum minimal amount
51. Rodin sculpture
52. Low points
55. Hearing aid
58. Essence
61. Alternative to pica
62. Leander's love
63. One of seven for Salome
64. Of sedate character
65. Pizzazz
66. Whirlpool

Down

1. Pet store purchase
2. Not include
3. Madison state
4. Back muscle, to gym regulars
5. More adroit
6. Aquatic mammal
7. German river
8. Appearance
9. War stat
10. Michaelmas daisy
11. Put a new price on
12. Sharp mountain spur
13. Far from prolix
18. Seat of King Olaf V's rule
19. On wheels
24. Agendum
26. Got mileage out of
27. Engage in self-pity
28. Mark replacement
29. Spurred (on)
30. Encircle with a band
32. Naysayer
33. Encouraged
34. Word with bump or jump
35. Proofreader's marking, perhaps
37. Dawn direction
38. Away from the water
39. Colored portion of the eye
44. Human being
45. Drying oven
46. They may get loaded at the baseball game
47. Grown-up
48. Female monster of Greek myth
49. Valuable violin
50. Sign of the Zodiac
53. Former Davis Cup coach
54. Point of honor settler
56. Sulfuric or hydrochloric follower
57. Depend (upon)
59. "The Simpsons" neighbor, Flanders
60. Blvd. relative

Puzzle 156

Across

1. You may be shown it
5. Catch sight of
9. Smoldering coal, e.g.
14. Teenage problem
15. Bang-up
16. Toast type
17. Grisham work
20. Green light
21. Lamb's alias
22. "Rocky III" fighter
23. A Met number
25. Goes ballistic
27. Defenseless victims or Bedard works
32. It may have complex stanza forms
33. First name among divas
34. Seasoning quantity
38. Memorable mission
40. Braying beast
41. Charlie's little sister
42. Trujillo locale
43. Frigid
45. Small quantity
46. McMurtry work
49. "Cabaret" city
52. Glazier's unit
53. Absorbed the cost of
54. Rickey need
57. Eagerly ready (with "up")
61. 1968 Richard Burton film

64. Archimedean machine
65. Bestial bellow
66. Joie de vivre
67. Popular Christmas gifts, up north
68. See at a distance
69. Place for brooding

Down

1. Holdings of some banks
2. "The Highwayman" singer Phil
3. ___, tens, hundreds
4. Kind of performance
5. Type of cracker
6. Tasty paste
7. Some years back
8. Canvasback kin
9. Set out on
10. Sea, across the sea
11. Dirigible
12. Movie critic Roger
13. They might send you down the river
18. Tenor Caruso
19. Dorothy, to Em
24. Blazing
26. Meat package letters
27. Kind of opera
28. Between engagements
29. Lacrimal droplet
30. Many are compact
31. Clear, as a drain

35. Brahms's "___Rhapsody"
36. Croatian, e.g.
37. Noted park name
39. Ponder
41. Movie divisions
43. Broadway hit
44. The use of figurative language
47. Defunct Texas team
48. Numb
49. Wails lustily
50. Mrs. Mertz
51. "Superman" star
55. Dark part of the moon
56. Psyche parts
58. Breathing rattle
59. Eventful times in history
60. Fender bend
62. Color of some diamonds
63. Child seat?

Puzzle 157

Across

1. Picks up
5. Equally distant
10. Circumstance's partner
14. Evangelical Roberts
15. Handy's "___ Street Blues"
16. Body partner
17. Male parent
18. Fabulist extraordinaire
19. Chlorophyllous organism
20. Component of momentum, perhaps
23. Frequently
24. Sch. auxiliary
25. G.W. Carver studied it
27. Word at an unveiling, perhaps
31. Type of lens
34. Ultimate purpose
36. It's after Monte
37. Earl Grey and others
38. Clay brick
40. "Othello" provocateur
44. Mortise-joint component
46. Ire
48. Concurrent program airing
52. Absconded with
53. Fanfare
54. Type or sort
56. Do sum math?
57. Looking like Porky?
64. Chicken style

66. Injurious acts
67. One of the martial arts
68. Poet Pound
69. Greece's Constantine II, for one
70. Length X width
71. It's overhead
72. "The Age of Innocence" actress
73. Symphonic silence

Down

1. Golly cousin
2. Famous canal
3. Scarlett's turf
4. Bob in the Olympics?
5. Sternward
6. Recreation for two
7. Intentionally skip meals
8. Medicinal plant
9. Changed the decor, in a way
10. Bible book, briefly
11. One of the others of 37-Across
12. Coffee amount, perhaps
13. County in Missouri or Nebraska
21. Birthstone for some
22. Word with corn or cracker
26. Embrocate
27. Hardly a rookie, briefly
28. Early afternoon
29. Classic TV mom Morgenstern

30. Like the home team, in baseball
32. Pictures on a small screen
33. Very small amount
35. English town on the Lune
39. Edmond O'Brien thriller
41. Commotion
42. Hair goo
43. Miner's pay dirt
45. Ms. Fitzgerald
47. Acts on one's curiosity
48. Object of Jimmy Buffett's search
49. Treat salt, in a way
50. Contemporary
51. Diacritical dot
55. DVD-player component
58. Like Jimi Hendrix's lady
59. Parched
60. Open a crack
61. As the driven snow
62. Mid-March day
63. Blame bearer
65. A wine container

Puzzle 158

Across

1. State flower of N.M.
6. Camp retreat
10. Baby seals, e.g.
14. Castaway's site, perhaps
15. Borodin opera prince
16. Mozart's Trojan princess
17. Trait of one displaying good judgment
20. Nonkosher
21. Unmatched
22. Defender of Troy
23. Demeanor
24. Word with deep or stir
25. En route on the QEII, e.g.
26. High school math course
32. Word with bar or days
34. Sea eagles
35. "Norma ___" (Sally Field film)
36. Shrink trailer
37. Deuce toppers
39. Post-larval insect
40. Do not delay
41. Regrets
42. Burns and Allen, e.g.
43. Brother-and-sister pop act
47. Intentions
48. Acoustic organ
49. Word with up or down
52. Acclaim
55. Range of vision
56. Of the highest quality, informally
57. They once hung over the Kremlin
60. Rombauer or "La Douce"
61. Baal, e.g.
62. Luster
63. Revolutionary Trotsky
64. ___ d'Azur
65. Fixes, as fences

Down

1. Historic conference site
2. Gestation stations
3. Darkroom object
4. Staff opening
5. The most you can get
6. Hippie coloring method
7. Old oath
8. Land east of Eden
9. Some high crimes
10. Auricles
11. 1997 Fonda role
12. Galileo's birthplace
13. Brat's forte
18. Headpiece?
19. Judges to be
24. Temporary trend
25. High-altitude habitation (Var.)
27. Race segment
28. Where to get down?
29. Honest
30. Engrossed
31. Some approvals
32. Knock out of the park
33. Military doctor's concern
37. Curry powder ingredient
38. Workout units
39. "___ favor, senor!"
41. Cause for celebration
42. Word with second or mile
44. Alligatorlike reptile
45. Kid
46. Turns into leather
50. Guideless
51. They're coming of age
52. TV Dr.
53. Stamp designation
54. It's loaded
55. It takes two people to tie it
56. Rubdown target
58. Pother
59. Doctrine

Puzzle 159

Across

1. Famous brother
5. Woodsy sites, often
10. Nosebag filler
14. "Mon ___!"
15. Papal garb
16. Black fly, e.g.
17. Feathered projectile
18. Squash squasher
19. Having the jitters, perhaps
20. Hit tune by 58-Across
23. Lobster trap
24. Something fishy?
25. Fall back
28. Drags one's feet
31. VSOP glass
33. ___ War, 1899-1902
35. Raison d'___
36. Hit tune by 58-Across
43. All-conquering thing
44. Rump
45. Helped someone cover up?
49. One beyond belief?
54. Yon maiden fair
55. "Ah, me!"
57. Wabbit hunter
58. Yarrow, Stookey, Travers
62. Smile up a storm
64. Rugged rocks
65. Prospectors' prizes
66. Cut the fat
67. ___ verte (graygreen)
68. Lessor's responsibility
69. Luck's title
70. Three-time PGA champ
71. Some Saint-Lo seasons

Down

1. Detox center candidate
2. Region of Nigeria
3. More hair-raising
4. "Here and Now" singer, Vandross
5. What a mama's boy needs to cut?
6. Elaborate song for solo voice
7. Like Rambo
8. Entreats earnestly
9. It can be delivered on Sunday
10. Curved molding
11. Indy winner, 1969
12. Game of pursuit
13. Chester White's home
21. Cover story?
22. X-ray relative
26. European capital
27. Propagated
29. One billion years, in geology
30. Variety of whale
32. Word in a Marines slogan
34. ER staff
36. Expression of general listlessness
37. Solitaire spot, perhaps
38. Making too much
39. Condition of some paint
40. Yunnan or Keemun, e.g.
41. It may be passed
42. Memorable Merman
46. Make lacework, in a way
47. Votes in
48. McGavin of "Kolchak: The Night Stalker"
50. Crime writer Leonard
51. Turkish hostelry
52. Unflustered
53. Secret meetings
56. Alley mark
59. Award for "60 Minutes"
60. Taj Mahal city
61. Betrayed, in a way
62. Liq. container
63. Romantic or Victorian, e.g.

Puzzle 160

Across

1. Word with tag or double
5. Answering-machine feature
9. Thrash about
14. Potent start
15. Europe's tallest volcano
16. Links' rara avis
17. Gas that's hard to ignore
18. It has its place in the Bible
19. Came around
20. Make calls
23. Playground rejoinder
24. Sheet at the police station
25. Word with media or hysteria
29. They're uncertain
31. Type of clock or number
33. Adventurous exploit
37. Tinker about
40. Tin Man's quest
42. "Fantasy Island" prop
43. Strauss selection?
44. Transplant hero
47. You may get a hand here
48. Daily ritual, below the border
49. Burglarize
51. "Live at Red Rocks" musician John
52. Multiple refusals
55. Declared
60. Really taut
63. Bringing death
66. Much of Mongolia
67. Mystique, e.g.
68. Key ring
69. Sterilizing apparatus
70. Overpriced, e.g.
71. Needs a bath badly, e.g.
72. Where subs are assembled
73. Concert halls

Down

1. South Pacific nation
2. Islamic prince (Var.)
3. Swinburne's "___ on Charlotte Bronte"
4. City in North Dakota
5. Drive back, as an attack
6. Permanently mark, in a way
7. Word of welcome
8. Former Turkish title
9. Cause of cowardice
10. It helps level the playing field?
11. Way back when
12. Classification
13. "Do the Right Thing" director
21. "___ won't be afraid" ("Stand by Me" lyric)
22. A birthstone
26. Nitrogen compound
27. Form of protest
28. Jerk
30. Forage storage
32. "The Splendid Splinter" Williams
33. Author's writer
34. Unsettlingly strange
35. Men of learning, e.g.
36. Some attempts at intimidation, in sports
38. Jungle home
39. Name that's quite fashionable
41. Razer's supply, perhaps
45. Backwoods interjection
46. "The Thieving Magpie" composer
50. Sheepish response
53. Burns film
54. Potbelly, e.g.
56. State since 1890
57. Certain priest of old
58. Sudden onrush
59. City since 1854
61. Troubles and misfortunes
62. First second son
63. A ways away
64. Had something
65. It's usually first into the tub

Puzzle 161

Across

1. Dungeness or hermit
5. Ovine exchanges
9. Basic-training activity
14. River through Leeds
15. Coiffure style
16. "Cat got your tongue?" e.g.
17. Protected, in a way
19. Disney pachyderm
20. Mel Brooks classic, 1974
22. Short map line?
23. Mom's order
24. Bronco catcher
28. Ahead of schedule
31. Light color?
34. When mammoths lived
36. Piddling amount
37. Turn gray
38. James Baldwin novel
41. In this location
42. Cyan finish
43. Expunged
44. They make periodical changes (Abbr.)
45. Nocturnal sound
47. Selfish folks
48. Trail the pack
49. Family name
51. Clark Gable film, 1938
59. Old Toyota
60. Kind of garden
61. Broadcasting
62. Teen follower
63. Mat victories
64. Modeler's wood
65. Went on horseback, e.g.
66. Entree go-with

Down

1. Low-___ diet
2. Iranian coin
3. Covent Garden ear pleaser
4. Auto pioneer Karl
5. Very well-done!
6. Highest point
7. Hubbubs
8. Place for lost change
9. Daily divider
10. Former juvenile
11. Hoarfrost
12. Male swans
13. Abbreviated medical plan
18. Small meat turnover (Var.)
21. Loaded with options
24. Like a ballerina
25. Needed liniment
26. Tiresias and Nostradamus, e.g.
27. Out of harm's way
29. "Roots" Emmy-winner
30. Beluga spawn, e.g.
31. Texas Hold 'em ploy
32. Funny Fudd
33. Title documents
35. "___ bragh!"
37. Elhi support groups
39. Tokyo's ex-name
40. He said, "The buck stops here!"
45. Largest desert
46. Exaggerated a part
48. Large-eyed lemur
50. Windy City destination
51. Popular salad
52. Fall gemstone
53. Construction beam
54. Benin neighbor
55. Spin backward?
56. Galba's 602
57. Reach the beach
58. "You're something ___!"
59. Woeful sound

Puzzle 162

Tough

Across

1. Some turkeys
5. Sweetened custard
9. Davidic verse
14. Shampoo additive, perhaps
15. Billion follower
16. More than a franchisee
17. Was philanthropic
18. Infection of a sebaceous gland
19. Surfer's stops
20. Sideshow attraction, perhaps
23. Borrower's burden
24. Early spring flowers
28. Park features, perhaps
32. Stock value, perhaps
33. Request legal recompense
34. Coat material, perhaps
37. Feeds the hogs
39. Stone made of silicon and oxygen
40. Some Muslims
42. Got off a horse, e.g.
43. Favorite's defeat
45. Swimming stroke
47. Third of September?
48. 1963 Paul Newman role
50. Firstborn
51. Vortices
53. Mr. Peanut accessory
55. Brit's dish, sometimes
61. They may be planted
64. Instinctive impulse
65. Alpine reverberation
66. Culpability
67. Utter indistinctly
68. Gad about
69. Rumor producers?
70. One of the Cartwrights
71. Start a pot

Down

1. Old witches
2. Distinctive flair
3. Observatory observation, perhaps
4. Make an effort to find
5. Dictatorial ones
6. Gracefully limber
7. Certain Indo-European
8. ___-do-well
9. They're not who they pretend to be
10. Make like a whirlpool
11. Pantry invader
12. "Malcolm X" director
13. Bride's new title
21. Norse deity who defeated Thor
22. Kingston Trio hit of '59
25. Tristan's love
26. The eyes have them
27. Last six lines of a sonnet, often
28. Company of performers
29. MC Hammer did it
30. Lowered in esteem
31. End of access
32. Hardly a libertine
35. Elmer ___
36. Interplanetary transport
38. Alan of "Shane"
41. Those who use currency
44. They believe in God
46. Knighted actor Guinness
49. Letters on a flattop
52. "If ___" (Beatles song)
53. It's after Monte
54. Breed of cattle
56. "Pipe down!"
57. Zeus' consort
58. PC screen image
59. Excellent, in slang
60. Unspecified quantity
61. "Ben-Hur" studio
62. French affirmative
63. Word describing Abner

Puzzle 163

Across

1. Street vernacular
6. Livorno currency, once
10. Certain construction beam
14. Black thrush
15. Teapot tempests?
16. Artist's inspiration
17. Alternate passage indicator, in a score
18. Where soldiers are made
20. Flabbergasted
22. Clothes line
23. ___ de la Cite
24. Weave go-with
25. Crackpot
28. "Look ___ ye leap"
29. Wax eloquent
31. Permeates moistly
33. Heady draft
34. Sneaky-laugh sound
36. Deck-planking wood
37. Concerns for ecologists
40. Aka Deseret
42. Hockey legend
43. A/C capacity measurement
44. Chinese-food order request, perhaps
46. Part of IV
48. "Shoo!" on the farm?
51. Socially-emerging young woman
52. It may be heroic

54. One-time White House nickname
55. It contains genetic info
56. Blistering
60. Ignore the alarm
62. Erode
63. Cubbyhole
64. Type of exam
65. More than double
66. Defeats regularly, in slang
67. Italy's Villa d'___
68. Divided, as real estate

Down

1. Offer comfort to
2. More opulent
3. Presuppose
4. Nuremberg negative
5. Flower shop purchases, sometimes
6. Famous tar pits
7. Words that bond
8. Type of float
9. Member of the Jetson's family
10. Computer that came in many colors
11. Crummy joints?
12. Dangerous reptile
13. Solfege syllables
19. World Series winners of 1908 and not since
21. City in Oklahoma
26. "___ lazy river ..."

27. "For shame!"
30. McCullough's "The ___ Birds"
32. Words to Brutus
33. Massage reactions, perhaps
35. Burial site for Abraham and Sarah
37. Talk and talk and talk ...
38. Squanders little by little (with "away")
39. "The Girl From Ipanema" saxophonist
40. Berlin connection
41. Musician's tapper
45. Comic's collection
47. Almost a home run
48. How some potatoes are served (with "au")
49. Ready for a commitment?
50. Made some lace
53. Lover of Daphnis
57. Rankles
58. Shipshape
59. Casino game
60. Lennon's mate
61. Formal promise

Puzzle 164

Across

1. Moat menace, briefly
5. On or about
10. Place for change
14. Word with happy or eleventh
15. Make into law
16. Verb with down or out
17. Shop sign
19. Naysayer
20. Freshman on the bench
21. Cry from a nest over water
23. Brit. honor
24. It cannot be returned
25. Make coffee, in a way
26. "Kalifornia" star
28. Consent concern
31. Word with space or soap
34. Sweet-smelling necklace
35. Part of some film reviews
36. Loony
40. King of entertainment
41. Industrial container
42. Usher's post, often
43. French appellation
44. Mr. with the Mrs. and Mrs.
47. Kyrgyzstan range
48. Test req.
49. High-tech defense initials
52. "Little Women" author
55. On a tilt
57. Dear partner
58. Bizarre
60. Philosopher Immanuel
61. Kind of range
62. Need an ice bag, e.g.
63. Vicinity
64. Eyesores, really
65. Unexpected slide

Down

1. It may be struck
2. Lounge lizards, e.g.
3. Trump
4. Some computer displays, briefly
5. Toyota model
6. Habituated
7. Unleash a diatribe
8. VI x L
9. Muscular
10. Best Actress, 1999
11. Make advances
12. Promising words?
13. Small combo
18. Mitchell clan
22. If it's a bust, it still qualifies as this
25. Landing on the water
26. Fiber source
27. Rio de la ___
28. Resigned remark
29. Kind of talk
30. Dueling sword
31. Middle East sultanate
32. ___ Alto, California
33. Dutch town or type of food
35. Marker
37. Certain United workers
38. "The Gift of the ___"
39. Minor but aggravating problem
44. Meal known by its initials
45. Sleeveless coat
46. Furlong's 7,920
47. Carrier from the left ventricle
49. Cheese and crackers, e.g.
50. Jawaharlal Nehru University state
51. Twiddled one's thumbs
52. "Puppy Love" singer
53. TV producer Norman
54. Nursing home aid, perhaps
55. Uncertain
56. "When ___ a lad ..."
59. Temper tantrum

Puzzle 165

Across

1. Bistro
5. Beliefs
11. Israeli weapon
14. Organic compound
15. It puts you in the slow lane
16. Play on words
17. Levelheaded
19. Beethoven's "Minuet ___"
20. Bookplate
21. Star of "The Day the Earth Stood Still"
23. Collars
24. Deal of fortune?
25. A piece of work
27. Place to pick up a Schwinn
30. Strong-willed type, according to the stars
31. "Backyards, Greenwich Village" artist
33. It's full of holes
34. Tribulations
36. Movie snack bar word, perhaps
38. It's heard on the roof
39. Greek sorceress
41. General drift
43. Travel stop
44. Missing one
46. Yankees leader

48. Dines go-with
49. "No way"
50. Lunar feature
52. Out of jeopardy
56. This may be over your head
57. Test under pressure
59. Joanne Woodward title role
60. So far
61. Film Dr.
62. Certain evergreen
63. Rubbed out, in a way
64. Say it ain't so

Down

1. Turn over
2. Dumb as ___
3. Chicken or turkey, e.g.
4. Storm's cause, perhaps
5. Target of an Avon representative
6. "___ the loneliest number"
7. Pate de foie ___
8. Fold, spindle, or mutilate, e.g.
9. US rail
10. Heavenly bodies
11. Undecided
12. New Mexico tribe

13. Pulitzer playwright William
18. Ski lift features
22. Private reply?
24. Smattering
25. One with more than 15 minutes of fame
26. Stands up to scrutiny
27. Ballerina balancer
28. Like ewe?
29. Sean of "The Game"
30. Bean town?
32. Hall's singing partner
35. "Now you ___, now you don't"
37. Like the pharaohs
40. Bening of "American Beauty"
42. Grumpy co-worker?
45. Abject fear
47. Called the game or separated fighters
49. Nick of "Cape Fear" (1991)
50. ___ de cuisine
51. Sitarist Shankar
52. Lukas of "Rambling Rose"
53. Rip in two
54. Julia's Brockovich
55. Wriggly and slippery, e.g.
58. Mountain in Crete

Puzzle 166

Across

1. Counterpart
5. Muscle contraction
10. Beginning of relief?
14. Allies' adversary
15. Type of black tea
16. Cap setting
17. Some checks
20. Gucci of fashion
21. Prefix for classical or Latin
22. Finish the course?
23. Opposite of deject
26. ___ Dawn Chong
28. Words with the chase
30. Some checks (With 49-Across)
33. Tourmaline, e.g.
34. Appease fully
35. Make a right
36. "Watermark" chanteuse
38. "Beauty and the Beast" character
40. Nursing a grudge
44. Vientiane native
46. Hebrides isle
48. Recess game
49. See 30-Across
54. Interior style
55. End of some Web addresses
56. Pains in the neck
57. Get behind, in a way
58. Gig implement
60. Dele undoer
62. Some checks
68. Jungian topics
69. Get ready for kickoff
70. Superior, for one
71. Adam's boy
72. Marching drum
73. Checked out with interest

Down

1. Make imperfect
2. Firefighter's tool
3. "Whether ___ nobler ..."
4. Executorial concern
5. Future fries
6. Make a long, grandiloquent speech
7. Bit of rap sheet shorthand
8. Elizabeth Barrett Browning work
9. Apportion
10. Take on moguls?
11. Coves
12. A frozen dessert
13. Memorable Moses portrayer
18. Baldwin, Guinness and others
19. Game often played with wooden balls
23. Good thing to have when competing
24. Legal claim
25. Type of ant
27. Artist's studio
29. Maui melody makers, briefly
31. Off-limits
32. Insurance promoter
37. Brand for Bowser
39. Bird with brownish plumage
41. Sheriff Taylor kept a cell for him
42. Spew fire and brimstone
43. Faberge handiworks
45. Kitchen cover-up
47. By order of
49. Sun-dried bricks
50. Section in a music store
51. Spotted wildcat
52. Corcoran of "Bachelor Father"
53. It lets off steam
59. It comes before Romans
61. Word with deck or measure
63. Silvery gray
64. Caribbean, e.g.
65. Vocal objection
66. Barely make (with "out")
67. Clearly embarrassed

Puzzle 167

Across

1. Word on a cornerstone, perhaps
5. Gift from China
10. Kind of loser
14. Car sound
15. Therapeutic plants
16. Like a world famous office
17. Stops shouting
20. Gave to another for care
21. Rear for rear, perhaps
22. Lawyers' grp.
23. Hearty brew
24. Kipling novel
27. Balkan republic (Var.)
31. Classified fodder
34. Out for the accused
36. Type of tea
37. Combat outfit
38. Increases the chance for a sale
41. Newsman Roger
42. Indigent
43. First symptoms, e.g.
44. '70s White House kid
45. Throw a monkey wrench into, e.g.
47. Sibilant sound
48. Dry, in Napa
49. Sound of satisfaction
51. Salts used medicinally
54. Largest city of Laos
60. Rejects a bid

62. It bonds models
63. Pointed arch
64. Place for dinars
65. Certain salamanders
66. Lessened
67. Absorbs gravy with bread, e.g.

Down

1. With the wherewithal
2. Atomic number 10
3. Eye used in spooky recipes
4. Phantom's passion
5. Where the Danube meets the Inn
6. Words with "Thanks"
7. All alternative
8. Transfer document
9. Sure-footed animal
10. Honorary Shawnee
11. Roman love poet
12. Census form query
13. Red or Cardinal, for short
18. Protocol
19. Southern constellation
23. Hospital staffer, e.g.
24. Word in a John Lennon tune title
25. Part of the small intestine
26. David Robinson was one in college
28. Japanese flavorings

29. One for whom play means work
30. India's first prime minister
31. Liqueur flavoring
32. Chops into cubes
33. Editor's markings
35. Unopened bloom
37. Samovar, e.g.
39. Heroic in scale, moviewise
40. Non-computer chip?
45. Actress Moore
46. Gave a negative review to
48. They stay ahead of heels
50. Sound investments?
51. Flange
52. Ill-gotten gains
53. Hare's tail
54. Old Chevy
55. Words with the doctor
56. Residential overhang
57. Voluminous do
58. Tide of minimum range
59. Seashore sights (Var.)
61. When do we want it?

Puzzle 168

Across

1. Deer enemy
5. Saucy
9. It causes one to hesitate
14. Not at hand
15. Induction rating
16. Like Audubon's interests
17. After-dinner wine
18. Lumpy masses
19. Invoice word
20. Cause of stubbornness, for some
23. Descriptive of an intimate dinner
26. Save the Tin Man again
27. Toy introduced in 1950
30. Vile Nile creatures
34. Hardly an Oscar candidate
35. Spew forth
36. Richard's veep
37. Great heavyweight
38. Baltimore-Philadelphia dir.
39. A question of identity
41. Millennia upon millennia
42. Notorious Bugs
44. It has a ball at the circus
45. Cimabue's "___ Trinita Madonna"
46. "Good grief!"
47. High-rise convenience, perhaps

50. Cut off from everyone else
52. Studies desperately
53. Pleasant climate
58. Kind of breeze
59. Region
60. Hybrid citrus fruit
64. French bread, once
65. Thomas, the clockmaker
66. Nursery rhyme vessel
67. Onward
68. First place
69. Laborious journey

Down

1. Infant fare
2. Craft in the tabloids
3. Deface
4. Like a literary Dodger
5. Walt Kelly character
6. Organic compound
7. Renaissance
8. It hangs from the fauld
9. Wrist bones
10. Partial superimposition
11. "La Boheme" role
12. Word with old or meter
13. Pot content
21. Kind of mask
22. Heavy barge
23. "Ain't That ___"
24. Short conversation?
25. Site of Twain's remains
28. Play on words
29. Put to work

31. Nap in Hermosillo
32. For the time being
33. Underwater detection instruments
36. Comfort in sorrow
39. One W of WWW
40. Hee follower
43. Unbudging
44. Practiced yellow journalism, perhaps
47. Jones' financial partner
48. Feeling of anxiety
49. Enter uninvited
51. Type of mob
53. Loud, hearty laugh
54. Prefix with phobia or bat
55. "Sanford and Son" co-producer
56. Head of France
57. 1944 chemistry Nobelist Otto
61. Long-jawed freshwater fish
62. Tell it like it isn't
63. Classification

Puzzle 169

Across

1. It may be full of lemons
6. "The ___" (sci-fi classic)
10. Elevator innovator
14. Tree exudation
15. Military assistant, e.g.
16. Moccasins' old kin
17. "Belay there!"
18. Clarinetist's need
19. Meagerly manages (with "out")
20. Little girls' ingredients?
23. Sea homonym
24. Gardner of "Show Boat"
25. Clemente or Mateo lead-in
26. Carte start
29. Spotless
32. Kind of air filter
35. Stout kin
36. Abstract style of the '60s
37. Linen color, perhaps
38. Below, poetically
41. Middle of Descartes' conclusion
42. Symbol of laziness
44. Despite the fact that, in short
45. College founded in 1440
46. Unharmed
50. Bastille Day season
51. British bathroom
52. Genetic stuff
53. About-to-be-grads
56. Pleasantly brief
60. Western tableland
62. Jazz man Hinton or Jackson
63. One with a promising future
64. Assert
65. Arsenal contents
66. Crop up
67. Like some turkey meat
68. "Lawrence of Arabia" director
69. Mend a split in one's pants, e.g.

Down

1. Fescue, for one
2. Casino show, perhaps
3. River to the Missouri
4. Traveler's need, maybe
5. Snare
6. Marine crustacean
7. Spoke with forked tongue
8. Black Sea port
9. Hospital room object
10. Cartel since 1960
11. Disassemble
12. Restaurant block
13. Serpentine sound
21. Bird-related
22. China lead-in
27. Florida city near Tampa
28. Rubinstein or Bruckner
29. Fry a little
30. Contemporary of Shelley
31. A driving concern?
32. 1946 Literature Nobelist Hermann
33. Critical success
34. Academician
39. "Our Town" author Wilder
40. Baskervilles dog
43. Seraphic topper
47. Type of behavior
48. Complete a sentence
49. Flag-waving org.
53. Round of four
54. Actress Witherspoon
55. Spread by scattering
57. Dove opposite
58. ___ mater
59. Donned
60. Steaming
61. ___ Marie Saint

Puzzle 170

Across

1. Cary Grant, originally
6. Man of many parts
11. Noisy dispute
14. Golf rarity
15. Piece of the pie
16. Commit a faux pas, e.g.
17. Old hands in the garden
19. Citrus suffix
20. Peak in the mythical war of the Giants
21. Plot set in the suburbs?
22. Comedian DeGeneres
24. Cooperstown's Ryan
26. "Brian's Song" character
27. Goon's blow-enhancers
31. Put down in writing?
32. Luau dish
33. Resign (with "down")
36. Kind of wind
37. Simpleton
40. Kooky
42. Glamorous Gardner
43. Defendant's part of the bargain?
45. Its floor is wet
47. Warren or Joyce Carol
49. Worst one to handle packages
53. Type of doll
55. Martini's partner
56. Pearl Mosque country
57. Guilty party, to a cop
58. Word oft shouted downtown
62. Prefix with ode or pod
63. Sign of nerves
66. Naval agreement?
67. Yankees skipper
68. One way to be lost
69. Was in front
70. Geisel's pen name
71. Daft

Down

1. Block brand
2. Cornstalk features
3. Seemingly forever
4. Purge
5. Mother ptarmigan
6. School of painters, c. 1908
7. Roil
8. Far from shocking
9. Spheroid
10. Put the lid back on
11. Houses and land
12. Court call
13. Some birds
18. Radio format
23. Caustic soaps
25. Christiania, today
26. Crash prelude, often
27. Radar sighting
28. Small brook
29. Physically fit
30. Make baby sounds
34. At any time
35. Third-and-long option
38. Concerning
39. Service charge
41. Gangland bigwigs
44. Their logo has four rings
46. Unpaid debts
48. Excitedly, in music
50. Champagne salutes
51. Long suits
52. Cosby TV series
53. Absolutely necessary
54. Deli phrase
57. Cole Porter's birthplace
59. Furthermore
60. Comic-book super-heroes
61. Brit's exclamation
64. Tribulation
65. Chum

Puzzle 171

Across

1. Help out in a scam
5. Designed for all school grades, in the U.S.
9. Once and again
14. Nominate
15. Move toward
16. Use a stationary bike
17. Start of a timely definition
20. Underhanded
21. Vast South American region
22. Mantel piece, perhaps
23. British bombshell Diana
24. Slugging stat
26. Have respect for
29. Causation study
34. Low dam
35. Switch words?
36. Stubbed item
37. Timely definition (Part 2)
41. Pythagorean P
42. Wayne Gretzky, until 1988
43. Take it on the chin
44. Tarnish
46. Selected
48. Shelley praise
49. Sticky stuff
50. Brit's baby carriage
53. Less calm
56. Fill in
59. End of the definition
62. Mississippi quartet
63. Aqua or cosmo trailer
64. Low tract
65. Newborn puppy
66. Has a balance
67. Petri dish medium

Down

1. Tamandua's diet
2. Keep a leaky boat afloat
3. TV trophy
4. Golf expendable
5. Make certain
6. Martin's screen partner
7. "Serves you right!"
8. Mashed locale
9. Map abbreviation, perhaps
10. Certain cottoneater
11. Clever thought
12. Supply for play pistols
13. Alternatively
18. Sikorsky or Stravinsky
19. Import duty, e.g.
23. It may be dished
25. Belly laugh
26. Bestow an honor upon
27. New ___, India
28. Director Forman
29. Script direction
30. Guided excursion
31. Others in Mexico
32. Barnyard honker
33. Red Sea country
35. Norse capital
38. Chivalrous Robin
39. Actress Brennan
40. Drifting ice sheet
45. Make someone do something
46. Footballer's footwear
47. Feel pain
49. Concluding dance movement
50. Expression of relief
51. Poison ivy symptom
52. End of many sanctuaries
54. Flintstone's pet
55. Chew on, as a bone
56. Hosiery problem
57. Where Bill Walton played college ball
58. Kind of belly
60. Prognosticator's forte, maybe
61. Eggs, scientifically

Puzzle 172

Across

1. Epistle writer
5. Temple's first husband
9. Bar fare
14. One-time Delhi queen
15. Prefix meaning "minute"
16. Beethoven dedicatee
17. Garden bloom
18. Film villain
19. Invoice word
20. Beat
23. Barking mammal
24. Food for a flicker
25. Woodstock gear
28. Buttercup relative
31. Cain raiser
34. Henhouse perch
36. .0000001 joule
37. Overlook
38. Beat
42. Glimpse
43. Tempest in a teapot
44. Slake
45. A Partridge portrayer
46. Marked for life
49. Allen wrench shape
50. Play parent for a night
51. Essayist's alias
53. Beat
60. Type of system or badge
61. Fiesta fare, perhaps
62. Frosty the Snowman accessory
63. Griffin part
64. Kitten's plaything
65. "The Camp Meeting" composer
66. Garson of "Madame Curie"
67. One of a matched set
68. Piggy-bank deposit

Down

1. Stuck-up one
2. Bern is on it
3. Word with military or heating
4. Shopping memos
5. Cuzco native
6. Distort, in a way
7. Stuart queen
8. Dig like a pig
9. Completely calm
10. Wide-eyed
11. Prom night wheels, briefly
12. "Clueless" exclamation
13. NYPD title
21. Tract of wasteland
22. Latin dance
25. Dangerous go-with
26. Large northern deer
27. Type of seed
29. Produce item
30. Precious metal, in Madrid
31. Writer Zola
32. Like some statistics or organs
33. Gas for Merman?
35. Place for pen pals?
37. Barn bird
39. Inheritance of the meek
40. Pharmaceuticals overseer, for short
41. Woody Allen's "___ Days"
46. Kind of pill
47. Winter aid for windshields
48. Nudges, in a way
50. Subway feature
52. Savory jelly
53. Juicy fruit
54. Compulsion
55. Imprint
56. Headless cabbage
57. One place to find your honey
58. Lead the bidding
59. Arboreal abode
60. "Little Women" woman

Puzzle 173

Across

1. Stretch for a VIP
5. Saturate
10. Abacus unit
14. Urgent memo letters
15. Gets warmer, in a game
16. Inner drive
17. Verbal error
20. Russian Tea Room decorations, perhaps
21. American impressionist Childe
22. Lost animated fish
23. Type of coincidence
24. Grocery store section
27. Escapee from Sodom
28. Wall Street abbr.
32. Topple over
33. High-pressure personality
35. Some plural endings
36. What delicious food seems to do
39. Crony
40. Fine partner
41. City in Montana
42. "The ___ the limit!"
44. Fjord relative
45. Yon partner
46. ___ and feathers
48. Nautical centerpiece
49. Illinois river city

52. Minerals found in copper deposits, sometimes
56. Set for battle
58. List on a detergent label, perhaps
59. Some Jewish months
60. Wife of a rajah
61. Camera attachment
62. Insolent
63. Sharp blow

Down

1. Young lady
2. Majorca, to a native
3. Hurt severely
4. Frazier, to Ali
5. Odious reputation
6. Urban newspaper section
7. "A Christmas Carol" cries
8. Press ending
9. Art lovers (Var.)
10. Inventor of a burner
11. Work units
12. Request from a thirsty Spaniard?
13. Form an opinion
18. Went to extremes
19. Lifeboat must
23. Displaying listlessness, e.g.

24. Grinds partner
25. In a vertical position
26. Shade of green
27. "Wonder Woman" Carter
29. It must be served, it's said
30. Hill count in Roma
31. English urban district
33. Morrison and Tennille
34. Surrounding
37. Adds commentary to
38. People living away from their place of work
43. Accent
45. Joan of Arc's crime
47. Helping hand
48. Eye makeups
49. He was converted on the road to Damascus
50. Scottish Gaelic
51. Good or bad sign
52. Heating measures, briefly
53. Marsh duck
54. Sicilian volcano
55. Transport commercially
57. Pay ending

Puzzle 174

Across

1. Red Sea port (Var.)
6. Counterfeit quarter, e.g.
10. Degrees sought on Wall St.
14. Soubise base
15. Places for runs?
16. Voice below soprano
17. Ultraviolet glower
19. Around the bend
20. Pecs display case
21. Expires
22. Lotto relative
23. Squared up
25. Revered remnant
27. Singer's first recording, often
28. 1952 and 1956 campaign name
31. Soldier's helmet, in slang
34. Got by
37. "Absolutely Fabulous" character
38. Tie up the phone, e.g.
41. Met by chance
43. Bachelor's pride
44. For ___ see (in plain view)
46. Rathskeller needs
48. Muscle contractions
50. Deplete
51. Chaotic happenings
55. Ball partner
57. Scout's discovery

59. Mythical god of discord and mischief
61. "The Honeymooners" role
64. Start for metric or bar
65. ___'acte (intermission)
66. Revise a manuscript, e.g.
68. Leave unacknowledged
69. Informal lead-in to "girl!"
70. "___ say more?"
71. Keeps company with
72. Carrel furniture
73. Called one's bluff

Down

1. Subcontracted (with "out")
2. One way to fall
3. Royal headwear
4. One of a short seven
5. Fibula's terminus
6. Place for hands
7. Sometimes they get the ax
8. Theater guide?
9. Starter's phrase
10. The human race
11. Kind of stock
12. Envelope abbr.
13. Hardly thrilling
18. Pretentious
24. ___ de plume
26. Use, as a chaise longue

29. Ranges of understanding
30. Reviews and corrects
32. Santa ___, Calif.
33. Small amount
35. Waft from the kitchen
36. Prime draft classification
38. Word with tank or range
39. Mountain climber's challenge
40. Like some formal events
42. Highest point
45. Souvenir-shop items
47. Erie mule
49. Voyager of legend
52. Winter windshield clearer
53. Within the legal area of play
54. Impassive
56. Actor Nick
58. What all good things must come to
59. Most people born in August
60. "Lean ___" (1989 film)
62. Dead-end jobs, e.g.
63. Hardwood used on boats
67. Teachers' org.

Puzzle 175

Across

1. New Testament book
5. Provide the grub
10. CD followers
14. Marshal Kane's deadline
15. Kicking partner
16. Give off
17. Abandoned queen of Carthage
18. Mechanical learning routines
19. Miami or London, e.g.
20. States dined, except Alaska and Hawaii?
23. Court order
24. Walker on a beat
25. Computer guru
28. Extol
30. Its symbol is an omega
33. Value system
34. Whiskey drink
35. Corn lily
36. Famous warblers making sawbucks?
39. Wine choice
40. Moreover
41. Up until now
42. Burdened beast
43. Units of wire thickness
44. Electorate
45. Big one in London
46. Big rig
47. Last one at the Round Table?
53. Gifted one
54. In the first place?
55. Dynamic start?
57. Top-of-the-line
58. Slowly, to Toscanini
59. Follow
60. Contest
61. Light-show source
62. Sphere's lack

Down

1. Popular joiner
2. Phone cord shape
3. Fuss
4. Gal pal of seven little ones
5. King thriller
6. In the clouds
7. Milosevic predecessor
8. Always
9. Prescription for burnout
10. Go over
11. Leave out
12. Pesky arachnid
13. It's fit for a pig
21. "Love Story" author Segal
22. Hebrew letter
25. One more than tri-
26. Morals standards
27. Fischer's game
28. Rich soil
29. Camera setting
30. Type of daisy
31. Human Resources person, at times
32. Sails' staffs
34. Order to a broker
35. Be behind
37. Precipitation type
38. David's great-grandmother
43. Blanc or Torme
44. Merchant
45. Jewel holder
46. An old one may need a key
47. Commandment word
48. Sparkling, for one
49. "Take ___ Train" (Duke Ellington)
50. Feathered females
51. Kind of hunter
52. Math subj.
53. Roll for a high roller
56. Seville cheer

Puzzle 176

Across

1. Frankenstein's gofer
5. Kitchen piece, perhaps
10. Turkish leader
14. Nonnegotiable item
15. German sub
16. Broadway production
17. Actor in scary roles
19. Bring down the house?
20. Were now?
21. Hale and Ladd
22. Lies low
23. Uninvited partygoer
25. Where Singaraja is
26. Kiss partner
27. Exclude from practice
30. Mythical monster
33. Suffix with patriot or manner
36. Like a sacker of Rome
38. Actor in scary roles
42. An alarm clock or rooster, e.g.
43. Photo ___ (camera sessions)
44. Track act
45. Underground growth
47. Norwegian metropolis
51. Package delivery org.
53. Hunting dog
56. "West Side Story" song
58. Items in a hold

60. Tasteless newspaper
61. Country on the Caspian
62. Actor in scary roles
64. After-bath powder, perhaps
65. Mountain ridge
66. ___ fixe
67. "Will there be anything ___?"
68. Editor's marks
69. Kevin Costner role

Down

1. Strike forcefully
2. Nom de ___ (pseudonym)
3. Pertaining to bone
4. 66 is a well-known one (Abbr.)
5. Bridal veil material, perhaps
6. On the train
7. Brought into the world
8. Phyllis' never-seen TV husband
9. Summer on the Cote d'Azur
10. Clock-changing month
11. Sword lilies
12. It follows "Purple" in a song title
13. Seafaring assents
18. Preppy cheer

22. In great need
24. Smooth and glossy
25. Stringed instrument
28. Tennis legend Chris
29. Chesapeake, for one
31. Brazilian vacation destination, for short
32. "Proud Mary" grp.
34. Tibetan guide
35. Spanish hands
37. Williams "Happy Days"
38. Scientist's site
39. Be obligated to
40. Seven and eleven, in Vegas
41. Classical prefix
46. "Doctor at Large" character
48. Walked with a purpose
49. Rental agreements
50. Saturnalias
52. From a time
54. Leers at
55. Promissory note
56. Wee parasite
57. Asian sea
58. Dick Francis book "Dead ___"
59. Away from the wind
62. Some university degs.
63. Jubilant cry in a card game

Puzzle 177

Across

1. Vaulted church section
5. Hair curlers?
10. Rivers or Lunden
14. Rhythmic pulse
15. Bye-bye, in Burgundy
16. Take apart
17. Garb for a rite of passage
19. Unenviable grades
20. Skirt insert
21. Rather formal
23. Weather word
26. Toast topper
28. Wake-up calls
29. Bumper sticker phrase, usually
30. Advised leader?
33. Folder fodder
34. Salts, in a way
35. "The Cask of Amontillado" author
36. They're from Splitsville
37. Kind of dog
38. Horse sound
39. Mr. Caesar
40. "A Certain State of Mind" author Norma
41. Witchlike old woman
42. Prefix for corn or angle
43. Latin being
44. Boarding house occupant
45. Like all living organisms
47. Swift pieces
48. Japanese straw mat
50. ___ and crafts
51. Horror-film helper
52. When one becomes eligible for college
58. Weightlifting exercise
59. Mortal
60. China lead-in
61. Piano pieces?
62. League constituents
63. ___ out a living (scraped by)

Down

1. Start of a kindergarten song
2. Garbanzo, for one
3. Maple product
4. Places for knickknacks
5. National League team
6. Move bit by bit
7. Grande or Bravo
8. Feline sound
9. Like some raisins
10. Land occupied by Israel since 1967 (Var.)
11. What's obtained upon 52-Across
12. Lemon and lime drinks
13. Too inquisitive
18. Benchmarks
22. Dumbbell turns
23. Least dangerous
24. Word on a bottle of snake oil
25. Address at 52-Across
26. Raised to the second power
27. Runs smoothly, as an engine
31. Like some "tunes"
32. Biblical outcasts
34. Put the whammy on someone
37. Old-fashioned illumination
38. Transverse beam
40. Place to find leaders
41. Word with Rica or Mesa
44. "The Honeymooners" episodes, today
46. Countesses' counterparts
48. Watch sound
49. Feverish condition
50. First lady's man
53. Lament
54. "I ___ lineman for the county"
55. Media attention, in slang
56. Verse form
57. Say yes, in a way

Puzzle 178

Across

1. Foul callers, briefly
5. Tale with a point
10. Famous loser in a 5-Across
14. Pawn taker, sometimes
15. Acclaim
16. Zatopek or Jannings
17. Transistor adjective
19. Front the money
20. Random choice
21. Computer signpost
22. Feel in the gut
23. Engine type
26. Turn in
29. Modicum
30. River into the Severn
31. City in South Korea
33. Word with punching or sleeping
36. Imaginary shell formed by the sky
40. Word with all or result
41. Variety of beet
42. Coward's confession?
43. Anglo-___ War
44. Slow reptile
46. Summer treat
51. Whiz
52. Jai ___
53. Lamb's call
56. Dyeing plant
57. Butcher's offerings
60. "___ Flanders"
61. Emulate Paul Revere
62. New York state canal
63. Congressional meeting (Abbr.)
64. Cumbersome
65. Entertainer Horne

Down

1. Heavenly bear
2. Space race target
3. Roly follower
4. One way to make tracks
5. Variety of grass
6. Role player
7. Voice of Daffy Duck
8. Short back muscle
9. Berlioz's "Les nuits d'___"
10. City not far from Butte
11. Change a contract, e.g.
12. Certain cycle
13. Mormon official
18. Noted Christian
22. Certain exercise
23. Exquisite
24. Relinquish, as control
25. Fireplace fodder
26. Word with course or horse
27. Without advantage or disadvantage
28. Recounted
31. Royal crown
32. Berne's river
33. Lahr or Parks
34. A salty lake
35. Hereditary factor
37. Look down on with disdain
38. "God shed His grace on ___"
39. Put on the payroll
43. They're in bone marrow
44. Warm and comfy
45. The "U" in ICU
46. Muslim teachers
47. It needs a good paddling
48. Monkeys' taboos
49. Silents actress Normand
50. Uriah Heep, by profession
53. Without clothes
54. Related by blood
55. On the Mediterranean, e.g.
57. It'll take you for a ride
58. Curved Alaskan knife
59. It may be smoked

Puzzle 179

Across

1. Small annoyance
5. They're supportive to a star
9. Institute
14. Louis-Philippe and others
15. Between ports
16. Brimless woman's hat
17. Unlikely place to find a star
20. Proposes
21. Delays
22. Bean-spillers
24. Vintner's valley, perhaps
25. Combustion byproduct
28. Correct a tire pull
30. Hindu prince
34. Quick to learn
35. Collections of reminiscences, e.g.
36. "___ of God"
37. Unlikely place to find a star
41. Not on all fours
42. Came down, as on a perch
43. Umbrage
44. Seldom seen
45. Herculean types
47. Tryout
48. Open partner
50. Seeming eternity
52. Obvious offensiveness
56. Malodor
60. Unlikely place to find a star
62. Emulate a horse, in a way
63. Location of an ancient garden
64. Cabbage concoction
65. "Dynasty" actress Emma
66. Something to break into
67. "Desire Under the ___"

Down

1. Handlebar feature
2. Forbidden thing
3. British isles
4. Popular souvenir item
5. Airport feature
6. Thick-brick connector
7. Splinter group
8. Very attractive
9. Throat ailment, perhaps
10. What an XXXL jacket is, for many
11. Blue tinged with green
12. Ladder segment
13. Danson and Williams
18. Greek letter
19. Fed. agent
23. Crate component
25. Curved sword
26. Haunt of a certain phantom
27. Last choice on some lists
29. "It Had to Be You" composer Jones
31. Warbucks' ward
32. Hoots, boos, raspberries, e.g.
33. Valued property
35. Colony soldier
36. What a star is paid to do
38. Freezing rain event
39. Zeno's home
40. Infamous New York penitentiary
45. Pursue
46. Applies acid to glass, in a way
47. Bloodthirsty fly
49. Handles for 25-Down
51. It's seen briefly at the end of a list?
52. Paycheck signer, typically
53. Goddess of the moon
54. Molecule maker
55. Former name of Tokyo (Var.)
57. Void partner
58. Study in a hurry
59. Chops down
61. Confident puzzle-solver's tool

Puzzle 180

Across

1. Anthem beginning
5. Chest muscles, for short
9. It's seen at the Olympics
14. Added up (to)
15. Jack-in-the-pulpit, e.g.
16. A status symbol
17. Poser
19. State one's views
20. Type of wrestler
21. Reeves of "Speed"
23. ___ del Plata (Argentinean resort)
24. Newly hatched hooter
25. Think quietly and inwardly
27. "Well!"
31. Hive members
32. Help wanted advertisement?
33. First name in masterpieces
35. Filly filler
36. Poser
39. Cutting thrust
41. Cooking fat
42. Insecticide banned since 1972
45. Thinly populated
47. Held by a third party, as money
50. Unventilated

52. 1836 battle site
53. Retrieve
54. Fancy footwear, once
57. Flaky mineral
58. Like Wingfield's menagerie
60. Poser
63. Ghastly strange
64. Con ___ (with vigor, in music)
65. Elbow-wrist connector
66. Stallone title role
67. Deadly snakes
68. It may be due, get the point?

Down

1. Scottish "Oh my!"
2. "According to what authority?"
3. Vials
4. Naval petty officers
5. Golf standard
6. Composer Satie
7. Quaintly attractive
8. Microscope sample
9. Elaborate decoration
10. One way to take a bough
11. Sustenance
12. Threatens
13. Puts forth effort

18. Dove's domicile
22. Homer's neighbor
24. Fourth qtr. followers
26. Rich soil
28. L.B.J.'s successor
29. Part of R.S.V.P.
30. Listlessness
34. Yemeni port
36. "Blue Suede Shoes" writer Perkins
37. Preoccupied with
38. Hwy.
39. Pitchman
40. Served raw
42. Blood count?
43. They may be eminent
44. Tangoing number
45. Drooped
46. Medium's method
48. Kind of old story
49. Coterie
51. Brazilian dance
55. Seafarers
56. Cutting sound
59. A Caesar
61. Calculator figs.
62. First name among legendary crooners

Puzzle 181

Across

1. Org. co-founded by Helen Keller
5. Nothing special
9. Transport with a gas engine
14. Farm wagon
15. Word with indigestion or test
16. Orderly grouping
17. "Tom Thumb" composer
18. Ragged, as a garment
20. Word with base or scene
22. Nipper's corp.
23. Kansas City Wizards org.
24. Group of islands belonging to Scotland
26. "Today I ____ man"
28. Kind of card
29. "Father Knows Best" family name
34. Coffee variety
36. Fare at a luau
37. Blues singer James
38. Want as a price
39. Mexican president, 1988-94
43. Siegfried's partner
44. For whom the bell tolls
46. Maiden name preceder
47. Ovine sign
49. Fragrant plant
51. Big English clock
52. Wing of a building
53. Flat-bottomed sled
58. ICU offering, hopefully
61. Malaysian export
63. Illustrious
64. Like some terriers
67. Gadgets for Tiger
68. Public persona
69. Prong
70. Pucker-producing
71. Islands near Fiji
72. British fellows
73. Colony members

Down

1. Covered by waves
2. Food list
3. Defensive stalwart, in football
4. Find after a long search
5. Overly full
6. Moderate orange-yellow color
7. Term of address
8. River in central Europe
9. Tussauds' honorific
10. Spherical shape
11. Hyde Park stroller
12. Viscount's superior
13. Turns silver to gold?
19. Former French colony
21. Succotash ingredients
25. Possessing wisdom
27. "... Women ____ From Venus"
30. Prefix for profit or dairy
31. Skin-and-bones sort
32. Siouan Indian
33. Negative votes
34. Damon of "Saving Private Ryan"
35. Labor Dept. section
40. Britain, to Caesar
41. Sign of the zodiac
42. Carved shoe
45. Before, poetically
48. Boat race
50. Tennis great Gibson
54. Upturned, as a box
55. Portends
56. Vigilant
57. Branch headquarters?
58. Twerp
59. It can move stars
60. Fishy capacity measure
62. Immature parasites
65. Dinosaur's start
66. Brazilian city

Puzzle 182

Treacherous

Across

1. Insane
4. Pipsqueak
9. Macho guy
14. Steak partner
15. Uncannily spooky
16. Dodge, as a question
17. Brigitte, for one
18. Inflexibility
19. Prepared potatoes, in a way
20. Hanks comedy
23. From the top
24. Command to a guest
25. NRC predecessor
28. The worse for wear, e.g.
31. Fundraising event, sometimes
33. Kraits' kin
36. Object of a quest
38. Massenet heroine
40. One of a Freudian trio
41. "___ Joe's"
42. Without getting results
44. Untouchable name
45. Baltic or Fifth
46. It may be taken up
49. Color to paint the town
50. Bro's foe, at times
52. '60s coloring method
56. 19th-century trade route
59. Woody Allen film
62. He lost to Dwight
63. "My Name is Asher ___"
64. Without delay
65. Actress Della
66. Wallach or Lilly
67. Rubbernecks
68. They provide prayer support
69. Gridiron divs.

Down

1. "___ tear has to fall"
2. Hard to get close to
3. Voice a formal objection
4. Mother of Calcutta
5. Dumbbell, e.g.
6. Therefore
7. Prison-movie event, perhaps
8. Salon specialties
9. Birthright
10. "Beyond Good and ___" (Nietzsche)
11. PC alternative
12. Suffix with lemon or lime
13. Homer's neighbor
21. Part of KJV
22. Subject to a draft
25. "... ___ worse than death"
26. Sewing machine innovator Howe
27. Irish and Welsh, e.g.
29. "Take ___ Train" (Duke Ellington)
30. Bear and Berra
32. More candid
33. Fragrant oil
34. What push comes to
35. Having divisions, as a window
37. Laze about
39. Some links
43. Streak, as in marble
47. Order to relax
48. Washington and Lincoln, e.g.
51. Devoid of any disguise
53. Windy City politician
54. Relinquish, as control
55. Hip swinger of note
56. Kind of bay
57. Oil port
58. Head for the hills
59. Half of a stitch
60. Air quality overseer (Abbr.)
61. Order companion

Puzzle 183

Across

1. Did a thespian's job
6. "You've Got a Friend ___"
10. Degs. for some execs
14. Fore or after attachment
15. Type of miss
16. Jocular Johnson
17. Having a high pH, e.g.
18. Rush hour, to radio stations
20. When a new day begins
22. Pigskin's perch
23. Something to bend on a human
24. Type of lab
25. "... ___ of thee"
28. Kathmandu-to-Calcutta dir.
29. Arcade pioneer
31. Future litigators' exams
33. Ukr., once
34. Burning result
36. Partner of odds
37. Phantasmagoric
40. Petroleum gp.
42. Nero's noon
43. Brazilian city, for short
44. English philosopher John
46. Presented, as a problem
48. Unannounced, as a quiz
51. Old hoops org.
52. It may be blown
54. Runner Sebastian
55. Marienbad, for one
56. Hero's sine qua non
60. Translator, of sorts
62. Frequently visited place
63. Soprano's solo, sometimes
64. Fancy fabric
65. Pandemonium's lack
66. Track tourney
67. Tend to the batter, in a way
68. "Cheers" character

Down

1. Some baseball stats
2. Abrades
3. Finals taker
4. Pennsylvania city
5. Iron?
6. Mrs. Gandhi
7. Geek
8. It can be filling
9. Senator of Watergate fame
10. It has its pluses and minuses
11. Former province of France
12. Place for a money order?
13. "Comprende?"
19. Same, along the Seine
21. Mathematical array
26. "Why, ___ be a pleasure!"
27. Steam train sound
30. Two-to-one, e.g.
32. Zaire's Mobutu Sese ___
33. Kind of bay
35. Concerning this, in legalese
37. Dessert choice, perhaps
38. Bit playfully, as a puppy
39. Circus attraction
40. Pay follower
41. Numbered compartment in a U.S. post office, briefly
45. Raison d'___
47. One who puts up points
48. Prefix meaning "false"
49. Started the bidding
50. Trifling
53. Egg shapes
57. Latin I verb
58. Big rig
59. Starchy tuber
60. Fugitive's flight
61. Fury

Puzzle 184

Across

1. Bank statement abbr.
5. Without ___ in the world
10. ___ facto
14. Where to wallow
15. Loafers' lack
16. Actress Talbot or Naldi
17. Unconventional sort
19. "Saturday Night Live" segment, e.g.
20. "Queen of Country"
21. Some Consumer Reports employees
23. What "I love" in an Irving Berlin song
24. Where Swansea is
25. Dr. of rap
26. Habitual troublemaker
29. College choice
32. "No mas" boxer
33. One billion years, in geology
34. Russia's ___ Mountains
35. Psychic letters hidden in the theme words
36. Poi need
37. Word with ball or shoe
38. Maryland and Montana, in France
40. "Land ___ alive!"
41. Superbowl XL team
43. I, abroad
44. Clean fish, in a way
45. Paradigms of sluggishness
48. Horrify
50. Set forth
52. Churlish one
53. Sponsor's spiel
55. Make a break for it
56. Facility west of Schiller Park
57. Gillette razor product
58. Sommer of "The Treasure Seekers"
59. Timberlake's boy band
60. Desideratum

Down

1. Like most radios
2. On or about
3. Eddie Haskell, to Beaver
4. Young star, perhaps
5. Type of skiing
6. Capital near Alexandria
7. 160 square rods
8. Portuguese king
9. "CHiPs" star
10. Moving to the rhythm
11. One place to get a Rocky Mountain high
12. Con's home
13. Mare fare
18. A Beatle
22. Hale of "Gilligan's Island"
24. Bends out of shape
26. Some museum exhibits
27. Knowledge gained through anecdote
28. Genesis son
29. Coffee holders
30. In ___ (going nowhere)
31. 11th U.S. president
32. "The Wreck of the Mary ___"
36. Papeete resident
38. Ben-Gurion Airport carrier
39. Tattles
40. Line of cliffs
42. Card game for two
43. Shortly, conversationally
45. Cruiser's rear
46. Singer Lenya or Lehmann
47. Ecuadorian money, once
48. French priest's title
49. Summer hangout, perhaps
50. Kill or put in stitches
51. Jones of jazz
54. Contented sighs

Puzzle 185

Across

1. Clothing accessories?
5. Cluster of feathers
9. Readies for surgery
14. Roller coaster cry
15. Manipulative one
16. Saudi Arabian money
17. Beatles classic
19. Phantom's passion
20. Back muscle, briefly
21. Closes in on
22. Having a sharp flavor
23. Carol opening
25. Vandalize
27. Unwelcome engine sounds
30. Do-to-do interval
33. Completely out of order
36. Request for repetition
38. Ball belle
39. Dramatic device
40. It's "positively" hidden four times in this puzzle
41. ___ ear and out the other
43. Half of a square
44. ___ B'rith
45. Type of situation
46. "Star Trek" trip
49. J.F.K. relative
51. White-plumed bird
53. Word with wrong or prime

57. Discombobulated
59. Old sleep aid?
62. It's inn stock
63. Lustrous fabric
64. Ensign's answer, perhaps
66. "This is only ___!"
67. Deserved a ticket
68. Part of Caesar's question
69. Hair curlers
70. Sniggler's haul
71. On the ball

Down

1. Theatrical Tharp
2. Winning
3. P.C. Wren's Beau
4. Rigidify
5. Soup holder
6. They may ask, "Where's the beef?"
7. Phobia
8. Surreptitious meeting
9. A prescription drug
10. Most likely to fall from a tree
11. Cosmetic coloring
12. Hair line
13. Leave helpless with laughter
18. Some real thing
24. Created a Web site?

26. Fall into decay
28. Actress lover of Charles II
29. One way to gather wool
31. Start of a Latin boast
32. Bacheller's Holden
33. Ukraine's capital
34. The younger Guthrie
35. Suit material, perhaps
37. "No way!" to a teen
41. Pulled hamstring, e.g.
42. Average
44. Quilting follower
47. Type of discrimination
48. Endowments for the arts
50. Manipulates muscles
52. Make fun of
54. Make a temporary stitch
55. Upper crust
56. Summer showing, often
57. "Immediately, if not sooner" letters
58. Museum that's called a gallery
60. Font makeup
61. It might be said to a dog
65. It might be said to a mouse

Puzzle 186

Across

1. Reprimand (with "out")
5. Bundle
10. Scoop contents
14. Nautical direction
15. Oktoberfest dance
16. Dear companion?
17. Bogart or Presley flick
19. Gambling, e.g.
20. Med. readout
21. Hatcher of "Desperate Housewives"
22. The Sorbonne and those like it
24. Stew
26. Hunky-dory
27. Hitch
34. They can be broken into bits
37. Water nymph, in mythology
38. Unusual shoe width
39. Kind of cloth
40. Actress Parker ___
41. "The Sweetest Taboo" singer
42. Positive reply from Popeye
43. Emerald, essentially
44. Positioned
45. It involves much giving and taking
48. "... ___ nation under God ..."
49. Motion detector, e.g.
53. More expensive
56. Fr. miss
58. "___ Sera, Sera"
59. Carry on
60. What adulterers do
63. "Verrrrry interesting" comedian Johnson
64. King of the long ball
65. Like some lingerie
66. Ran, as dyes
67. With ___ in sight
68. Suit to ___

Down

1. Prepares beans, in a way
2. Homologous
3. Pie piece
4. Stage
5. Iron-recycling organ
6. Old and gray
7. Pre-college, to American textbook publishers
8. Wanted poster abbr., perhaps
9. Type of basketball shot
10. Call forth
11. First name among moonwalkers
12. Address forthrightly
13. They're found in pockets and seams
18. Dumas swashbuckler
23. Heavy string
25. Treasury agents
28. Campbell's competitor
29. Course that doesn't require much studying
30. Output
31. Undiluted, as liquor
32. Turn over
33. Mind
34. Ho-hum
35. Fluctuate repeatedly
36. Wedding cake part
40. The perennial perennial youth
41. Omen
43. Nota ___
44. Villainous expression
46. Put in alphabetical order, e.g.
47. Santa Catalina or Coney
50. Sit on one's heels
51. Gold unit
52. Cover the gray again
53. Colorless
54. Rank below marquess
55. Go in on a hand
56. Lunar plain
57. City on the Rhône
61. Philosopher ___ Tzu
62. It follows cray

Puzzle 187

Across

1. Northern Norwegian, historically speaking
5. Cement ingredient
9. Bills
13. Prima donna performances
15. Object of veneration
16. Inactive
17. Scotland Yard yard?
18. Cold War weapon
20. Masseur's offering
22. Panama pronoun
23. Final stage
24. Crones
25. Fixed payments, as for students
27. Many a GI
29. Dueler's choice
31. Kind of treatment
32. Israeli flier
34. Way out West, once
39. "Ben-Hur" setting
40. Atty. group
41. Algonquian tribe
42. Economic elite
46. Kind of quarter
47. Corp. ladder topper
48. Goad
50. It holds fortified swine?
51. Where drinks come at a price
55. Spinnaker support
57. Well-chosen

58. Site of the Tell legend
59. Cattle place in the boonies
62. One between second and third
65. River through Hades
66. Ike's partner, once
67. Biblical author
68. Spots for 18-Across
69. Paradise lost
70. Some sandwich breads
71. Without a mixer

Down

1. Creche figure
2. Tiler's calculation
3. Begin a night in the woods, perhaps
4. Coat for the slopes
5. Appendage
6. First name in despots
7. Painter of water lilies
8. Hard to get
9. Dead heat
10. Jingle writers
11. Rather dull
12. Transports
14. Suit fabric
19. Subject
21. FedEx rival
25. Saltwater catch
26. Noteworthy period of history
27. Llama land

28. Box-office bomb
30. Latin shortcut
33. Real sucker
35. Utter breathlessly
36. Alexander the Great's teacher
37. Dollar portion
38. "Algiers" actress Lamarr
43. Refute
44. Less couth
45. Sport for heavyweights
49. R&B singer Lou
51. Social position
52. Plant louse
53. Item used in curling
54. Posh
56. Mug for a chug
59. Bus. Degree holders
60. "Slow down!"
61. Place for a clutch
63. Campaigned
64. Miner's bonanza

Puzzle 188

Across

1. Like some decisions
5. It has its reservations
10. Gardener's need
14. Formerly faddish doll
15. Kind of house or glasses
16. Leigh Hunt's "___ Ben Adhem"
17. Ampule kin
18. Experienced know-it-all
20. Loud and discordant
22. Consummate
23. Purposely stay just out of reach, e.g.
24. Holiday season
26. Involuntary muscle contraction
28. KFC side dish
30. On pins and needles
34. Kind of top
36. Sea eagle
37. Koran chapter
38. Galena or cinnabar, e.g.
39. Comforts
42. Word in a Debussy title
43. "The Nazarene" author Sholem
45. "And the earth ___ without form"
46. Poked fun at
48. Feel affection for
49. Support in shenanigans
51. Performs "Stairway to Heaven," e.g.
52. Plant appendages
54. "Island of the Blue Dolphins" author

56. Wing-shaped
59. Some comics
62. Numbskull
65. Shade of hosiery
66. ___ Domini
67. Monte ___ (Monaco principality)
68. Bypass
69. Coral habitat
70. Gather for oneself
71. Certain NCO

Down

1. Guns it
2. Reached the tarmac
3. Wisenheimer
4. Most sacred
5. Elias and Gordie
6. Expounds upon
7. Word with litmus or acid
8. Literary "before"
9. It's spoken in Vientiane
10. They're placed on horses
11. Philharmonic instrument
12. 29th state
13. Calm by deception, perhaps
19. Bit of truth decay
21. Women, to hard-boiled detectives
24. DEA agent
25. Man or woman with a title?
26. Stretch of shallow water

27. Zoroastrian living in India
29. Break it and you may be out on the street
31. Not the brightest people
32. Unintelligible writing to me
33. Bolt units
35. Martin's TV sidekick
40. Hands-on classes
41. Wailing warning
44. Known
47. Most daring
50. Utterly destroys, as an automobile
53. Penultimate letter
55. Wainscots (Var.)
56. Purim's month
57. Clair de ___
58. Bancroft or Boleyn
59. Title word in a Doris Day song
60. Stuffed shirt
61. Apartment building employee (Abbr.)
63. TV producer?
64. Type of sandwich

Puzzle 189

Across

1. Interstate hauler
5. Calcutta misters
9. Coffee preference
14. Clay clump, e.g.
15. Cistercian or Trappist
16. End of "the end of"
17. Tenacious bug?
20. "How sexy!"
21. Phrase of distress
22. Certain compass pt.
23. Disappoint
26. Curious bug?
31. Open-air rooms
34. Pro ___
35. Nastase of the courts
36. Beehive, for one
38. Skirmish
40. Hannibal's challenge
41. Jazzman's lick
45. Sun features
46. Comical bug?
49. Schedules
50. Razor-billed bird
53. Square-dance step or call
57. Complain
59. Squirm-producing bugs?
62. Evening wrap
63. Canine from Kansas
64. Desiccated
65. Aspirations
66. ___ Mawr
67. Lazy Susan, essentially

Down

1. Offspring
2. Pop's John
3. Dayan of Israel
4. Pastoral poem
5. Happy face icon
6. Kind of cuff
7. Playable serves
8. Where stars shine
9. Nymph loved by Apollo
10. Wife of Geraint
11. Hand over
12. Environs
13. Jamie of "M*A*S*H"
18. Troubadour's offering
19. "Who cares?"
24. Some forensic evidence
25. Mel of baseball
26. Before the rest
27. Thin and weak
28. To boot
29. Happy tune
30. Wine sediment
31. Melville captain
32. Imaginary narrative
33. Ready for the pickin'
37. The Beaver State
39. Exhausts, as a supply
42. "When Will ___ Loved" (Everly Brothers)
43. Groupie
44. On edge
47. Word on some doors
48. "The Far Side" cartoonist

50. "Li'l" one of comics
51. Extreme
52. "Sometimes a Great Notion" author
53. SOUPCON
54. Having knowledge of
55. Telegram punctuation word
56. Any of the Antilles
58. Boom support
60. Gamblers' option, briefly
61. Negative link

Puzzle 190

Across

1. Infamous Colombian city
5. Hogwash
9. "Lou Grant" star
14. Islands off Ireland
15. Untraceable author, for short
16. Oak-tree-to-be
17. "Dead ___" (Francis book)
18. Become prominent
19. The in things
20. Hangover remedy
23. Retirement home residents (with "the")
24. Director Bergman
28. Weekly stipend, e.g.
29. Colonial insect
31. Not missing any marbles
32. Impassive
35. Deplume, in a way
37. Passing word?
38. Politically moderate
41. When the French fry?
42. Island known for immigration
43. Towel material
44. Utah ski resort
46. "To Kill a Mockingbird" author
47. It's loaded with cash
48. Job-hunter's offering
50. Asserts without proof
54. Just average
57. Workers, as opposed to management
60. Painter of melting watches
61. Statue's bottom

62. John who wrote "Butterfield 8"
63. Poet Khayyam
64. Arthurian maid
65. Well-worn
66. Musical silence
67. Some numbered rds.

Down

1. Hidden supply
2. "He's ___ nowhere man ..." (Beatles)
3. Web-footed aquatic bird
4. Daring
5. Sot
6. Oneness
7. Fridge raider's quest, perhaps
8. Dummy's seat
9. Brother of Moses
10. Rocker Boz
11. Eggy drink
12. Before, in an old syllable
13. IV givers
21. Delphi figure
22. You can dig it
25. "Key to the city" presenter
26. Words with bend or lend
27. Prepared
29. Oscar-nominated song of 1966
30. Some party snacks
32. Apply jam
33. Appellation
34. "Golden Boy" playwright
35. Amundsen's quest

36. It may let off steam
39. Actress Burstyn
40. Show appreciation to
45. Goddess of the dawn
47. Touted trumpeter
49. Diego Rivera work
50. Hammond product
51. Jack's adversary
52. "___ Venner" (Oliver Wendell Holmes novel)
53. Seasonal transports
55. Nose-wrinkling stimulus
56. Renown
57. Arced toss
58. "Eureka!"
59. Blackball

Puzzle 191

Across

1. In this manner
5. Exclusive group of people
10. Lot measurement
14. Harangue
15. Paris fighter
16. Type of tide
17. Yachting to Hawaii, e.g.
18. British pokeys
19. Bull's-eye piercer
20. Classic children's book
23. Electrical pioneer Nikola
24. Theme pronoun
25. Some fasteners
28. Do a slow burn
30. Smeltery input
32. Theme pronoun
33. "Lord, is ___?" (Last Supper question)
34. Unedited, as data
35. Mia Farrow classic
40. Slangy name for a stranger
41. Absorbed, as a loss
42. That's a moray!
43. Eldritch
46. Pestilent fly
49. Royal name
50. Fab attachment
52. Emulate Pac-Man
54. Streep classic
57. Put down, as tiles
59. Sharp
60. Fertilizer ingredient
61. Instrument made from African blackwood, often

62. Like some surgery
63. Circus performer
64. Without
65. Company vehicles, collectively
66. Amoco rival

Down

1. Open land
2. Corned beef dishes
3. Misgiving
4. Like an overcast night
5. Consequently
6. Hate with a passion
7. Act without restraint
8. Rapidity
9. Decide with a coin
10. Type of condor
11. Use a sponge twice, e.g.
12. Auditory apparatus
13. Qualified
21. Motorized shop tool
22. Journalist's question
26. Say the Paternoster
27. Create seams, e.g.
29. Defender of Castle Grayskull
31. Hemingway title word
33. Anger
35. Member of Rampur royalty
36. Wedding or birthday, e.g.
37. Irregular
38. Type of tree by the ocean?
39. Despite the fact that
40. Kind of pie

44. Positive electrodes, perhaps
45. Siesta
46. Student, at times
47. Evening event
48. Sports banquet hosts, e.g.
51. Get repeated value from
53. High points
55. Football game segment
56. Popular breath mint
57. ___ Alamos
58. Camel hair fabric

Puzzle 192

Across

1. Divulge a secret
5. Sainted mother of Constantine
11. Roll of dough?
14. Mythical mischief-maker
15. Not involving questions of right or wrong
16. Cheer for a toreador
17. Sheep genus
18. Picture book?
19. Pool table success
20. Creepy crawler
22. Card game for a sot?
24. Thorny bunch
25. Singer Ives
26. Stonecutter
29. Some medical buildings
32. Stamp-making org.
33. Sharp emotional attacks
36. Pulitzer-winning Akins
37. Enjoy Aspen, perhaps
38. Pythagorean proposition
39. Legal org.
40. Jack and Bobby's brother
41. Spoke from the soapbox
42. Limo destination, sometimes
43. Knitted garment
45. In a wild and crazy way
46. Ceremony
47. Some hotel amenities
50. "Filthy" money
52. Creepy creature
56. Commit a faux pas, perhaps
57. Bookworm
59. Dashing style
60. Nabokov novel

61. Elegant fur
62. Apartment, e.g.
63. Pencil stump, e.g.
64. Treats a broken bone
65. Rajah's mate

Down

1. Group voting the same way
2. All-conquering thing
3. Related (to)
4. Informal cafes
5. Hinged fasteners
6. Host a show
7. Noblemen
8. Toledo's body of water
9. Preschooler's dread
10. Selflessness
11. Creepy crawler
12. Certain astringent
13. Contradict
21. Electron-deficient atom, perhaps
23. Keats praised one
25. Run, as ink
26. Essential items
27. Lopsided
28. Creepy sidler
29. Heart
30. Computer-programming language
31. Disreputable
33. Number of storied bears
34. Listen and pay attention
35. Decay
38. One with an unsteady gait
42. French chemist and vaccine developer

44. Radial fill
45. Chess units
47. Hawkins of Dogpatch
48. Contraction between looks and everything
49. Kramden's collections
50. Supermarket meat label, perhaps
51. Language of Pakistan
52. Scottish caps
53. Arm bone
54. Past participle of lie
55. Prefix for bodies
58. Before, in poesy

Puzzle 193

Across

1. Doesn't keep up
5. Positive attitude
10. "Of ___ are you speaking?"
14. Southwest crockpot
15. Clownish act
16. Council Bluffs is there
17. Takes a sharp turn
20. Estimated time of arrival
21. Large serving bowls
22. Free pass, in sports
23. Brimless cap
24. Answer to a charge
27. Hemingway title word
28. Follower of the Gospels
32. Seeks entry, in a way (with 43-Across)
35. Napoleon III, to Napoleon I
37. Start of Mr. Rogers' song
38. Trailblazer
40. Linguistic suffix
41. Nervy?
43. See 32-Across
45. It might need surgery
46. Atty. ___
47. Stone made of hydrated silica
48. Peer among peers
51. Linen liturgical vestment
53. Changed to suit
56. Up to now
60. Orbits
62. Give off
63. Split land
64. First name in mysteries
65. Some four-footed mothers
66. Golf great Sam
67. Exploit

Down

1. Almighty one
2. Moises of baseball
3. Filler for some guns
4. Common balloon ballast
5. Socioeconomic class
6. Kick in for a hand
7. Utmost degree
8. Ate sparingly
9. Come about
10. Intercept a conversation, in a way
11. Cutting edge creator
12. "The Virginian" author Wister
13. Setting for many sci-fi films
18. What light indicates
19. It may be picked
23. Kitchen gizmo
24. Form request, sometimes
25. Metric unit of capacity, stateside
26. Follow logically
27. "Well, well, well!"
29. Nestling's cry
30. Magnetic unit
31. Crestless wave
33. Evian attraction
34. Up to, colloquially
35. Paleo- opposite
36. Show fallibility
39. One billion years, in geology
42. Culls
44. It needs to be pushed to get started
46. Certain relative
49. Result of a Google search
50. Malodors
51. In front
52. Carry with effort
53. Made a hole in one
54. South American capital
55. Not a full cut
56. Duke Ellington's "Take ___ Train"
57. Fairway warning
58. Up to the task
59. Cattail, e.g.
61. Three, in Napoli

Puzzle 194

Across

1. First part of a Florida city
5. First place of habitation
9. Valerie Harper series
14. ___ elephant (part of a tot's lesson)
15. Western postwar alliance
16. Invisible emanations
17. Start of a quip
20. Solder or soldier material
21. Riles
22. Lose
23. Word with pick or pack
24. Right-turn command
25. Directions word
26. Quip (Part 2)
33. Shaker ___, OH
34. Indeterminate number
35. Taj Mahal's locale
36. Husbands and wives
39. Steak go-with
40. Nebraska natives
41. Over again
42. Punching tool
43. Hospital lines
44. Quip (Part 3)
50. Shrewdly tricky
51. "___ So Fine" (The Chiffons)
52. Hagen of Broadway
53. Sightlessness

57. "Gone With the Wind" estate
58. Fiddle stick?
59. End of the quip
62. Having to do with bees
63. Huck's transport
64. Vogue competitor
65. Takes ten
66. Gaelic tongue
67. Welfare state?

Down

1. Michael Jackson hit
2. Kind of pool or park
3. Optometrist's concern
4. Indonesian islands
5. Menu heading
6. Less lit
7. Pilots' approximations, briefly
8. "Ripley's Believe It or ___!"
9. Michelin introduced it in 1946
10. Close-mouthed singing
11. Like some vaccines
12. Kind of bank or base
13. Like a fireplace floor
18. Something to take in
19. Post of propriety
25. Transport for Tarzan
27. Like caramel
28. Half of a Washington city

29. Unkind nickname for a corpulent man
30. Teamwork spoiler
31. Poet's preposition
32. ___ Palmas
36. Longtime Chinese leader
37. Raggedy doll
38. Business-card abbr.
39. Off-kilter
40. Egg container
42. One of the black keys
43. Sound like a broken record
45. People with the most people
46. Shucks
47. Marriageable
48. Actor Peter of "The Lion in Winter"
49. Kowtowed
53. Slightly open
54. Casual dissent
55. Some sashes
56. Exam for jrs., in the U.S.
57. Peter the Great, e.g.
60. Vexation
61. Half a score

Puzzle 195

Across

1. Pelican protrusion
5. Use a sickle
9. Prefix with red or structure
14. A rhyme scheme
15. First name in courtroom fiction
16. Take it easy
17. Familiar sign
18. Part of an old English Christmas feast
19. Up
20. Figure from a popular nursery rhyme
23. East or west leadin
24. Behind (with "of")
25. Model's asset
27. Surrealist Salvador
30. They have a glow about them
33. American humane org.
37. Adversity
39. "Do I ___ second?"
41. D.D.E., informally
42. Haughty one
43. Lottery winner's locale?
46. Scary sound for a balloonist
47. Spread the gospel
48. Brit. medals
50. Villains do it, typically
52. Brings about
57. Unwelcome fruit part, perhaps

59. Tenacious one
62. Eyes
64. Some intestinal divisions
65. Building location
66. "M*A*S*H" extra
67. Approach
68. Social suffixes
69. Eyelid swellings
70. Match makers
71. Conde ___

Down

1. Some opera voices
2. Skip the restaurant
3. 1945's "Little Boy," for short
4. Phi Beta ___
5. Noted mother of twins
6. Greek cupid
7. Jai ___
8. Lasting dos
9. Modern Persians
10. Novel
11. Dances accompanied with guitar music
12. Turkish liqueur
13. Terminated ruthlessly
21. Type of PC screen
22. Siberia's second largest city
26. Detroit gridders
28. Spot for an ocelot
29. Annoyed
31. Some ring stats

32. The Concordes, initially
33. Almanzo's dog
34. Brandy flavor
35. Business school topic
36. Indo-European
38. Poor grades
40. They make do without
44. "The Cosby Show" character
45. What AAA contractors do, often
49. Good sign for scalpers
51. Archaeologist's find, perhaps
53. Dye used as a toner
54. Guard dog breed
55. They fly and have tails
56. Look at, in the Bible
57. Short dogs, for short
58. "New Jack City" actor
60. Type of club
61. Radiator output
63. Tell a tall tale

Puzzle 196

Across

1. Obeys the green light
5. Dummkopfs
10. Charitable offerings
14. First name in a Tolstoy novel
15. Unwelcome kitchen visitor
16. Partiality
17. July 4th entree, perhaps
19. Farm insects
20. Prayer
21. Front-runner
23. Copy machine need
24. Expression of displeasure
26. Hunky-dory
28. Tots give them to get attention
29. Just one of those things?
30. Cum laude modifier
32. Road shape
33. Medium pace
34. Timberland
35. July 4th beverage, perhaps
37. More than whimper
40. Wilderness rarity
41. Snowball of literature
44. Variety of salts
45. Saucy
46. Train-sound syllable
47. Flow stopper
48. Chipmunk snack

50. Wonder Woman alias
51. Trade diplomat
53. Sight in the west
54. Be revolting?
55. July 4th dressing, perhaps
58. Singer Redding
59. Central artery
60. Pointing devices
61. Revolutionary computer game
62. San Francisco player, briefly
63. Years in Madrid

Down

1. Inquisition collar (Var.)
2. Burdensome
3. Many have twists
4. Disrespects verbally
5. Like some cereal
6. Alley-___
7. Atomize
8. Yellow and black cat
9. Shakespearean title character
10. In ___ way (suffering)
11. Family tree
12. Dowagers
13. Bacon sound
18. Neither companion
22. Prunus dulcis fruit
24. Liquor serving, perhaps
25. One at a wedding reception

27. Krazy of the comics
29. Cream was one
31. Common verb
33. Wendy's pitchman, once
34. Royal decree
35. Reporter's question, often
36. Threadbare
37. You may make it in the morning
38. Lack of transparency
39. Effortless learning procedure
41. Introduce gradually
42. "Rhinoceros" playwright Eugene
43. Chin beards trimmed into a point
45. Hoi follower
46. Movie house
49. Castro, for one
50. "Well, that's completely obvious!"
52. Where worms may be served
53. An unwanted lasting impression
54. CD-___
56. Keats subject
57. Summer, to a Frenchman

Puzzle 197

ΩAcross

1. Portoferraio's locale
5. Dish for Twist
10. Tumultuous sitdown
14. Jerusalem Mount
15. Roomy size
16. Tear asunder
17. Words with "here I come"
19. Often used Latin abbreviation
20. Severely simple
21. Reflexive pronoun
23. Horse course
24. Odorize by burning
26. Cake feature
29. Piper's due
30. Spot for shots
34. Low in fat
35. Approximately
37. Eruption fallout
38. They're hot south of the border
39. Move aimlessly
40. "Last chance!"
42. Acronymic computer truism
43. It may be light or grand
44. Back muscle, to weightlifters
45. They sometimes accompany ejections
46. Respond to, as information

48. ___ Salvador, El Salvador
49. Brunei's island
52. Priest's simple ceremony
56. On tenterhooks
57. When to call me?
60. Editor's option
61. Certain Alaskan
62. First of 13 popes
63. Sniggler's haul
64. "The Winding Stair" poet
65. Masher's look

Down

1. Book of the Bible
2. In ___ of
3. Parts of Phyllis Diller's wardrobe
4. Words with now
5. Denzel Washington film
6. Infrequent
7. Caterer's vessel
8. Psyche division
9. Admit
10. Find a buyer beforehand
11. A type of beer
12. Shape of the old pigskin
13. Filthy lucre
18. Orbital period
22. Ivan and Peter
24. Camel string

25. Shoelace place
26. Steppe sister?
27. Fable composer
28. A name for the God of the Old Testament
29. Grapefruit relative
31. Initiate
32. English teacher's concern
33. It was opened before Windows
35. Homo sapiens
36. "... ___ the fields we go"
38. Use caller ID
41. They are often juggled
42. Saloon
45. Act the sycophant (with "over")
47. It's here before tomorrow
48. Puts first things first
49. Beseeched
50. A type of arch
51. Paper-towel unit
52. Stumblebum
53. "The Morning Watch" author
54. Clog, e.g.
55. Prepare paint
58. Adult beverage
59. A vote for

Puzzle 198

Across

1. Great time or great noise
6. With the bow, musically
10. Where electrons orbit
14. Long-handled server
15. Closed circuit
16. Profligate
17. TV studio sign
18. Wagner work
20. Bizet work
22. Like TV's Gilligan
23. Acapulco acknowledgements
24. Dine
26. Palindromic fictional twin
27. Waitress with Sam and Coach
29. Some luxurious fabrics
34. Washstand pitcher
37. Min. fractions
39. Columbus' birthplace
40. Puccini work, translated
43. Mindless
44. Culinary directive
45. Whispers sweet nothings
46. It's good for what ails you
48. Cream of the crop
50. 007's creator Fleming
52. Rocky hill
53. Word with sheet or session

56. Bad way to be caught
61. Strauss work
63. Verdi work
65. Unit of length for Noah
66. Medicinal plant
67. Put safely away
68. Steadily reduce, in a way
69. Stages
70. Eschew the mouse
71. Dissuade

Down

1. Alliances
2. Kauai porch
3. Some Jewish months
4. ___ to none (long odds)
5. Mother of renown
6. Monopoly portion?
7. Suite section
8. Cagney role
9. Theme of this puzzle
10. Medea's getaway craft
11. Mountain lake
12. "Grapes of Wrath" escapee
13. Repair
19. Minority
21. Certain hospital employee
25. Commoners in ancient Rome, informally
27. Construction-site sight

28. Extremely sharp or intense
30. Third canonical hour
31. Compressed data
32. ___ contendere
33. Verbalizes
34. Nabob of the Near East
35. Decrease gradually
36. Red-clad cheese
38. Clown's height enhancer
41. Situated toward the middle
42. Some musical groups
47. Most nimble
49. Made an outline
51. Like mesh
53. "Lost in Space" figure
54. Ammonia compound
55. Falk of "Columbo"
56. Europe and Asia boundary
57. World's longest river
58. In a state of eager anticipation
59. Afflictions and troubles
60. Desist
62. Tackle box item
64. Run up debt

Puzzle 199

Across

1. What a spy may write in
5. Soldier's lullaby
9. Handles hardship
14. A song for one
15. Cylinder you may see in the country
16. Persona's reverse
17. Burn slightly
18. Etc. relative
19. Thematic element
20. It stings
22. Natural smoke detector
24. Roar of a Spanish crowd
25. It may double your dough
27. Detective novelist Erle Stanley
29. "A Room With a View" novelist
31. Lendl or Reitman
32. Send sky-high
33. Seagoing vessel, in myth
35. Dear one of advice
39. Luau loop
40. Carnivorous birds
43. Piece of mine?
44. List type
46. It may wind up on a dock
47. City on the Ruhr
49. Expert, in slang
51. Some reed players
53. Official discharge

56. Fry lightly
57. In the past
58. Invigorates (with "up")
60. Like many a winter road
63. Like fresh lettuce
65. Burghoff's TV co-star
67. On a slow boat to China, e.g.
68. Unearthly
69. Stir turbulently
70. Unit of pressure
71. Rudder's locale
72. Marquee
73. Ink's color, to Shakespeare

Down

1. Carry partner
2. Embossed snack
3. Journal theft? (goes both ways)
4. Sincere
5. Fly over the equator?
6. British islet
7. Word with game or pension
8. Male escorts working alone? (goes both ways)
9. Tourist's tote
10. Words of protest from Yoko?
11. Rock climber's spike
12. Rousseau work
13. Comparatively unthreatened
21. Faster's opposite?

23. Relish
26. Certain acrobatic bar? (goes both ways)
28. Evidence type, briefly
29. Sensed
30. Stick in the fridge?
34. Abbr. in some directions
36. Head honchos weep? (goes both ways)
37. "The Outcasts of Poker Flat" author Harte
38. Strong desires
41. What a question might do
42. Olympic site of 1988
45. Be in hock
48. Place firmly
50. Occur
52. Certain volcanic rock
53. Pennant chases
54. Fine-feathered specimen
55. River viewed from Amboise
59. Blackthorn
61. White knight, stereotypically
62. "The one that got away," say
64. Poitier title role
66. Strident noise

Puzzle 200

Across

1. Damsel's plea
7. Baby's berth
11. Grimalkin, e.g.
14. Covert comments
15. German auto firm
16. Lord's Prayer opener
17. Presiding officer
19. Spooky sighting
20. Gwyneth's mom
21. Stock car feature
23. Row partner
26. Vast multitude
28. Noted groundhog's name
29. Scandal suffix
30. 20-year sleeper
31. Takes into one's family
33. One of a Freudian trio
34. Brolly alternatives
35. "Little Caesar" gangster
36. Gizmos
38. "You said it!" (in '60s slang)
41. Petty of "A League of Their Own"
42. Umps' counterparts
43. Unproductive bother
44. Coronary procedure
46. Legolas of Middle Earth, e.g.
47. Cherry handle

48. The third can shock you
49. Purchase for a 1950s home, perhaps
51. Went with
52. Approach to an article
54. The key for making change?
56. Part of Tina Turner's revue
57. Second-stringer
62. New prefix
63. Moldy cheese
64. Typesetting mistakes
65. Equivalent of 1,000 rin, once
66. British knights
67. Air lane

Down

1. Yolk encloser
2. Eruption fallout
3. Itinerary word
4. Fit for consumption
5. First name among country crooners
6. Catch a glimpse of
7. Drive-in employees of old
8. Artifices
9. Terse vow
10. Pickle
11. One glued to the tube
12. Up on

13. Creatures of folklore
18. Deontology, e.g.
22. Memorable era
23. Like good burgundy
24. "Othello" evildoer
25. Informer
27. Tax on imports
30. Salad ingredient, sometimes
32. Aggressive remarks
34. Olympus Mons locale
37. Factotum, e.g.
38. Enjoy with gusto
39. Some English readings
40. City on Norton Sound
42. Get back to the task at hand
44. Smart as a whip
45. Ruth was one
47. Cooking wine
50. Word with tube or ear
51. "Downtown" singer
53. Eases off
55. Leaves dumbfounded
58. Ransom ___ Olds
59. Animal's gullet
60. Due date, briefly
61. Hope unit

Puzzle 201

Across

1. Hardly modern
6. Cartoon supply company
10. Edicts
14. D-Day beach
15. Manifesto writer
16. "Scram!"
17. CAP
19. Many a former Yugoslavian
20. Editor's override
21. Carbon-14 determination
22. Dolphins' domain
23. Neophyte
24. TEE
27. Hosp. staffers
29. Perseveres
30. Best supporting actress for "Girl, Interrupted"
33. Some push-ups
35. Top layer?
38. SHORTS
42. Asian holiday
43. Mouth-related
44. Bears Hall of Famer Mike
45. Raise
48. Immigrants' prep class, perhaps
49. SOCKS
53. Painter with a museum in St. Petersburg
57. "The Luck of Roaring Camp" writer
58. Nemo's harpoonist
59. It may come after life
60. Big name in 1970s gymnastics
61. SNEAKS
64. Roman poet
65. Massage aids
66. Place for outdoor dining, perhaps
67. Mr. America's pride, perhaps
68. Jubilation
69. Candid

Down

1. Awaken
2. Handed or headed start
3. Long candle
4. Pretentious speech
5. It may go for a dip in the ocean
6. South-of-the-border buddy
7. Caravan member
8. X-ray follow-up, perhaps
9. Phone no. addition
10. Help out
11. Low blow
12. The Velvet Fog
13. Film based on a Ferber novel
18. Falls behind
22. Common title
25. Thrash about
26. River under the Brooklyn Bridge
28. Aquarium implement
30. Type of stream
31. "Bravo!" relative
32. Sluggish
33. Result of labor?
34. Color TV pioneer
36. "A mouse!"
37. Org. for U.S. cryptologists
39. Supreme leader?
40. They might be sq.
41. Tusked beast
46. Pieces of eight?
47. '50s campaign name
48. Vortex
49. Battle cry
50. Bisect
51. Approach to an article
52. Actress Witherspoon
54. Major blood supplier
55. "E pluribus unum," e.g.
56. Reassuring phrase
61. Gear tooth
62. Be indisposed
63. Sunscreen meas.

Puzzle 202

Sudoku Puzzles

Fill in the numbers 1 through 9 one time in each row,
column, and 3-x-3 box within the grid. See Chapter 3 for
more information on Sudoku puzzles, especially the
target (round) puzzles in the Treacherous section.

Easy

				3	6		9	5
3			9		4		7	
	9	7						
	3	1	6					
			2		1			
					9	5	4	
						2	5	
	1		4		7			8
4	6		5	9				

Puzzle 203

			6			1	7	
	8			4	1	5		
	3			2		4		
			3	9	4		2	
				5				
	4		2	6	7			
		1		7			5	
		3	4	1			8	
	2	9			3			

Puzzle 204

		1	8		6	9		
4		5						
	2		4	3				
9			7	2		5		
	8						1	
		2		9	8		7	6
				8	4		3	
						8		1
		4	3		2	7		

Puzzle 205

		5		2		3		
6	3		4					9
			3				7	
2						8	9	
8		4				6		1
	9	3						5
	4				5			
1					8		5	4
		6		9		7		

Puzzle 206

						3	6	4
7		2		4				
1	6		9		3			5
					5	6	4	2
9	8	5	2					
2			6		1		5	8
				2		7		6
6		7						

Puzzle 207

			4			1		9
4			7			5	8	2
	2		6		9	8	7	
5								3
	1	9	3		5		2	
1	6	5			8			7
8		3			7			

Puzzle 200

Tricky

			9		2			8
2		7	3			1	9	
			1		5		3	
		4		9	3			
	6		7		1		2	
			8	2		7		
	4		2		8			
	1	6			7	2		9
5								

Puzzle 209

	7			5		1	8	
		4	2					6
9	8							
8	9		5	2				
4								3
				4	3		5	8
							4	1
3					5	8		
	5	8		9			7	

Puzzle 210

3		4				1		8
	6		9		3		2	
		6	8		2	7		
5	2						1	6
		1	3		5	9		
	3		7		1		5	
6		7				2		3

Puzzle 211

				6			1	5
			4		7		8	
	6			9				2
	5		2		1			7
		3				9		
8			9		4		3	
3				1			6	
	4		7		9			
2	1			4				

Puzzle 212

2			5		8			
	1	8	4					
	6							2
6			9	7		5		
		4	8		3	9		
	2		5	6				1
3						9		
				9	6	3		
		6		1				7

Puzzle 213

7	8		4					
	3			8		9	7	
		9	3	2			6	
1	5							
		2				5		
							3	8
	1			7	8	6		
	2	7		9			8	
					4		1	9

Puzzle 214

1		2		9	6			
					2	9		
9			4					3
	4			1		6	2	
		8				3		
	2	9		6			8	
5					9			8
		4	1					
			6	7		4		5

Puzzle 215

		3	5	9				1
		5			2		8	
	7		4	8				
4		8						
	6						7	
						1		9
				4	7		3	
	3		8			2		
1				2	3	5		

Puzzle 216

		2				1	5	3
		9	8				7	
5			3	6		9		
	4			2				7
8				1			9	
		6		3	9			1
	9				8	5		
3	2	8				7		

Puzzle 217

2		6						
	3				8			1
	5	9	4			8		
				2				9
	1	8	6		9	7	3	
9				7				
		5			7	2	6	
3			9				1	
						9		5

Puzzle 218

4	1	8			3			9
	5						7	
		6	2			4		
3			4				6	
			5		1			
	2				9			7
		5			2	1		
	6						9	
9			1			2	5	4

Puzzle 219

7			9	7	5			8
			9	7	5			
9		6				5		4
		9	5		7	8		
	7						4	
		3	2		6	7		
2		5				6		7
			1	5	9			
4								3

Puzzle 220

			8		6			
6				3		7		
	5	2					4	6
4				2				
	9	1				6	2	
				9				5
2	4					8	1	
		7		4				3
			1		3			

Puzzle 221

6		9	2		4	1		3
		3		6		9		
1								7
		1	5		6	2		
		4	8		9	3		
8								9
		7		9		4		
9		5	3		1	8		6

Puzzle 222

Tough

		5			4		2	
9				6			3	7
	3	8				9		
		3		9				
		4	5		3	7		
				1		6		
		9				3	7	
3	4			2				8
	5		3			1		

Puzzle 223

Puzzle 224

19	11			17	11	11		4
	13						12	17
		15		16	19			
5		18					17	8
13	6		26			13		
							7	
3	22				16		13	14
		10		18				
7	9				15			

Puzzle 225

Puzzle 226

		1					3	5
2			9		3	8	1	
		4					9	7
			8	2				
6								9
				3	9			
		3				5		
3	7		1					8
1		8				4		

Puzzle 227

1	7					3		
		2			9	7		
	8	9				5	2	
	9		4				1	
	5				8		4	
	1	6				9	5	
		4	1			8		
9	4						7	6

Puzzle 228

	1			9				7
7			4		1	9		5
		7	5			1		
	5		7		2		4	
			6	7	3			
	3		8		7		9	
				5		7	1	9
6		5	1		5		7	8
	7	1	9				2	

Puzzle 229

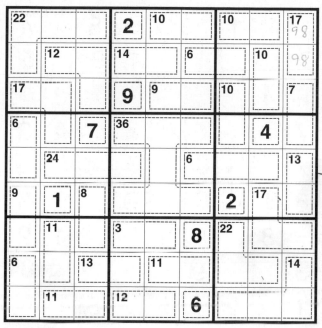

Puzzle 230

		1		3		8		4
					6			9
2	4						3	
7			2				4	3
		4				2		
6	1				9			7
	8						1	2
3			9					
1		9		5		3		

Puzzle 231

Puzzle 232

30		6		11		18		12
			8	10			14	
5	9	6		14				1
		17	9	9		5	10
15	10			19			
	2	9		10		4	11
6	21		17		3	4		
5		13	11		32		
			10		9		

Puzzle 233

Puzzle 234

Puzzle 235

6			3		9			4
		2			1		5	9
	9		7			1		
	6	4						2
5						4	6	
		3			2		4	
2	1		4			9		
4			6		8			5

Puzzle 236

	8			4			1	
			8		1			
7		4	6		5			
	6	1				9	4	
8								1
	4	3				5	7	
			5		6	4		3
			7		4			
	5			2			9	

Puzzle 237

Puzzle 238

Puzzle 239

Treacherous

		9	4	7			8	
7				3			5	
8					2	6		
2					3		1	
	4						3	
	1		5					2
		6	3					7
	7			2				8
	5			8	1	3		

Puzzle 240

			6		3			
	7		4		1		5	
8		3				1		6
		8		5		2		
4								7
		9		7		4		
1		7				5		9
	3		7		9		4	
			2		5			

Puzzle 241

		6			2			4
	5						1	
3		8			4	2		
		5			6			3
7	1						2	5
6			5			4		
		3	7			8		2
	2						4	
5			8			1		

Puzzle 242

					2	7	6	
6				1			5	2
			3	7				
	4			3			2	
		6	2		7	1		
	9			8			7	
				5	9			
3	7			6				4
	6	8	4					

Puzzle 243

7	5		9		6		4	8
				7				
9	4						1	5
			5		8			
6								3
			2		7			
4	6						7	9
				8				
5	1		7		2		6	4

Puzzle 244

		1		4		8		5
						1	4	
	2	8		1	3		7	
								9
5			4		9			7
6								
	9		1	2		6	3	
	6	4						
1		3		6		2		

Puzzle 245

17	12	11		11	8	14		
		8					19	9
11			13		6			
	12	10		15	15	6		16
7		6	10			2	11	
	8				9			10
4	15		4	10		12	21	
		23		10	8			5
17								

Puzzle 246

		2		8	4		1	
				7				
	5				9	6		
	3	5		2			6	
9	2						8	7
	6			1		3	4	
		4	8				3	
				5				
	8		4	9		2		

Puzzle 247

3								4
		2	4		6		8	
								2
		8	5		4	2		
	1						3	
		4	3	2	9	7		
7								
	4		9		8	6		
9								8

Puzzle 248

Puzzle 249

Puzzle 250

Puzzle 251

Puzzle 252

					2	1		
8	3	2	4	1	9			
				6			3	2
7			3		6			8
	2						6	
5			6		1			4
		7		5				
4			2	8	3			5
	8		9					

Puzzle 253

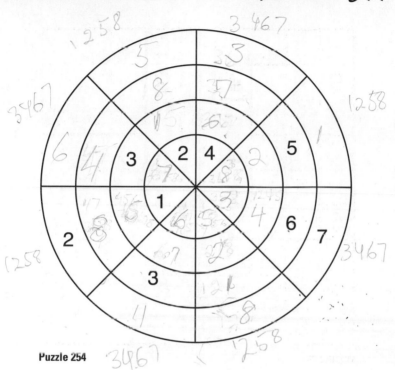

Puzzle 254

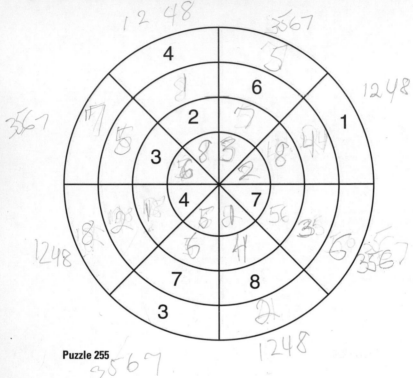

Puzzle 255

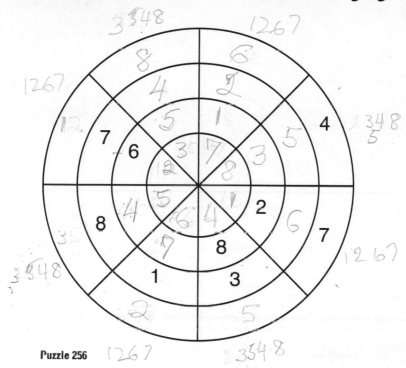

Puzzle 256

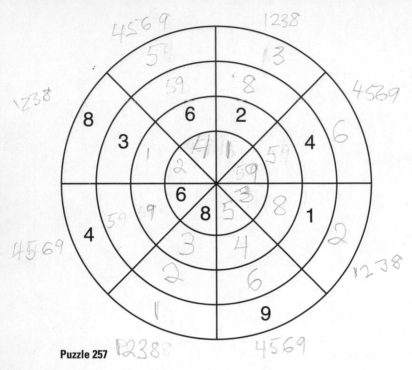

Puzzle 257

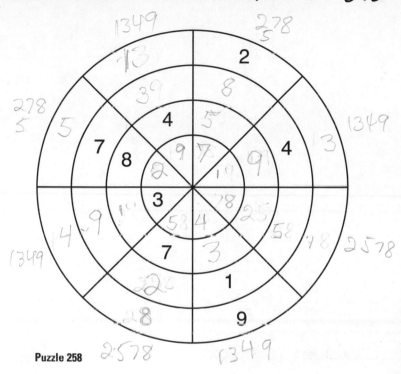

Puzzle 258

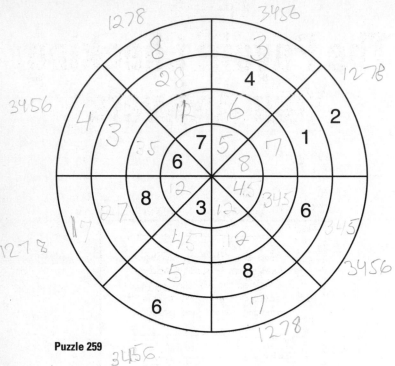

Puzzle 259

Part III
The Payoff: Checking Your Answers

The 5th Wave   By Rich Tennant

In this part . . .

I twould be downright cruel to omit this part from any puzzle book. Even if you're certain you've completed a certain puzzle or answered a riddle exactly the right way, you want the satisfaction of seeing your accomplishment in print, right? And face it: Everyone has those days when they just can't get the final few entries to the crossword puzzle or when a seemingly unsolvable logic puzzle threatens to keep them awake all night.

I don't want to be accused of causing sleep deprivation, so here are the answers you need. Just promise me you won't crack this part open until you've given your puzzle of choice a run for the money!

Chapter 5

Answers

• •

*P*lease do not read through this chapter until you've worked on the puzzles in Chapter 4!

Puzzle 1
Once. After that, the mathematician would be subtracting ten from 90, then 80, then 70 . . .

Puzzle 2
Three wise men

Puzzle 3
They were part of a set of triplets, the third child being a daughter

Puzzle 4
5 + 5 4 5 = 550 (add one diagonal line to the second "+" to make it a "4")

Puzzle 5
Alexander juggled the gold as he crossed the bridge, keeping at least one piece in the air at all times.

Puzzle 6
One person stands on one corner of the handkerchief and closes a door. The second person stands on the corner of the handkerchief protruding under the door. With the door between them, they cannot possibly touch.

Puzzle 7
The person is on tracks in a railroad tunnel walking toward the train and is close to the end when the oncoming train is discovered. The person must then run forward to clear the tunnel before the train enters.

Puzzle 8
You send the container with one of your locks securing the container. Your acquaintance receives the container, and without trying to open it, attaches his lock next to your lock. He then sends the container back to you. You use your key to unlock your lock, remove it, and send the container back to your acquaintance with only his lock on the container. He can then open the container using his own key to his own lock.

Puzzle 9
The man said: "I will be drowned."

Puzzle 10
The word is STARTLING and the word sequence is:
STARTING - STARING - STRING - STING - SING - SIN - IN - I

Puzzle 11
A hole in the ground

Puzzle 12
A goose

Puzzle 13
A fire

Puzzle 14
A yardstick

Puzzle 15
The future

Puzzle 16
Tomorrow

Puzzle 17
Stairs

Puzzle 18
Your breath

Puzzle 19
The letter "i"

Puzzle 20
4, positioned like this: WW
WW

Puzzle 21
Raise and raze

Puzzle 22
Taking any eight of the nine coins, load the scale with four coins on either side. Whenever two sides are equal, the remaining coin is the fake.

Puzzle 23
Noon

Puzzle 24
Bookkeeper (oo-kk-ee) and sweet-toothed (ee-tt-oo)

Puzzle 25
Answer: Nothing

Puzzle 26
LAUGH AND THE WORLD LAUGHS WITH YOU. SNORE AND YOU SLEEP ALONE.

Puzzle 27
BE CAREFUL OF YOUR THOUGHTS. THEY MAY BECOME
WORDS AT ANY MOMENT.

Puzzle 28
SHUN IDLENESS. IT IS THE RUST THAT ATTACHES ITSELF
TO THE MOST BRILLIANT METALS.

Puzzle 29
IF I TAKE CARE OF MY CHARACTER, MY REPUTATION
WILL TAKE CARE OF ITSELF.

Puzzle 30
HE WHO ESTABLISHES HIS ARGUMENT BY NOISE AND
COMMAND SHOWS THAT HIS REASON IS WEAK.

Puzzle 31
WHENEVER I FEEL LIKE EXERCISING, I LIE DOWN UNTIL
THE FEELING PASSES.

Puzzle 32
TRUST YOUR OWN INSTINCT. YOUR MISTAKES MIGHT AS
WELL BE YOUR OWN INSTEAD OF SOMEONE ELSES.

Puzzle 33
THE ONLY PEOPLE WHO LISTEN TO BOTH SIDES OF A
FAMILY QUARREL ARE THE NEXT DOOR NEIGHBORS.

Puzzle 34
ALL THE BEAUTIFUL SENTIMENTS IN THE WORLD
WEIGH LESS THAN A SINGLE LOVELY ACTION.

Puzzle 35
THERE'S NOTHING IN THE MIDDLE OF THE ROAD BUT
YELLOW STRIPES AND DEAD ARMADILLOS.

Puzzle 36
THE GEM CANNOT BE POLISHED WITHOUT FRICTION,
NOR MAN PERFECTED WITHOUT TRIALS.

Puzzle 37
REMEMBER, WHEN THE PEACOCK STRUTS HIS STUFF HE
SHOWS HIS BACKSIDE TO HALF THE WORLD.

Puzzle 38
LACK OF WILL POWER AND DRIVE CAUSE MORE FAIL-
URES THAN LACK OF INTELLIGENCE AND ABILITY.

Puzzle 39
BELIEVE IT OR NOT, ONCE UPON A TIME, ALL MEMBERS
OF THE FAMILY HAD BREAKFAST TOGETHER.

Puzzle 40
IF YOU WILL SPEND MORE TIME SHARPENING THE AX,
YOU'LL SPEND LESS TIME CHOPPING WOOD.

Puzzle 41
THE WORSHIP MOST ACCEPTABLE TO GOD COMES
FROM A THANKFUL AND CHEERFUL HEART.

Puzzle 42
THE LAND OF MILK AND HONEY HAS ITS DRAWBACKS.
YOU CAN GET KICKED BY A COW AND STUNG BY A BEE.

Puzzle 43
WHEN A MAN SEES THE HANDWRITING ON THE WALL,
THERE IS PROBABLY A CHILD IN THE FAMILY.

Puzzle 44
PERSONALITY CAN OPEN DOORS BUT ONLY CHARAC-
TER CAN KEEP THEM OPEN.

Puzzle 45
GOD'S TOMORROW WILL BE BETTER THAN ANY YES-
TERDAY YOU HAVE EVER KNOWN.

Puzzle 46
FOUR THINGS DO NOT COME BACK; THE SPOKEN WORD,
THE SHOT ARROW, THE PAST LIFE AND THE NEGLECTED
OPPORTUNITY.

Puzzle 47
I FINALLY KNOW WHAT DISTINGUISHES MAN FROM THE
BEASTS - FINANCIAL WORRIES.

Puzzle 48
NO PASSION SO EFFECTUALLY ROBS THE MIND OF ALL
ITS POWERS OF ACTING AND REASONING AS FEAR.

Puzzle 49
BRAVERY IS THE CAPACITY TO PERFORM PROPERLY
EVEN WHEN SCARED HALF TO DEATH.

Puzzle 50
OPPORTUNITY IS MISSED BY MOST PEOPLE BECAUSE IT
IS DRESSED IN OVERALLS AND LOOKS LIKE WORK.

Puzzle 51
LIVES

Puzzle 52
CO-STAR

Puzzle 53
SORES

Puzzle 54
SECURE

Puzzle 55
LISTEN

Puzzle 56
THEY SEE

Puzzle 57
THEIRS

Puzzle 58
SOBER

Puzzle 59
SPEND IT

Puzzle 60
CHEATING

Puzzle 61
KITCHEN

Puzzle 62
DEBIT CARD

Puzzle 63
DATE'S UP

Puzzle 64
THE CLASSROOM

Puzzle 65
CAR INSURANCE

Puzzle 66
DETECT THIEVES

Puzzle 67
ELEVEN PLUS TWO

Puzzle 68
THE DESERT REGION

Puzzle 69
PAID ME EVERY CENT

Puzzle 70
CASH LOST IN 'EM

Puzzle 71
ELECTION RECOUNTS

Puzzle 72
DREAM FOR CUE BALLS

Puzzle 73
PUBLIC RELATIONS

Puzzle 74
NEW YEAR'S RESOLUTION

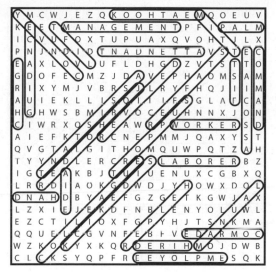

Puzzle 75

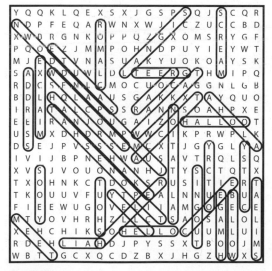

Puzzle 76

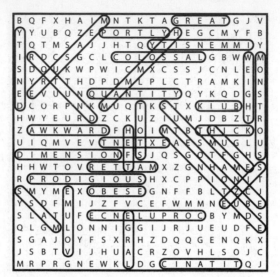

Puzzle 77

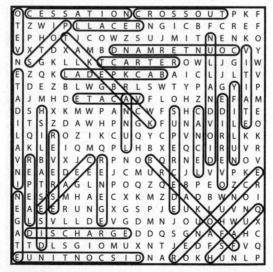

Puzzle 78

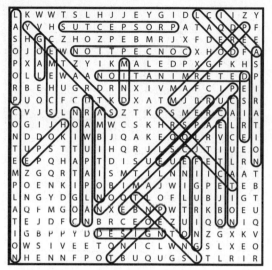

Puzzle 79

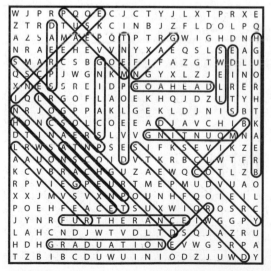

Puzzle 80

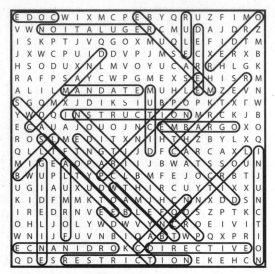

Puzzle 81

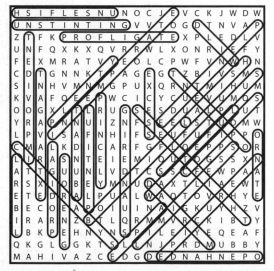

Puzzle 82

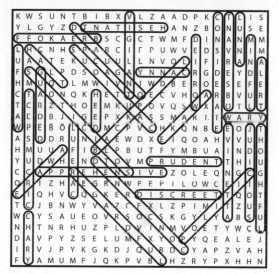

Puzzle 83

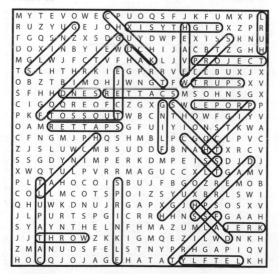

Puzzle 84

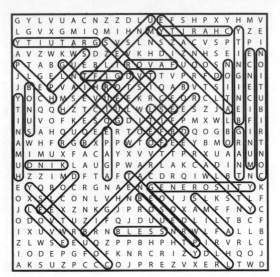

Puzzle 85

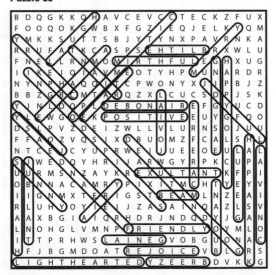

Puzzle 86

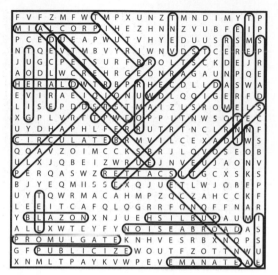

Puzzle 87

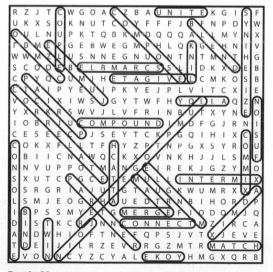

Puzzle 88

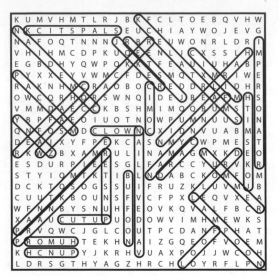

Puzzle 89

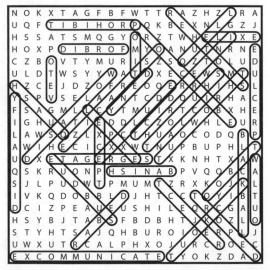

Puzzle 90

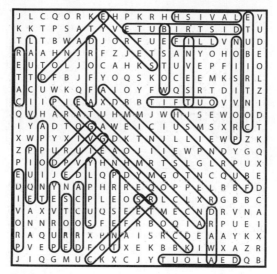

Puzzle 91

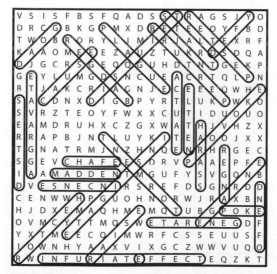

Puzzle 92

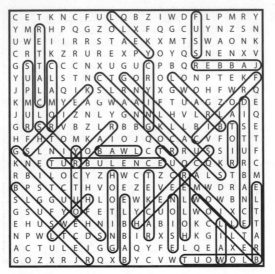

Puzzle 93

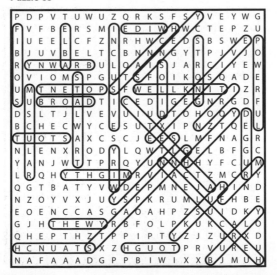

Puzzle 94

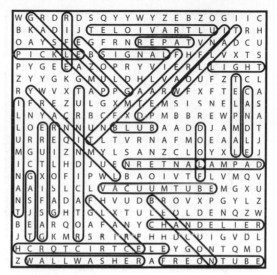

Puzzle 95

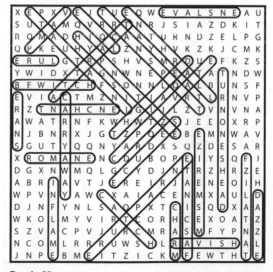

Puzzle 96

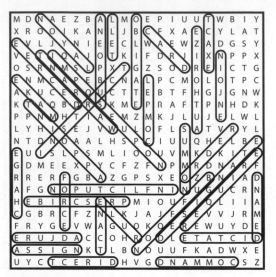

Puzzle 97

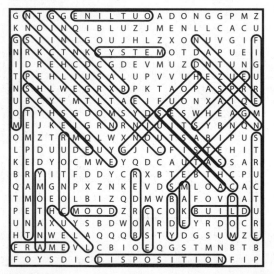

Puzzle 98

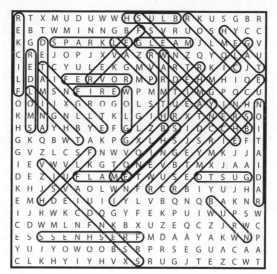

Puzzle 99

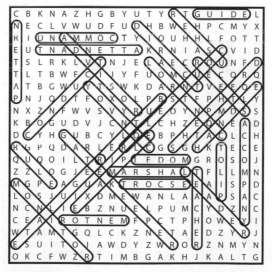

Puzzle 100

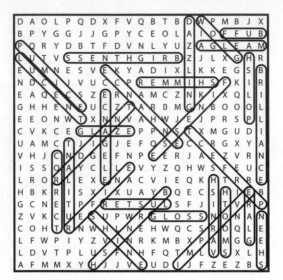

Puzzle 101

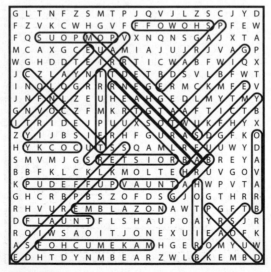

Puzzle 102

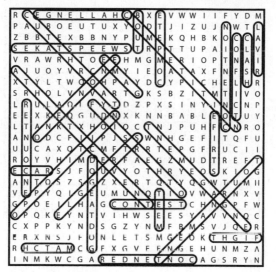

Puzzle 103

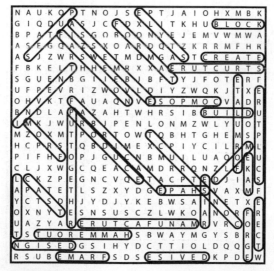

Puzzle 104

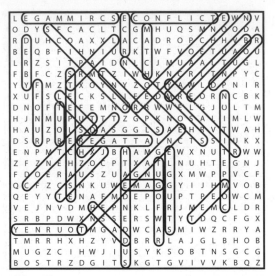

Puzzle 105

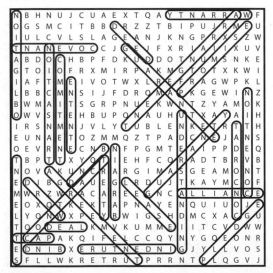

Puzzle 106

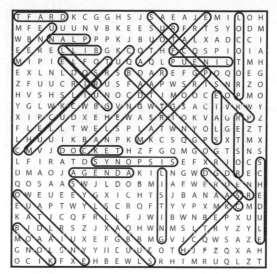

Puzzle 107

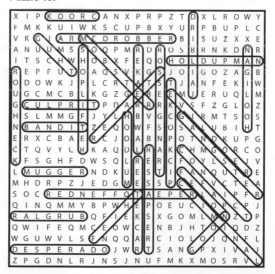

Puzzle 108

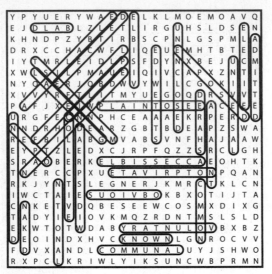

Puzzle 109

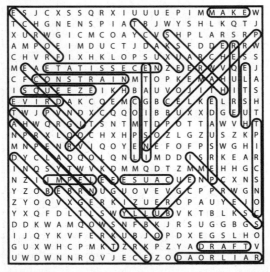

Puzzle 110

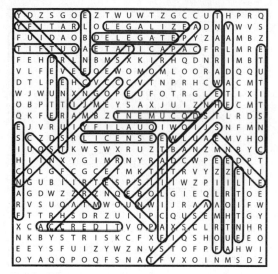

Puzzle 111

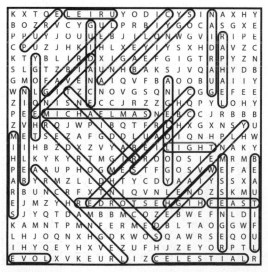

Puzzle 112

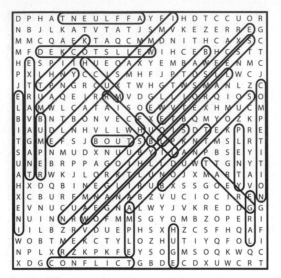

Puzzle 113

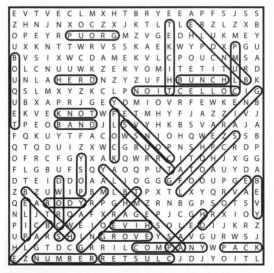

Puzzle 114

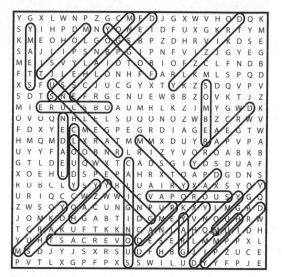

Puzzle 115

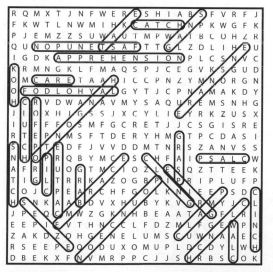

Puzzle 116

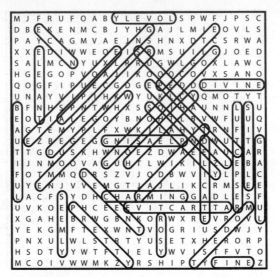

Puzzle 117

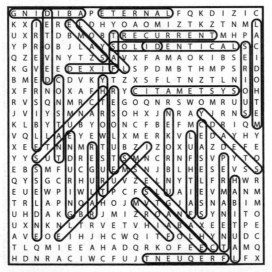

Puzzle 118

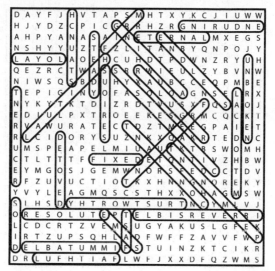

Puzzle 119

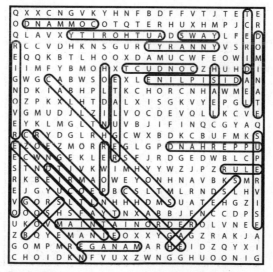

Puzzle 120

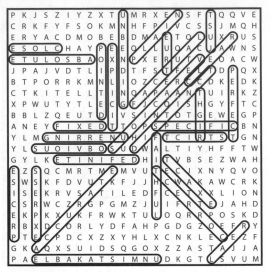

Puzzle 121

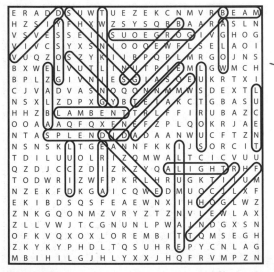

Puzzle 122

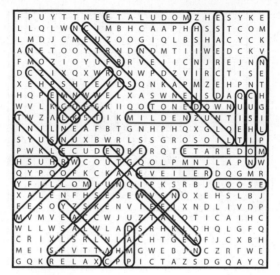

Puzzle 123

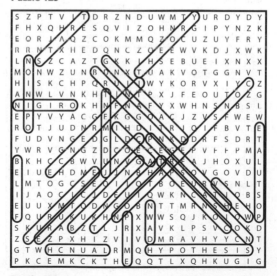

Puzzle 124

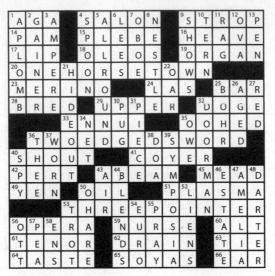

Puzzle 125

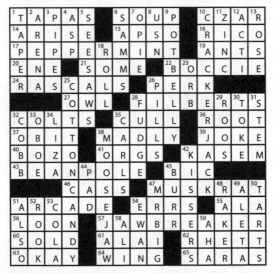

Puzzle 126

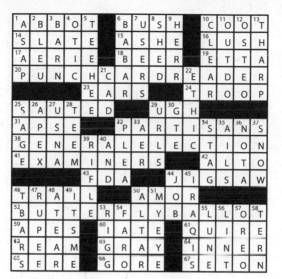

Puzzle 127

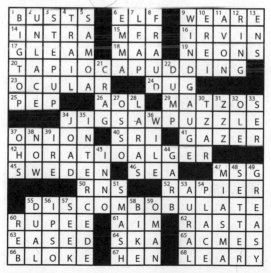

Puzzle 128

Puzzle 129

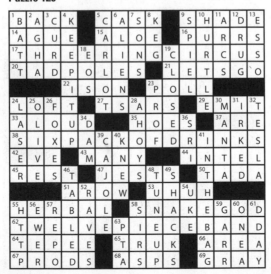

Puzzle 130

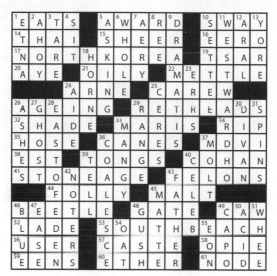

Puzzle 131

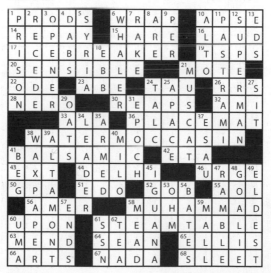

Puzzle 132

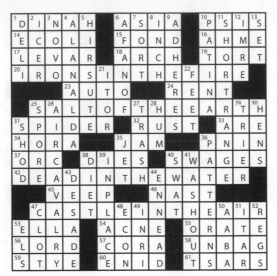

Puzzle 133

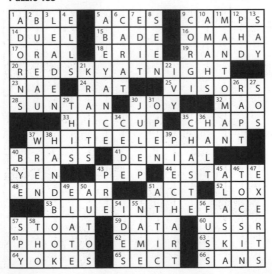

Puzzle 134

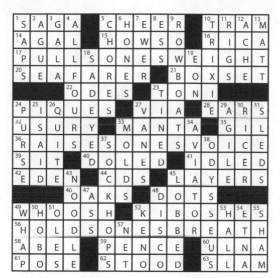

Puzzle 135

Puzzle 136

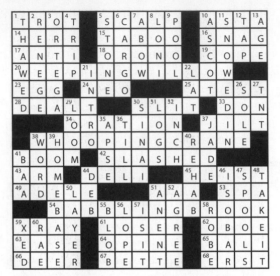

Puzzle 137

Puzzle 138

Puzzle 139

Puzzle 140

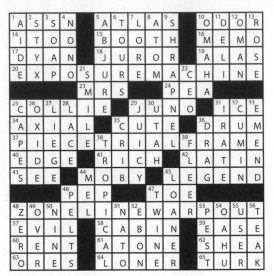

Puzzle 141

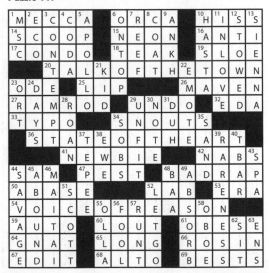

Puzzle 142

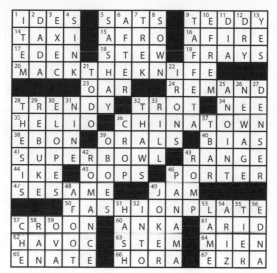

Puzzle 143

Puzzle 144

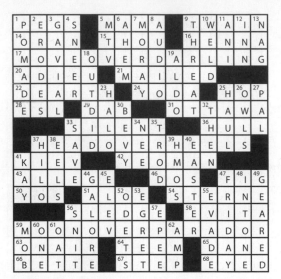

Puzzle 145

Puzzle 146

Puzzle 147

Puzzle 148

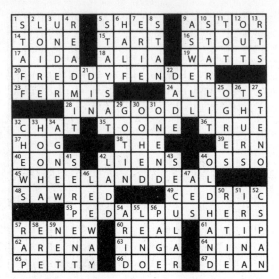

Puzzle 149

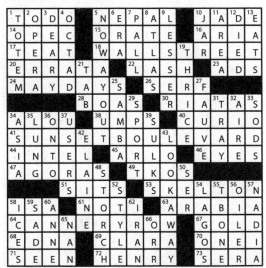

Puzzle 150

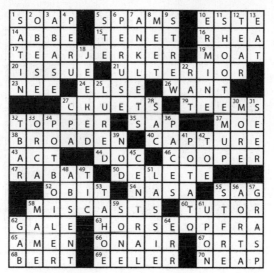

Puzzle 151

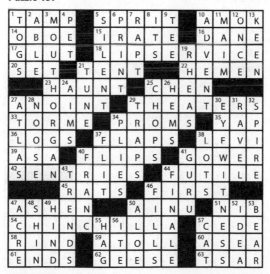

Puzzle 152

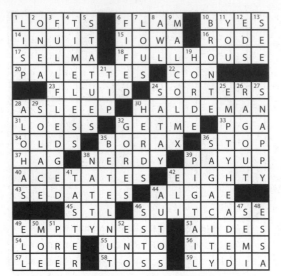

Puzzle 153

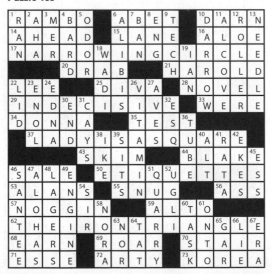

Puzzle 154

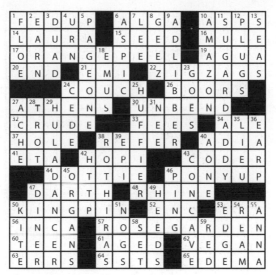

Puzzle 155

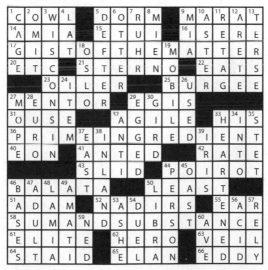

Puzzle 156

Puzzle 157

D	O	O	R		S	P	O	T		E	M	B	E	R
A	C	N	E		A	O	N	E		M	E	L	B	A
T	H	E	P	E	L	I	C	A	N	B	R	I	E	F
A	S	S	E	N	T		E	L	I	A		M	R	T
			A	R	I	A		E	R	U	P	T	S	
S	I	T	T	I	N	G	D	U	C	K	S			
O	D	E		C	E	L	I	N	E		D	A	S	H
A	L	A	M	O		A	S	S		S	A	L	L	Y
P	E	R	U		A	R	C	T	I	C		T	A	D
			L	O	N	E	S	O	M	E	D	O	V	E
B	E	R	L	I	N			P	A	N	E			
A	T	E		L	I	M	E		G	E	A	R	E	D
W	H	E	R	E	E	A	G	L	E	S	D	A	R	E
L	E	V	E	R		R	O	A	R		E	L	A	N
S	L	E	D	S		E	S	P	Y		N	E	S	T

Puzzle 158

G	E	T	S		A	S	F	A	R		P	O	M	P
O	R	A	L		B	E	A	L	E		S	O	U	L
S	I	R	E		A	E	S	O	P		A	L	G	A
H	E	A	D	O	F	S	T	E	A	M		O	F	T
			P	T	A		P	E	A	N	U	T		
V	O	I	L	A		W	I	D	E	A	N	G	L	E
E	N	D	A	L	L		C	A	R	L	O			
T	E	A	S		A	D	O	B	E		I	A	G	O
			T	E	N	O	N		D	A	N	D	E	R
S	I	M	U	L	C	A	S	T		S	T	O	L	E
H	O	O	P	L	A			I	L	K				
A	D	D		A	S	F	A	T	A	S	A	P	I	G
K	I	E	V		T	O	R	T	S		J	U	D	O
E	Z	R	A		E	X	I	L	E		A	R	E	A
R	E	N	T		R	Y	D	E	R		R	E	S	T

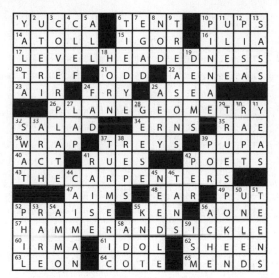

Puzzle 159

Puzzle 160

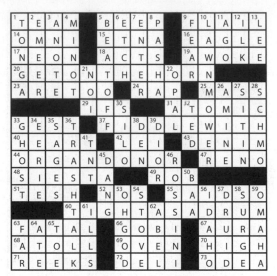

Puzzle 161

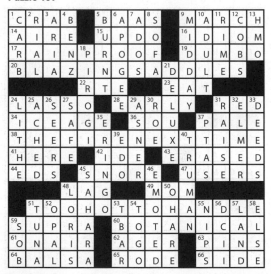

Puzzle 162

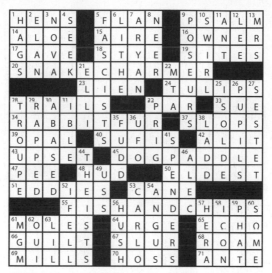

Puzzle 163

Puzzle 164

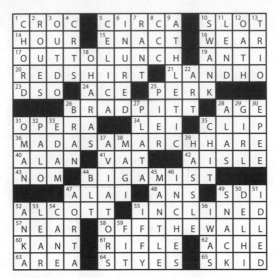

Puzzle 165

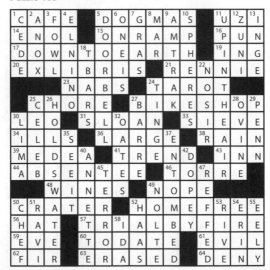

Puzzle 166

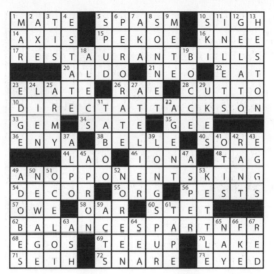

Puzzle 167

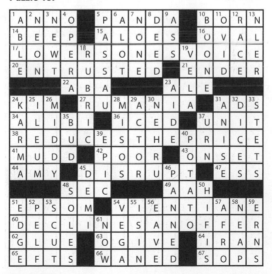

Puzzle 168

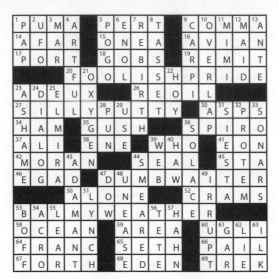

Puzzle 169

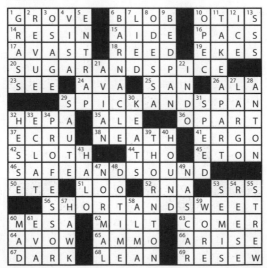

Puzzle 170

Puzzle 171

Puzzle 172

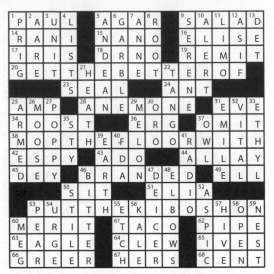

Puzzle 173

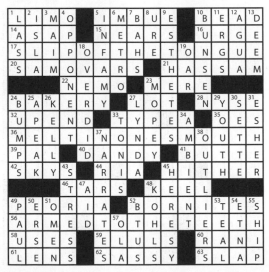

Puzzle 174

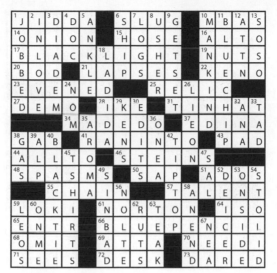

Puzzle 175

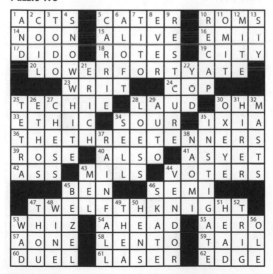

Puzzle 176

Puzzle 177

Puzzle 178

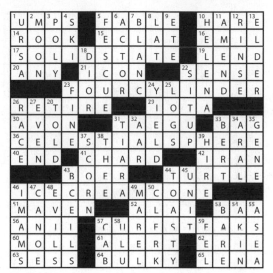

Puzzle 179

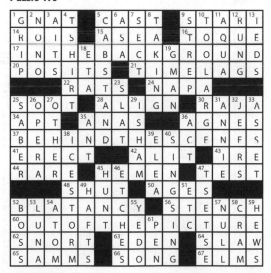

Puzzle 180

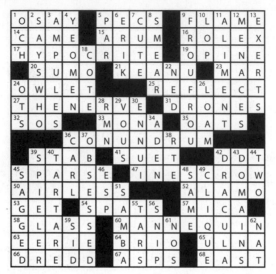

Puzzle 181

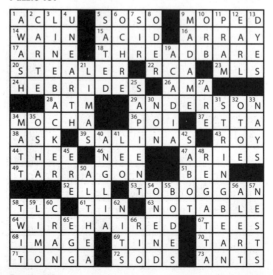

Puzzle 182

Puzzle 183

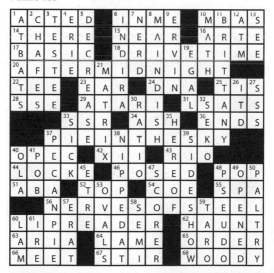

Puzzle 184

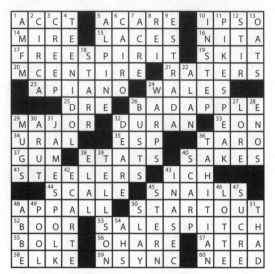

Puzzle 185

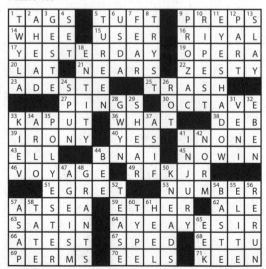

Puzzle 186

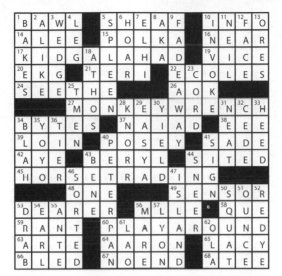

Puzzle 187

Puzzle 188

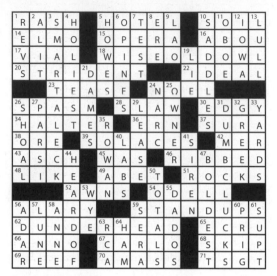

Puzzle 189

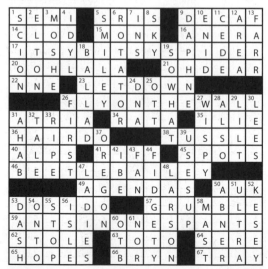

Puzzle 190

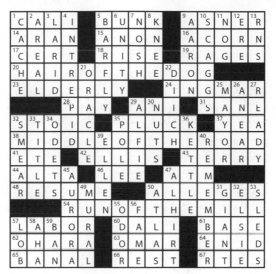

Puzzle 191

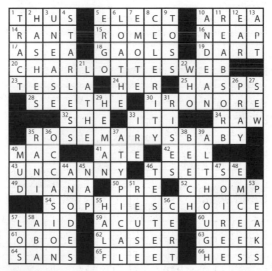

Puzzle 192

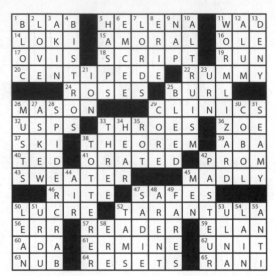

Puzzle 193

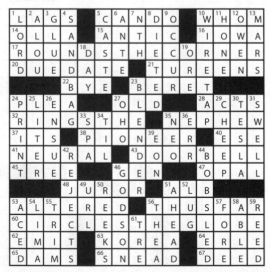

Puzzle 194

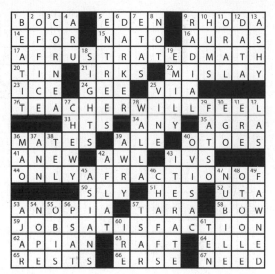

Puzzle 195

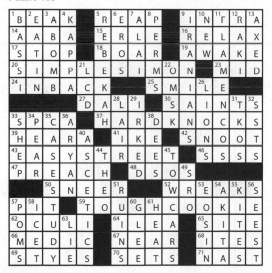

Puzzle 196

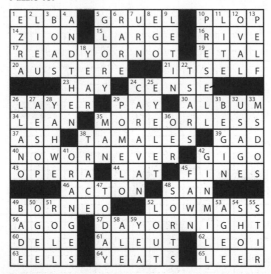

Puzzle 197

Puzzle 198

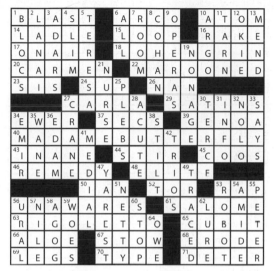

Puzzle 199

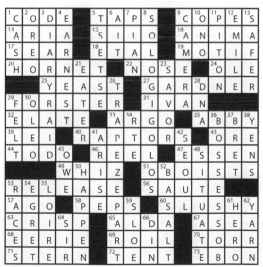

Puzzle 200

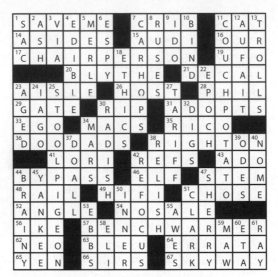

Puzzle 201

Puzzle 202

1	2	4	7	3	6	8	9	5
3	5	8	9	1	4	6	7	2
6	9	7	8	5	2	4	1	3
8	3	1	6	4	5	7	2	9
9	4	5	2	7	1	3	8	6
2	7	6	3	8	9	5	4	1
7	8	9	1	6	3	2	5	4
5	1	3	4	2	7	9	6	8
4	6	2	5	9	8	1	3	7

Puzzle 203

2	5	4	6	3	9	1	7	8
9	8	6	7	4	1	5	3	2
1	3	7	8	2	5	4	9	6
6	1	5	3	9	4	8	2	7
7	9	2	1	5	8	6	4	3
3	4	8	2	6	7	9	1	5
8	6	1	9	7	2	3	5	4
5	7	3	4	1	6	2	8	9
4	2	9	5	8	3	7	6	1

Puzzle 204

3	7	1	8	5	6	9	2	4
4	9	5	2	1	7	3	6	8
6	2	8	4	3	9	1	5	7
9	4	6	7	2	1	5	8	3
5	8	7	6	4	3	2	1	9
1	3	2	5	9	8	4	7	6
7	5	9	1	8	4	6	3	2
2	6	3	9	7	5	8	4	1
8	1	4	3	6	2	7	9	5

Puzzle 205

9	7	5	8	2	1	3	4	6
6	3	2	4	5	7	1	8	9
4	1	8	3	6	9	5	7	2
2	6	1	5	4	3	8	9	7
8	5	4	9	7	2	6	3	1
7	9	3	1	8	6	4	2	5
3	4	9	7	1	5	2	6	8
1	2	7	6	3	8	9	5	4
5	8	6	2	9	4	7	1	3

Puzzle 206

8	5	9	7	1	2	3	6	4
7	3	2	5	4	6	8	9	1
1	6	4	9	8	3	2	7	5
3	7	1	8	9	5	6	4	2
4	2	6	1	3	7	5	8	9
9	8	5	2	6	4	1	3	7
2	9	3	6	7	1	4	5	8
5	4	8	3	2	9	7	1	6
6	1	7	4	5	8	9	2	3

Puzzle 207

6	7	8	4	5	2	1	3	9
9	5	2	8	3	1	7	6	4
4	3	1	7	9	6	5	8	2
3	2	4	6	1	9	8	7	5
5	8	6	2	7	4	9	1	3
7	1	9	3	8	5	4	2	6
1	6	5	9	2	8	3	4	7
2	9	7	1	4	3	6	5	8
8	4	3	5	6	7	2	9	1

Puzzle 208

4	3	1	9	6	2	5	7	8
2	5	7	3	8	4	1	9	6
6	8	9	1	7	5	4	3	2
7	2	4	5	9	3	8	6	1
3	6	8	7	4	1	9	2	5
1	9	5	8	2	6	7	4	3
9	4	3	2	5	8	6	1	7
8	1	6	4	3	7	2	5	9
5	7	2	6	1	9	3	8	4

Puzzle 209

2	7	6	3	5	9	1	8	4
5	3	4	2	8	1	7	9	6
9	8	1	4	6	7	2	3	5
8	9	3	5	2	6	4	1	7
4	1	5	9	7	8	6	2	3
6	2	7	1	4	3	9	5	8
7	6	9	8	3	2	5	4	1
3	4	2	7	1	5	8	6	9
1	5	8	6	9	4	3	7	2

Puzzle 210

3	5	4	6	2	7	1	9	8
1	6	8	9	4	3	5	2	7
2	7	9	1	5	8	3	6	4
9	4	6	8	1	2	7	3	5
5	2	3	4	7	9	8	1	6
7	8	1	3	6	5	9	4	2
8	9	5	2	3	6	4	7	1
4	3	2	7	8	1	6	5	9
6	1	7	5	9	4	2	8	3

Puzzle 211

7	8	9	3	6	2	4	1	5
1	3	2	4	5	7	6	8	9
5	6	4	1	9	8	3	7	2
9	5	6	2	3	1	8	4	7
4	7	3	5	8	6	9	2	1
8	2	1	9	7	4	5	3	6
3	9	7	8	1	5	2	6	4
6	4	8	7	2	9	1	5	3
2	1	5	6	4	3	7	9	8

Puzzle 212

2	3	7	6	5	1	8	4	9
9	1	8	4	7	2	5	6	3
4	6	5	9	3	8	7	1	2
6	8	3	1	9	7	2	5	4
1	5	4	8	2	3	9	7	6
7	2	9	5	6	4	3	8	1
3	4	2	7	8	6	1	9	5
5	7	1	2	4	9	6	3	8
8	9	6	3	1	5	4	2	7

Puzzle 213

7	8	6	4	1	9	2	5	3
2	3	1	6	8	5	9	7	4
5	4	9	3	2	7	8	6	1
1	5	8	9	6	3	4	2	7
3	7	2	8	4	1	5	9	6
6	9	4	7	5	2	1	3	8
9	1	3	5	7	8	6	4	2
4	2	7	1	9	6	3	8	5
8	6	5	2	3	4	7	1	9

Puzzle 214

1	3	2	7	9	6	8	5	4
4	8	7	5	3	2	9	1	6
9	5	6	4	8	1	2	7	3
3	4	5	8	1	7	6	2	9
6	1	8	9	2	5	3	4	7
7	2	9	3	6	4	5	8	1
5	7	3	2	4	9	1	6	8
8	6	4	1	5	3	7	9	2
2	9	1	6	7	8	4	3	5

Puzzle 215

8	4	3	5	9	6	7	2	1
9	1	5	3	7	2	4	8	6
6	7	2	4	8	1	9	5	3
4	9	8	7	1	5	3	6	2
2	6	1	9	3	4	8	7	5
3	5	7	2	6	8	1	4	9
5	2	9	1	4	7	6	3	8
7	3	6	8	5	9	2	1	4
1	8	4	6	2	3	5	9	7

Puzzle 216

6	8	2	7	9	4	1	5	3
1	3	9	8	5	2	6	7	4
5	7	4	3	6	1	9	2	8
9	4	3	5	2	6	8	1	7
2	1	5	9	8	7	3	4	6
8	6	7	4	1	3	2	9	5
7	5	6	2	3	9	4	8	1
4	9	1	6	7	8	5	3	2
3	2	8	1	4	5	7	6	9

Puzzle 217

2	8	6	7	1	5	3	9	4
7	3	4	2	9	8	6	5	1
1	5	9	4	3	6	8	2	7
6	7	3	8	2	1	5	4	9
5	1	8	6	4	9	7	3	2
9	4	2	5	7	3	1	8	6
4	9	5	1	8	7	2	6	3
3	6	7	9	5	2	4	1	8
8	2	1	3	6	4	9	7	5

Puzzle 218

4	1	8	6	7	3	5	2	9
2	5	3	9	4	8	6	7	1
7	9	6	2	1	5	4	8	3
3	8	1	4	2	7	9	6	5
6	7	9	5	3	1	8	4	2
5	2	4	8	6	9	3	1	7
8	4	5	7	9	2	1	3	6
1	6	2	3	5	4	7	9	8
9	3	7	1	8	6	2	5	4

Puzzle 219

7	5	1	6	2	4	9	3	8
8	3	4	9	7	5	2	6	1
9	2	6	3	1	8	5	7	4
1	4	9	5	3	7	8	2	6
6	7	2	8	9	1	3	4	5
5	8	3	2	4	6	7	1	9
2	1	5	4	8	3	6	9	7
3	6	7	1	5	9	4	8	2
4	9	8	7	6	2	1	5	3

Puzzle 220

3	7	4	8	5	6	2	9	1
6	1	9	4	3	2	7	5	8
8	5	2	9	1	7	3	4	6
4	3	6	5	2	1	9	8	7
5	9	1	3	7	8	6	2	4
7	2	8	6	9	4	1	3	5
2	4	3	7	6	5	8	1	9
1	8	7	2	4	9	5	6	3
9	6	5	1	8	3	4	7	2

Puzzle 221

6	7	9	2	8	4	1	5	3
4	5	3	1	6	7	9	8	2
1	8	2	9	3	5	6	4	7
7	3	1	5	4	6	2	9	8
2	9	8	7	1	3	5	6	4
5	6	4	8	2	9	3	7	1
8	1	6	4	5	2	7	3	9
3	2	7	6	9	8	4	1	5
9	4	5	3	7	1	8	2	6

Puzzle 222

6	7	5	9	3	4	8	2	1
9	1	2	8	6	5	4	3	7
4	3	8	2	7	1	9	5	6
1	8	3	6	9	7	2	4	5
2	6	4	5	8	3	7	1	9
5	9	7	4	1	2	6	8	3
8	2	9	1	5	6	3	7	4
3	4	1	7	2	9	5	6	8
7	5	6	3	4	8	1	9	2

Puzzle 223

1	2	6	4	9	8	7	3	5
5	6	4	7	2	3	1	9	8
8	3	9	5	7	1	6	4	2
4	7	2	9	1	5	3	8	6
3	9	1	8	4	6	2	5	7
9	5	7	6	3	2	8	1	4
6	1	3	2	8	4	5	7	9
2	4	8	1	5	7	9	6	3
7	8	5	3	6	9	4	2	1

Puzzle 224

8	3	1	7	9	2	5	6	4
6	4	2	3	5	8	1	7	9
5	7	9	6	4	1	2	3	8
3	2	8	4	1	5	6	9	7
4	5	6	9	2	7	3	8	1
9	1	7	8	3	6	4	5	2
1	8	5	2	6	9	7	4	3
2	9	4	5	7	3	8	1	6
7	6	3	1	8	4	9	2	5

Puzzle 225

6	2	9	7	3	1	4	5	8
3	8	4	9	5	2	1	7	6
5	1	7	4	6	8	3	9	2
1	9	2	5	7	6	8	3	4
7	4	1	2	8	3	5	6	9
9	6	8	3	4	7	2	1	5
8	5	3	6	9	4	7	2	1
2	3	5	8	1	9	6	4	7
4	7	6	1	2	5	9	8	3

Puzzle 226

7	9	1	4	6	8	2	3	5
2	5	6	9	7	3	8	1	4
8	1	4	3	5	2	6	9	7
4	6	9	8	2	7	3	5	1
6	3	5	2	1	4	7	8	9
5	8	7	6	3	9	1	4	2
9	4	3	7	8	1	5	2	6
3	7	2	1	4	5	9	6	8
1	2	8	5	9	6	4	7	3

Puzzle 227

1	7	5	2	4	6	3	9	8
5	3	2	8	1	9	7	6	4
4	8	9	6	7	3	5	2	1
2	9	3	4	8	7	6	1	5
3	6	7	9	5	1	4	8	2
7	5	1	3	6	8	2	4	9
8	1	6	7	2	4	9	5	3
6	2	4	1	9	5	8	3	7
9	4	8	5	3	2	1	7	6

Puzzle 228

4	1	5	3	6	9	2	8	7
7	8	2	4	3	1	9	6	5
9	6	7	5	2	8	1	3	4
1	5	6	7	9	2	8	4	3
2	9	8	6	7	3	4	5	1
5	3	4	8	1	7	6	9	2
8	4	3	2	5	6	7	1	9
6	2	9	1	4	5	3	7	8
3	7	1	9	8	4	5	2	6

Puzzle 229

9	5	1	2	3	7	4	6	8
7	4	2	6	8	1	5	3	9
8	3	6	9	4	5	1	7	2
2	6	7	8	1	3	9	4	5
4	8	9	7	5	2	3	1	6
3	1	5	4	6	9	2	8	7
6	9	3	1	2	8	7	5	4
1	2	8	5	7	4	6	9	3
5	7	4	3	9	6	8	2	1

Puzzle 230

9	7	1	5	3	2	8	6	4
8	5	3	4	7	6	1	2	9
2	4	6	1	9	8	7	3	5
7	9	8	2	1	5	6	4	3
5	3	4	6	8	7	2	9	1
6	1	2	3	4	9	5	8	7
4	8	5	7	6	3	9	1	2
3	6	7	9	2	1	4	5	8
1	2	9	8	5	4	3	7	6

Puzzle 231

4	3	9	6	1	5	7	2	8
2	4	6	3	7	8	5	1	9
3	2	4	7	8	9	6	5	1
9	8	2	5	4	1	3	7	6
8	5	1	2	3	7	9	6	4
5	6	7	1	2	4	8	9	3
7	1	3	9	6	2	4	8	5
1	9	8	4	5	6	2	3	7
6	7	5	8	9	3	1	4	2

Puzzle 232

Puzzle 233

5	1	4	2	3	8	6	9	7
9	7	8	1	4	6	3	2	5
2	3	6	7	9	5	8	4	1
3	6	9	8	1	7	2	5	4
8	4	1	5	2	3	9	7	6
7	2	5	4	6	9	1	3	8
6	5	7	9	8	2	4	1	3
4	9	3	6	5	1	7	8	2
1	8	2	3	7	4	5	6	9

Puzzle 234

4	3	9	1	5	8	6	7	2
6	8	7	0	3	2	1	4	5
2	5	1	4	6	7	3	9	8
7	1	5	2	9	6	4	8	3
9	6	3	8	4	1	5	2	7
8	4	2	3	7	5	9	1	6
5	9	4	7	8	3	2	6	1
1	7	6	5	2	4	8	3	9
3	2	8	6	1	9	7	5	4

Puzzle 235

2	3	4	7	8	6	9	1	5
5	8	7	9	1	3	4	2	6
6	9	1	2	4	5	3	8	7
3	4	2	8	7	1	6	5	9
8	7	9	5	6	2	1	3	4
1	6	5	4	3	9	8	7	2
9	2	3	1	5	4	7	6	8
4	1	8	6	2	7	5	9	3
7	5	6	3	9	8	2	4	1

6	8	1	3	5	9	7	2	4
7	4	2	8	6	1	3	5	9
3	9	5	7	2	4	1	8	6
9	6	4	1	8	3	5	7	2
1	2	7	5	4	6	8	9	3
5	3	8	2	9	7	4	6	1
8	5	3	9	1	2	6	4	7
2	1	6	4	7	5	9	3	8
4	7	9	6	3	8	2	1	5

Puzzle 236

3	8	6	9	4	2	7	1	5
5	9	2	8	7	1	3	6	4
7	1	4	6	3	5	8	2	9
2	6	1	3	5	7	9	4	8
8	7	5	4	6	9	2	3	1
9	4	3	2	1	8	5	7	6
1	2	7	5	9	6	4	8	3
6	3	9	7	8	4	1	5	2
4	5	8	1	2	3	6	9	7

Puzzle 237

3	1	5	4	6	8	2	7	9
9	7	6	5	2	1	3	4	8
8	2	4	7	9	3	6	5	1
5	8	7	3	4	9	1	2	6
2	6	3	1	8	7	5	9	4
4	9	1	2	5	6	7	8	3
1	5	2	9	3	4	8	6	7
7	4	8	6	1	2	9	3	5
6	3	9	8	7	5	4	1	2

Puzzle 238

5	4	3	7	1	2	8	9	6
9	7	1	5	6	8	4	2	3
6	3	2	8	4	9	1	7	5
8	1	7	6	3	4	9	5	2
7	2	4	1	9	5	3	6	8
4	6	5	9	8	7	2	3	1
1	5	9	4	2	3	6	8	7
2	9	8	3	7	6	5	1	4
3	8	6	2	5	1	7	4	9

Puzzle 239

1	6	9	4	7	5	2	8	3
7	2	4	6	3	8	9	5	1
8	3	5	1	9	2	6	7	4
2	9	7	8	6	3	4	1	5
5	4	8	2	1	9	7	3	6
6	1	3	5	4	7	8	9	2
9	8	6	3	5	4	1	2	7
3	7	1	9	2	6	5	4	8
4	5	2	7	8	1	3	6	9

Puzzle 240

5	9	1	6	8	3	7	2	4
2	7	6	4	9	1	3	5	8
8	4	3	5	2	7	1	9	6
7	1	8	9	5	4	2	6	3
4	5	2	3	6	8	9	1	7
3	6	9	1	7	2	4	8	5
1	2	7	8	4	6	5	3	9
6	3	5	7	1	9	8	4	2
9	8	4	2	3	5	6	7	1

Puzzle 241

1	7	6	9	8	2	5	3	4
2	5	4	3	6	7	9	1	8
3	9	8	1	5	4	2	7	6
4	8	5	2	1	6	7	9	3
7	1	9	4	3	8	6	2	5
6	3	2	5	7	9	4	8	1
9	6	3	7	4	1	8	5	2
8	2	1	6	9	5	3	4	7
5	4	7	8	2	3	1	6	9

Puzzle 242

1	8	4	5	9	2	7	6	3
6	3	7	8	1	4	9	5	2
5	2	9	3	7	6	8	4	1
7	4	1	9	3	5	6	2	8
8	5	6	2	4	7	1	3	9
2	9	3	6	8	1	4	7	5
4	1	2	7	5	9	3	8	6
3	7	5	1	6	8	2	9	4
9	6	8	4	2	3	5	1	7

Puzzle 243

7	5	3	9	1	6	2	4	8
2	8	1	4	7	5	9	3	6
9	4	6	8	2	3	7	1	5
1	9	4	5	3	8	6	2	7
6	2	7	1	4	9	5	8	3
8	3	5	2	6	7	4	9	1
4	6	2	3	5	1	8	7	9
3	7	9	6	8	4	1	5	2
5	1	8	7	9	2	3	6	4

Puzzle 244

9	3	1	7	4	6	8	2	5
7	5	6	2	9	8	1	4	3
4	2	8	5	1	3	9	7	6
3	8	7	6	5	2	4	1	9
5	1	2	4	8	9	3	6	7
6	4	9	3	7	1	5	8	2
8	9	5	1	2	7	6	3	4
2	6	4	8	3	5	7	9	1
1	7	3	9	6	4	2	5	8

Puzzle 245

8	6	1	3	9	4	7	2	5
9	4	5	7	2	1	3	6	8
7	2	3	5	8	6	9	4	1
4	3	8	2	6	7	5	1	9
5	9	6	1	4	8	2	3	7
2	1	7	9	5	3	6	8	4
3	5	2	4	1	9	8	7	6
1	8	9	6	7	2	4	5	3
6	7	4	8	3	5	1	9	2

Puzzle 246

6	7	2	5	8	4	9	1	3
3	4	9	1	7	6	8	2	5
1	5	8	2	3	9	6	7	4
4	3	5	7	2	8	1	6	9
9	2	1	6	4	3	5	8	7
8	6	7	9	1	5	3	4	2
5	9	4	8	6	2	7	3	1
2	1	6	3	5	7	4	9	8
7	8	3	4	9	1	2	5	6

Puzzle 247

3	9	1	7	8	2	5	6	4
5	7	2	4	3	6	9	8	1
4	8	7	6	9	1	3	5	2
6	3	8	5	1	4	2	9	7
2	1	9	8	5	7	4	3	6
8	6	4	3	2	9	7	1	5
7	2	3	1	6	5	8	4	9
1	4	5	9	7	8	6	2	3
9	5	6	2	4	3	1	7	8

Puzzle 248

5	2	3	1	6	4	7	8	9
4	6	8	5	9	3	2	1	7
9	1	7	3	8	6	5	4	2
7	9	1	4	2	8	6	3	5
8	5	2	6	1	7	3	9	4
3	7	5	9	4	2	1	6	8
6	3	4	7	5	9	8	2	1
1	8	9	2	3	5	4	7	6
2	4	6	8	7	1	9	5	3

Puzzle 249

7	4	3	9	6	2	5	8	1
1	8	4	2	9	5	7	3	6
6	9	1	5	7	3	8	4	2
5	7	6	3	2	4	1	9	8
3	5	8	4	1	9	2	6	7
2	3	9	6	8	7	4	1	5
8	1	2	7	4	6	9	5	3
9	6	7	1	5	8	3	2	4
4	2	5	8	3	1	6	7	9

Puzzle 250

9	7	4	3	1	2	5	8	6
1	5	2	6	8	4	3	9	7
2	1	8	7	5	9	6	4	3
8	6	9	4	2	3	7	1	5
4	3	1	9	6	5	2	7	8
7	4	6	5	3	8	9	2	1
5	9	3	8	7	1	4	6	2
3	8	7	2	4	6	1	5	9
6	2	5	1	9	7	8	3	4

Puzzle 251

4	2	9	7	6	8	5	1	3
5	1	6	4	3	2	7	8	9
9	7	8	3	5	1	6	2	4
3	6	2	5	7	9	1	4	8
6	8	4	1	9	3	2	7	5
7	5	1	6	8	4	9	3	2
1	4	3	9	2	7	8	5	6
2	9	7	8	4	5	3	6	1
8	3	5	2	1	6	4	9	7

Puzzle 252

6	7	5	8	3	2	1	4	9
8	3	2	4	1	9	6	5	7
1	4	9	5	6	7	8	3	2
7	5	1	3	4	6	9	2	8
3	2	4	7	9	8	5	6	1
5	9	8	6	2	1	3	7	4
9	6	7	1	5	4	2	8	3
4	1	6	2	8	3	7	9	5
2	8	3	9	7	5	4	1	6

Puzzle 253

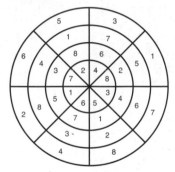

Puzzle 254

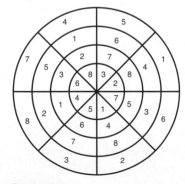

Puzzle 255

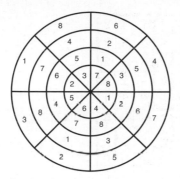

Puzzle 256

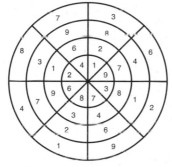

Puzzle 257

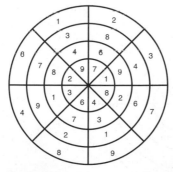

Puzzle 258

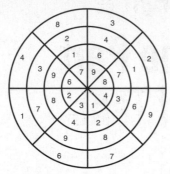

Puzzle 259

Part IV
The Part of Tens

The 5th Wave   By Rich Tennant

"No wrong answers — please! Not easy make erasures."

In this part . . .

My hope is that the information and puzzles in this book inspire you to make playtime part of your daily (or almost-daily) schedule for the rest of your life. The benefits are great, and the process should be nothing but fun.

Here, I offer two short chapters to complete the inspiration: one that lists ten additional types of puzzles and games you may want to discover (or rediscover); and one that suggests ten ways to become a better puzzler.

Chapter 6

Ten Other Types of Puzzles and Games to Keep Your Mind Fit

*T*he hardest part of writing this chapter was deciding what to include and what to leave out. There are so many great puzzles and games to keep your mind pumping that the list is pretty much endless. The most important consideration when deciding how to spend your precious free time is *fun:* Whatever you do has to be interesting enough to get your mental gears cranking, and enjoyable enough to keep you coming back for more.

To make sure you're really keeping your gray matter on its toes, try something new every chance you get. You may just discover some new favorites!

Ogling Optical Illusions

Optical illusion puzzles are great fun and can be really tricky. They test your powers of perception, as well as your eyesight. If you prefer your puzzles in hard-copy form, you can find books of optical illusions. If you're willing to do some puzzling online, you can find lots of optical illusion puzzles. I like Web sites such as www.brain bashers.com (click on Illusions), www.optical-illu-sionist.com, and www.eyetricks.com/illusions.

Tackling Letter Equations

Letter equations are well-known phrases or facts in which key words have been replaced with just their first letters. They're called *equations* because they often (but not always) contain a number and an equal sign. For example, a fairly easy one to figure out is

>   7 = D in a W

The answer is *7 days in a week.* A bit more challenging letter equation is something like

>   15 M on a D M C

The answer is *15 men on a dead man's chest.* An example of a fact-based letter equation is

>   88 = K on a P

The answer is *88 keys on a piano.* The phrases are often easier to figure out than the facts, which can be well-known to some people but seem obscure to others.

Solving Math Puzzles

What? Solve math problems for fun? Am I nuts?

No, not completely. I happen to know that when grades aren't involved, and when you're seeing the math problems in a context other than a textbook, they can be downright enjoyable to solve. Math is a true test of logic, and doing math puzzles on a regular basis builds your memory (so you don't stumble the next time you need to know what 7×6 equals).

Assembling Jigsaw Puzzles

Find a good surface so you can spread out the pieces, make sure the lighting is right, and get to work. You can choose an image that appeals to you, the number of pieces you want to work with (300, 500, 1,000, or even more), and even whether you want to work in one dimension or three. Assembling a jigsaw puzzle is a great way to spend a rainy day, but you don't have to wait for foul weather to enjoy the peace of mind that comes from concentrating on such a compact activity.

Building Models

Maybe as a kid you spent hours putting together model cars, ships, and planes. If so, or even if you've never touched a model kit in your life, this activity has no age limit. The stuff kids learn from constructing models is great stuff for adults to re-learn: how to focus on one project, follow detailed instructions, and get your fingers to maneuver precisely. A wide variety of model options is available; type "toy models" into your favorite search engine to see what I mean.

Playing Electronic Games

If you're more apt to spend your free time in front of a computer screen than grappling with the pieces of a model airplane, you have lots of computer game options that will challenge your mind — not just your ability to destroy alien warships.

If you're a fan of a particular type of puzzle, including the kinds featured in this book, you're bound to find lots of online versions by using your favorite search engine. Filling in a crossword or a sudoku grid certainly has a different feel on a computer screen than on paper, but you may find that you actually prefer the electronic versions: no erasers required.

Playing Chess

Chess, the granddaddy of strategy games, forces you to think logically; to be successful, you have to consider the outcomes of each possible move. Playing often enough may also boost your memory power because you start to memorize board layouts (so you don't have to walk through each possible move — you remember the outcomes from having seen a certain board layout before).

If you've never played chess before, don't let yourself be intimidated; the rules aren't complicated, and after a few games you'll have a good handle on basic strategy. You may want to play with someone whose chess experience is roughly equivalent to yours — you're both more likely to enjoy the experience and stick with it.

Strategizing with Scrabble

This game is sort of like one big word scramble puzzle, but with some competition built in. You don't have to be a walking dictionary to enjoy Scrabble; you can use some basic strategies (such as placing words where they accrue double or triple points) to make even short words pay off.

If you're a word lover, Scrabble's a great game to try. And if you play often enough that you start feeling a little bored with it, look up "Scrabble variations" online for suggestions of ways to shake up the rules to make the game even more challenging.

Conquering Card Games

These days, thanks to Texas Hold'em and the World Poker Tour, it seems like the only people playing cards have money on their minds. But I'm here to remind you that playing cards can be fun even if no cash is involved. Games such as hearts, pinochle, and bridge involve strategy and can be good mental workouts — as well as great excuses to get together with family and friends.

Working Up a Sweat

As I mention in Chapter 1, keeping your brain healthy requires paying attention to your body as well. Exercise — especially of the aerobic kind — seems to be crucial to mental fitness. So don't assume that sitting on your couch doing crosswords and math puzzles is all you need to keep your synapses in tip-top shape. You need to get up and move as well.

I won't even try to guess what type of exercise is best for you — your current health is a big consideration, and having fun is key if you want to stick with it. But if you're in good health, keep in mind that exercising doesn't have to mean being tied to a treadmill. Playing a sport — basketball, volleyball, soccer, even golf — is a great way to challenge your body, improve your coordination, build strategy skills, and socialize.

Chapter 7

Ten Ways to Be a Better Puzzler

*Y*ou probably don't plan to go pro with your puzzling (although I won't discourage you if you decide to try — it's worked out pretty well for me!). But anything worth your time is worth doing well. In this chapter, I outline some easy ways to step up your game so your brain gets the maximum benefit (and pleasure) from your puzzling pursuits.

Practice, Practice, Practice!

Unless the folks at Mensa know you by name, you're probably not going to pick up a sudoku grid for the first time and solve it in a matter of minutes. Believe me: Some of the puzzles in this book are *really* hard! They're supposed to be — I want you to be challenged. So don't get frustrated if the going is tough initially. With practice, I promise you'll see results.

Figure Out Your Puzzle Editor's Style

The person responsible for the puzzles in a certain newspaper, book, or Web site is called the *puzzle editor,* and getting familiar with that person's style can help you solve the puzzles. This is particularly true with crossword puzzles. The difficulty level of a crossword puzzle depends on how the clues are written.

For this reason, when you first start working puzzles, focus on puzzles published in the same source. This book is a great example because, as its puzzle editor, my style dominates throughout. After you work a handful of puzzles in this book, you'll likely start to figure out some of my tricks and quirks. Doing so should make solving each subsequent puzzle slightly easier.

Mix It Up

Even if your goal is to master a certain type of puzzle, you'll reap benefits from working a variety of puzzles along the way. Any challenging puzzle should help get your synapses in gear and improve your strategic thinking. And stepping away from your particular puzzle of choice once in a while may allow you to gain a new perspective and be even more successful when you return to it.

Create the Right Environment

The "right environment" depends on your preferences and, perhaps, on the type of puzzle you're working. For me, these things are essential:

- ✔ A comfortable chair

- ✔ Silence or soft music

- ✔ Good lighting

- ✔ Easy access to resources when necessary (such as when working a crossword)

- ✔ Ample time to complete the puzzle — or at least to make a good effort

Sever Ties with Your TV

If you want to spend more time puzzling, but time seems elusive, challenge yourself to shut off your TV completely for one week. Yes, I'm serious! I'm not suggesting that you never watch it again, but eliminating it from your schedule for one week may be eye-opening. Even if you think you don't spend a lot of time watching it, you may be shocked at how much time you free up by removing it altogether.

Listen to Classical Music

Studies suggest that listening to classical music may help to improve brain function. Some people find that classical music is the perfect background while working puzzles. If you're one of those people, it's possible you'll perform better — and increase the health benefits of your puzzling efforts to boot.

Hone Your Concentration

The suggestion to hone your concentration is a natural follow-up to creating the right environment for puzzling, turning off your TV, and listening to classical music. If you follow those three suggestions, you'll give yourself a leg up in the concentration department.

Exercise Your Memory

No running shoes required here: I'm talking about doing simple things every day to actively improve your memory. Following are a few suggestions:

- ✔ Write a shopping list, but don't carry it to the store. Instead, try to memorize the items you've written and recall them as you're shopping.

- ✔ Actively practice remembering names. One way to do so is to notice the names of people who help you at the grocery store, the pharmacy, or a restaurant. Thank each person by name, and then make yourself recall that name several minutes after you leave the establishment.

- ✔ Become a storyteller. Work on recalling details about events in your life and sharing them out loud with family members and friends. Most people can recall events more clearly if they tell someone else about them, so speak up!

Improve Your Physical Health

It's no surprise that mental health and physical health often go hand in hand. As you care for your body, you're caring for your brain as well, so make sure you pay attention to the basics:

- Get enough sleep.
- Eat healthy foods.
- Exercise.

Shake Up Your Routines

I'm not just talking about trying new puzzles here, although that's important too (see the earlier section "Mix It Up"). I'm talking about breaking out of ruts and taking simple steps to wake up your brain cells. Routines are crucial to accomplishing the things you have to do each day, but they can also drain your energy. So whenever possible, shake them up. Here are a few simple suggestions:

- Use your nondominant hand to eat, drink, brush your teeth, or do other simple tasks.
- Take a different route to work.
- Use part of your lunch break to stretch or go for a walk.
- If you usually turn the TV on at a certain time each day, keep it off until a program comes on that you really want to see. Do something active in the meantime.

- Prepare a new food, or order something new at your favorite restaurant.

- Call or e-mail someone you haven't spoken to in a long time.